Rarotonga
& the Cook Islands
a travel survival kit

Tony Wheeler
Nancy Keller

Rarotonga & the Cook Islands - a travel survival kit
   2nd edition

Published by
   Lonely Planet Publications
   Head Office: PO Box 617, Hawthorn, Vic 3122, Australia
   US Office: PO Box 2001A, Berkeley, CA 94702, USA

Printed by
   Singapore National Printers, Singapore

Photographs by
   Lawrance Bailey/Cocophotos (LB/C)
      Donald Cole/Cook Islands Tourist Authority (DC/CITA)
      Cook Islands Tourist Authority (CITA)
      Nancy Keller (NK)
      Tony Wheeler (TW)

      Portraits/flower page: Cook Islands Tourist Authority & Tony Wheeler
      Front cover: fishing from the reef, Mangaia - Tony Wheeler

Illustrations
   Historical: William Wyatt Gill, from *Cannibals and Converts, From Darkness to Light in Polynesia* and
      Cook Islands Customs, all published by the Institute of Pacific Studies, University of the South Pacific.

First Published
   December 1986

This Edition
   September 1989

National Library of Australia Cataloguing in Publication Data

Wheeler, Tony
   Rarotonga & the Cook Islands, a travel survival kit.

   2nd ed.
   Includes index.
   ISBN 0 86442 038 2

   1. Cook Island - Description and travel - Guide-books.
   I. Title.

919.6'2304
© Copyright Tony Wheeler, 1989

Tony Wheeler

Born in England, Tony spent his school years in Pakistan, the West Indies and the USA, returning to England to do a university degree in engineering. After a short spell as an automotive design engineer he returned to university to do an MBA, then dropped out on the Asia overland trail with his wife Maureen. They set up Lonely Planet in the mid-70s and have been travelling, writing and publishing guidebooks ever since. Travel for Tony and Maureen is now considerably enlivened by their children Tashi and Kieran, both of whom came to the Cook Islands during the research of the 1st edition of this book.

Nancy Keller

Born and brought up in California, Nancy earned BA degrees in history and social science, working along the way in a variety of occupations. In the '70s she worked in the alternative press doing every aspect of newspaper work from holding down the editor's chair to delivering the papers. She then returned to university to earn a master's degree in journalism, finally graduating in 1986 after many breaks for extended stays on the west coast of Mexico. Since then she's been travelling and writing in Mexico, Israel, Egypt, Europe and now the South Pacific.

Lonely Planet Credits

Editor	Debbie Rossdale
Design, cover design	Margaret Jung
Typesetting	Gaylene Miller

This Edition

Tony Wheeler researched the 1st edition of this book while Nancy Keller took over for the 2nd. Nancy would like to thank Lawrance Bailey of Cocophotos in Avarua for his photographic assistance. On the island of Mauke thanks must go to Nan Greenwood, the Carr family, to Nane who showed her around and to CAO Tautara Purea. On Mitiaro Nane Pokoati was a great help. On Atiu thanks to the Puruto family, especially Papa Puruto but not forgetting Piri, Junior, Ricky and Piripa. Or their falling-apart scooter and their kitchen table in Muri where Nancy did much of the work in this book. Thanks also to Andrea Eimke and her husband Juergen, who helped to make her stay on Atiu one of the best times she had in the Cooks.

On Aitutaki, thanks to Teata Makirere and the lovely Persian couple, to Moko Kavana, Aussie Admiral Ben Grummels and the many others who shared stories of their beautiful island. Back on Raro thanks to Dorice Reid and the staff of the Cook Islands Tourist Authority and Mr Toru. Thanks to Pauline Napa and the staff of Stars Travel (especially Melynnda Schedewie and Maria) and to Exham Wichman. Finally her deepest thanks to Papa Tangaroa Kainuku of Takitumu for his insights into the islands' history and culture.

Tony would like to repeat his thanks from the 1st edition to the people who helped him while he was in the Cooks. Particularly to Roger Malcolm on Atiu and for the information he has sent subsequently. And to Rick Welland on Rarotonga for his illustrations. Thanks must also go to the travellers who have written to us with suggestions, corrections and improvements. Thanks to:

Wayne Blake, A T Cusick (Aus), Frances Dunn (Aus), Kurt Eder (O), Y Gausla (Nl), Dr A P Hansen (Aus), Ase Jespersen, Lothar Kirsch (D), Deborah McCormick (USA), J Millward (Aus), James Millward (Aus), Ruth Park (Can), Neville Pearson, Junius Powell (USA), Dorice Reid, Marian Steele (Aus), Robert Stephenson (Aus), Lewis Warren (USA), Malcolm Wellings (Can), Cecelia Wiley (USA), D J Woods (NZ)

Aus – Australia, Can – Canada, D – Germany, Nl – Netherlands, NZ – New Zealand, O – Austria, USA – USA

And the Next

Things change, prices go up, good places go bad and bad ones go bankrupt. So if you find things better, worse or simply different please write and tell us about it. As usual good letters will be rewarded with a free copy of the next edition or an alternative Lonely Planet guidebook if you prefer.

Contents

The tiny and remote Cook Islands are Polynesia in a conveniently handy, though widely scattered, package. They offer something for nearly everyone. Rarotonga, the main island, has modern resort facilities, fine beaches, excellent restaurants, spectacular coral reefs, a wide variety of accommodation possibilities and good entertainment; all on an island just 32 km around. Furthermore it's a spectacularly beautiful island, a mountainous high island like Tahiti, cloaked in dense jungle. 'Raro' is also the entry point for 99% of visitors to the Cooks as it is the location for the international airport.

Rarotonga is only the starting point for exploring the Cook Islands. From 'Raro' you can fly or, if you're feeling hardy and adventurous and have time to spare, ship to the other islands of the southern group. Spectacularly beautiful Aitutaki is by far the best known with its huge lagoon fringed with tiny, picture-postcard islets. Aitutaki is a combination of high island and atoll and is a frequent nominee for any 'most beautiful island in the Pacific'

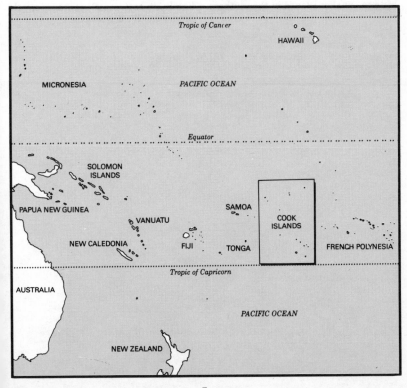

award. If Raro is the Tahiti of the Cooks then Aitutaki is the Bora Bora.

Few visitors go further than these two principal islands but that's a great shame because some of the others are equally interesting. Atiu and Mangaia are geological curiosities with a fringing, raised fossil reef known as a *makatea*. On both islands the *makatea* is a weirdly beautiful area of razor-sharp coral formations absolutely riddled with limestone caves. Stalactites and stalagmites may seem a strange thing to find on a tropical island but the caves are full of them. There's also a cave on Atiu inhabited by a tiny, unique swallow known as the *kopeka* and the island has countless burial caves. Mauke and Mitiaro, smaller islands in the southern group, also have a fringing *makatea* and can be visited from Rarotonga.

Finally there are the remote islands of the northern group, accessible only by the infrequent inter-island trading ships. These are the classic low atolls of the Pacific and you need time and persistence to explore them.

Of course islands aren't all there is to the Cooks, there are also the Cook Islanders themselves. Some say these handsome, easy-going people are the friendliest folk in the Pacific. They certainly have some of the most spectacular dancers and an evening at an Aitutaki 'island night' or a raucous Friday night at the Banana Court Bar in Rarotonga is an experience to remember. 'The Cooks are like Tahiti as it was 20 years ago,' say the promoters. It's a great place.

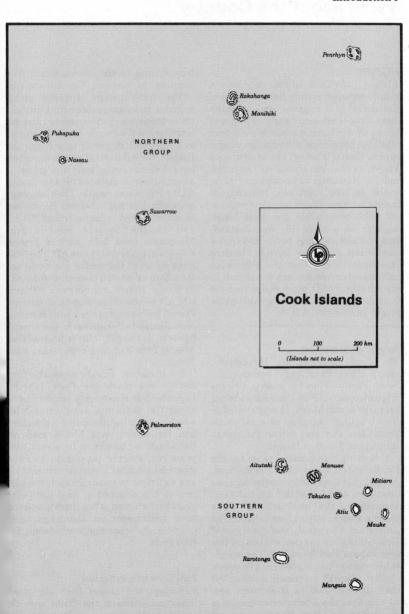

Penrhyn

Rakahanga
Manihiki

Pukapuka

NORTHERN
GROUP

Nassau

Suwarrow

Cook Islands

0   100   200 km

(Islands not to scale)

Palmerston

Aitutaki   Manuae

Mitiaro

Takutea

Atiu

SOUTHERN
GROUP

Mauke

Rarotonga

Mangaia

Facts about the Country

HISTORY

Although the Cook Islands only have a clearly recorded history from the time of the arrival of Europeans, archaeologists have discovered many early *marae* and traces of early settlements from a time when the population of Rarotonga was far greater than it is today. The ancient road known as the *Ara Metua* still encircles most of Rarotonga today and may be as much as 1000 years old. Rarotongans insist that their island was the jumping-off point from which the great Maori voyages were made to New Zealand. Indeed Rarotonga may be the Hawaikii of Polynesian migration legends. Modern historians believe that the Polynesian migrations moved through the islands in the 5th century AD, much earlier than the legends which date the first arrivals on the island around 1200 AD.

Polynesian Settlement

The Cook Islanders are Polynesians, people of the 'many' (*poly*) islands of the South Pacific. They are Maoris, like the original settlers of New Zealand, and their language is also Maori, closely related to the language of the original New Zealanders and also to the Polynesian language of Tahiti or Hawaii.

It is thought that 40,000 years ago the Pacific region was totally uninhabited. Around that time people started to move down from Asia and settled Australia and Melanesia – the 'black islands' which include modern Papua New Guinea. The Australian Aboriginals and the tribes of New Guinea are the descendants of this first wave of Pacific settlers. The islands of Micronesia ('tiny islands') and Polynesia ('many islands') remained uninhabited until around 5000 to 6000 years ago. At this time the Austronesian people of South-East Asia started to move beyond New Guinea to the islands which now comprise the Solomons, Vanuatu and Fiji.

The Austronesian language group includes the languages of South-East Asia (from Indonesian to Vietnamese) and the languages of the Pacific which developed as a sub-group as people moved into the Pacific. Around 1500 BC people moved on from Fiji to Tonga and this group is assumed to have included the ancestors of all the Polynesian people. Their language gradually diverged to become Polynesian as settlers moved to Samoa around 300 BC and to the Society Islands and Marquesas (now both part of French Polynesia) in the early years AD. The final great waves of Polynesian migration are thought to have taken place around 400 AD to Easter Island and between 500 and 800 AD to the other islands of modern French Polynesia, the Cook Islands and to New Zealand. Pukapuka in the Cooks, however, is thought to have been settled directly from Samoa or even earlier from Tonga.

It's uncertain exactly when the first settlers did reach the Cook Islands. Legends trace Rarotongan ancestry back about 600 years but early ceremonial adzes found on the islands are much older and the ancient Ara Metua road on Rarotonga is thought to be about 1000 years old. For the population to have grown from a small initial settlement to a size sufficient to construct such a major project it is assumed at least 500 years must have elapsed. Thus there may have been settlements on Rarotonga, and probably the other southern islands, for 1500 years.

Early Cook Islands Society

Rarotonga has always been the most important island of the Cooks and it's assumed the culture of its early in habitants was largely duplicated on the other islands.

Pre-European Rarotonga was divided into districts headed by a hierarchy of chiefs the most important of whom was the *ariki*. The districts were divided into *tapere* populated by a related group known as *ngati* and headed by a lesser chief known as a *mataiapo*. *Tapere* were typically around 150 hectares in area and had a population of 100 to 200. Each *tapere* had its own religious ceremonial ground or *marae*. The *koutu* was a similar centre, used for meetings and political functions. Larger *marae* and *koutu* served entire districts.

Although in some respects this pattern of relationship and land ownership was firmly established in other ways it was quite flexible. The line of chieftainship, for example, was not totally based on the male line and early European visitors gravely misunderstood the Rarotongan system by trying to translate what they observed into purely European terms. Hereditary titles could also be created and an *ariki* who became particularly powerful might have to create *rangatira* titles as a reward for his faithful supporters.

A chief's control over his people was related to his *mana*, a sort of supernatural power which he was felt to possess. A person's *mana* came not only from his birth but also from his achievements and status. *Mana* could not only be gained it could also be lost. An *ariki* who became unpopular (for example by interfering excessively in the distribution of crops) might suddenly find that his followers perceived a dramatic decline in his *mana*, which could even lead to his losing control.

Control of *tapu* was a powerful weapon for an *ariki*. Certain activities were *tapu* or forbidden for supernatural reasons and since a chief could often decide what was or was not *tapu* this gave him considerable power. It was the people's strong belief in an *ariki*'s combination of inherent *mana* and control of *tapu* which made the *ariki* so powerful and allowed them to exert control over their people without necessarily having the physical means to exert their will. Unfortunately the early missionaries failed to fully understand the structure of the Rarotongan society and virtually ignored the operations of the pre-European religion.

The islands were not as extensively cultivated as the first missionaries' reports may have indicated and many crops were disastrously susceptible to the occasional severe hurricanes. A bad storm could completely destroy an island's crops and lead to terrible famines until replanting could be completed.

European Explorers

The Spanish explorers Alvaro de Mendana and Pedro Quiros were the first Europeans to sight islands in the group in 1595. They sailed through the northern group and stopped at Pukapuka. In his expeditions of 1773 and 1777 Captain James Cook explored much of the group although, remarkably, he never sighted the largest island, Rarotonga. That honour was left to the mutineers on *HMS Bounty* who touched upon Rarotonga in 1789. The mutiny actually took place after the *Bounty* sailed from Aitutaki. Those modern historians who place the blame for the famous event on the seductive qualities of Polynesian women, as opposed to Captain Bligh's cruelty, possibly had the Cook Islanders in mind! From Rarotonga the mutineers sailed on to Pitcairn Island in their search for a refuge where they would not be reached by the long arm of the British navy.

Cook, following what was virtually an English tradition of attaching truly terrible names to truly exotic places, dubbed the group the Hervey Islands. Later, a Russian cartographer renamed them, with an equal lack of inspiration, the Cook Islands. It was not until the islands were annexed by New Zealand that the whole southern and northern group were known by the one name.

Missionaries

Missionaries followed the explorers and the Reverend John Williams made his first appearance at the island of Aitutaki in 1821. He left two Polynesian 'teachers' behind and when he returned two years later they had made remarkable progress. Indeed the conversion of the Cook Islanders, generally accomplished in its initial stages by Polynesian converts, went far faster and more easily than it had done in the Society Islands, from where the missionaries generally came.

Papeiha, the most successful of these original missionaries, was moved to Rarotonga in 1823 and he laboured there for the rest of his life. In that period the missionaries totally swept across the islands and established a religious control which has held strong to this very day. They did their best to completely wipe out the original island religion and traditions, establishing what was virtually a religious police state. The height of their power was from 1835 to 1880 when their rigid and fiercely enforced laws were backed up by a system where fines on wrongdoers were split between the police and judges. Naturally this turned police work into an extremely lucrative profession and in parts of Rarotonga one person in every six was in the police force, ready and willing to turn in their neighbours for a cut in the proceeds. The missionary 'Blue Laws' included strict limitations on what you could do and where you could go on a Sunday. There was even a law requiring any man who walked with an arm around a woman after dark to carry a light in his other hand!

Although their influence was huge, the missionaries left the actual government of the islands to the native chiefs or *ariki*. Therefore while Rarotonga, the headquarters for the London Missionary Society, became an important centre for the group it was not a government centre. The individual Cook Islands remained as separate and independent entities. Due to their relative isolation, small populations, lack of economic importance, and their generally poor harbour facilities the islands were largely neglected and ignored by traders, whalers and the European powers. The missionaries also worked hard at keeping other Europeans at arm's length.

The fact that the *ariki* system of government, the traditional land in-

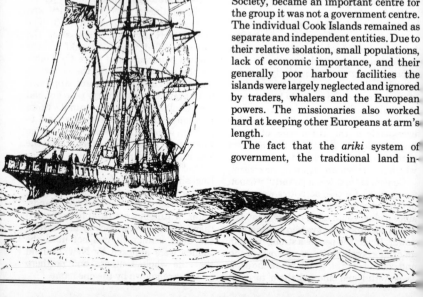

Mission ship
John Williams

heritance system, the native language and many other cultural attributes remained intact shows that the missionaries did not completely obliterate the original island culture, despite the drastic changes they brought. Even the old religion, which had been abandoned by the entire population as far as the missionaries knew, continued to survive among a select few.

Cannibalism

At one time the Cook Islanders certainly practised cannibalism. Although the early islanders rarely ate meat (their pigs were poor specimens and difficult to breed) there were plenty of fish and cannibalism was not, as it has been in some areas of the world, a protein supplement. It appears that in the Cooks it was an activity more closely associated with the supernatural acquisition of the *mana* or power of one's adversaries. It was also a way of exacting revenge: to eat your defeated opponent was probably the most telling indignity you could subject him to. The pioneering missionary William Wyatt Gill reported the following cannibal recipe:

The long spear, inserted at the fundament, ran through the body, appearing again with the neck. As on a spit, the body was slowly singed over a fire, in order that the entire cuticle and all the hair might be removed. The intestines were next taken out, washed in sea-water, wrapped up in singed banana leaves (a singed banana-leaf, like oil-silk, retains liquid), cooked and eaten, this being the invariable perquisite of those who prepared the feast. The body was cooked, as pigs now are, in an oven specially set apart, red-hot basaltic stones, wrapped in leaves, being placed inside to insure its being equally done. The best joint was the thigh.

If you really want to learn something about the practice of cannibalism in the Cooks, read *Cannibals & Converts* by Maretu (see Books section), who is the only author who has written not only as a historian but also a participant!

Disease, Population Decline & Slavers

The missionaries intended to bring far more than just Christianity to the islands of Polynesia: they planned to bring peace, an end to cannibalism and infanticide and a general improvement in living standards. Unfortunately they also brought previously unknown diseases and destroyed the islanders' traditional culture. The consequences were a drastic and long lasting population decline. The poor Cook Islanders took the onslaught of deadly new diseases as a message from above to abandon their old religion and fall in with the new.

Undoubtedly the diseases would have soon arrived – courtesy of traders and whalers – whether or not the missionaries had brought them, but the statistics are nevertheless horrifying. When the missionaries first arrived in Rarotonga in 1823 the population was probably around 6000 to 7000 (it's around 10,000 today). The first major assault on this population was the arrival of dysentery, from Tahiti, in 1830. It killed nearly 1000 people in a single year. A whole series of common European diseases, from whooping cough to measles, smallpox and influenza, followed. Each was previously unknown in the Cooks and each took a terrible toll.

Throughout the 19th century deaths exceeded births and by 1854, when an accurate census was finally taken, the population of Rarotonga was less than 2500, a decline of about two-thirds! By 1867 the population had dropped to 1856 and although migration from other islands began to create an artificial increase in the population of Rarotonga the decline in the group's total population did not start to level out until the late 19th century. It was not until early this century that a real increase in population began.

The trend of emigrating from the outer islands to Rarotonga that commenced in the 19th century continued, so that although the population decline on Rarotonga slowed it was only at the expense of a greater decline on other islands. Many islanders left for work on other Pacific islands, particularly Tahiti, but also on various plantation islands established by European traders. This migration continues to the present day as islanders move first to Rarotonga and then on, usually to New Zealand or Australia.

Disease was not the only cause of the drop in population. The new housing designs introduced by the missionaries were damp and poorly ventilated and probably contributed to the death rate. In addition, a brutal Peruvian slave trade took a terrible toll on the islands of the northern group, although the trade lasted a mere seven months from late 1862 to 1863. At first the traders may have genuinely operated as labour recruiters but they quickly turned to subterfuge and outright kidnapping to round up their human cargoes. The Cook Islands were not the only ones visited by the traders but Tongareva (Penrhyn) was their very first port of call and it has been estimated that three-quarters of the population was taken. Rakahanga and Pukapuka were also victims of the slavers.

Few of the recruits, whether they went freely, as many did in the beginning, or through baser methods, ever returned to the islands. Over 90% either died in transit to Peru, died in Peru, or died while being repatriated. At the time of repatriation efforts Peru was suffering from a terrible smallpox epidemic and many Polynesians died from this while travelling back and, far worse, brought the disease back to their islands. One ship left Peru with 29 islanders and landed 15 smallpox-infected survivors on the island of Nukuhiva (French Polynesia); the subsequent epidemic killed nearly 1000 people on Nukuhiva and a further 500 on a neighbouring island.

The islanders' limited contact with westerners and the fact that what little contact they had experienced had been relatively benign was a major factor in why they were easy prey for the South Americans. As the missionary William Wyatt Gill commented:

Their simplicity of character, their kindness to visitors, their utter ignorance of the depths of depravity and deceit in the hearts of wicked white men, render them the easy dupes of designing characters.

Protectorate & Annexation

Despite their considerable influence via the missionaries the British did not formally take control of the Cook Islands until 1888. In that year the islands were declared a British protectorate by a Captain Bourke who arrived off Rarotonga in the warship *HMS Hyacinth*. To some extent this inevitable, although reluctant, extension of British control was due to fears that the French might decide to extend their power from neighbouring Tahiti in the Society Islands.

It's indicative of the hasty manner in which the British finally took over the islands that they failed to make a firm decision on just which islands would be included in the protectorate. The unfortunate Captain Bourke also managed to get the ceremony wrong and technically *annex* the islands rather than simply bring them under British protection! This caused some embarrassment and the process later had to be reversed in the southern islands where he had hoisted the flag, although for some reason Aitutaki remained annexed. One by one the others islands in the southern and northern groups were brought under British control.

The first British Resident, F J Moss, arrived in 1891 but his period in the islands was not a great success. In part this was due to his basic failure to understand the complexities of the *ariki* system, and the inappropriate application of European economic assumptions to a wholly different system. Moss was given the shove with some lack of ceremony in 1898 and the new Resident, W E Gudgeon adopted a totally different method of running the islands. He ruled with an iron hand but his methods were also far from universally successful.

In the late 1890s the question of whether the islands should be associated with Britain or New Zealand was batted back and forth. Finally in 1900 Rarotonga and the other main southern islands were annexed to New Zealand and the net was widened to encompass all the southern and northern islands in 1901.

Population & Economics

A major problem facing the islands during the early years of British power was the steadily declining population. The combination of disease, slavery and migration meant that the population of the islands had fallen to less than half the pre-contact level. Gudgeon, whose opinion of the islanders under his charge was far from complimentary, was convinced they were a dying race. Finally in the early part of this century the population started to slowly increase, although there were continuing migration losses, first to Tahiti and later to New Zealand.

Economics was another major problem and an answer to the islands' economic difficulties is still far away. Prior to their takeover the New Zealand government was convinced that the Cooks could easily be made self-sufficient but this turned out to be a frequently repeated fallacy. The easy-going Polynesian nature, combined with shipping difficulties which continue to this day, defeated all attempts to tap the obvious agricultural richness of the islands, particularly the volcanic islands of the south.

The difficulty of improving the economic situation in the islands was felt by some officials to be related to the *ariki* system and land ownership patterns. Since land was traditionally controlled by the *ariki*, commoners did not have land to grow produce and the *ariki* often preferred to leave land unused rather than set a precedent for use by outsiders. The power of the *ariki* has gradually been weakened

Makea Takau, Queen of Rarotonga
at annexation

but they wield a lot of influence even today and the land ownership system is still a major disincentive to improving the use of agricultural land.

Independence

During WW II the USA built airstrips on Penrhyn and Aitutaki, but the Cooks remained a quietly forgotten New Zealand dependency. In the 1960s it was belatedly realised that colonies were becoming an aberration and the path to independence was plotted with considerable haste. In 1965 the Cook Islands became internally self-governing but foreign policy and defence were left to New Zealand. The continuing problem of the population drain accelerated after independence.

The close links with New Zealand have precluded the Cook Islands from taking a seat in the United Nations, and it has to be admitted that a country with a population of less than 20,000 is bound to face considerable difficulties in achieving real self-sufficiency in the modern world. The Cook Islanders derive a number of benefits from their semi-independence from New Zealand including New Zealand citizenship and the right to come and go from New Zealand at will. Not only is the population of Cook Islanders in New Zealand actually greater than in the islands themselves but it's also a very important source of income for the nation.

Elections in 1968 brought Albert Henry, leader of the Cook Islands Party and a prime mover in the push for independence, to power. In 1972 he was once again elected prime minister and in January 1974 he was knighted by Her Majesty the Queen. Sir Albert was an Aitutakian and it's said that the people of this island are such keen arguers and debaters that they'll get themselves into trouble simply for the joy of talking their way out of it. With the 1978 elections Sir Albert got himself into deep trouble.

The problem revolved around the great number of Cook Islanders living overseas, principally in New Zealand. Sir Albert feared that the forthcoming election was going to be a close one and dreamt up the ingenious plan of organising a series of charter flights from Auckland, New Zealand to Rarotonga, bringing back hordes of Cook Islanders for a short vacation and a quick visit to the polling booths – where they would gratefully vote for the provider of their free tickets. It worked a treat: 445 Cook Islanders were flown back by the Australian airline Ansett at a cost of $290,000 and Sir Albert was duly re-elected.

Then came the protests of electoral fraud, a High Court case followed and eventually Sir Albert was kicked out of office by the Chief Justice for misappropriation of public funds. In 1980 he was stripped of his knighthood and in early 1981 he died, some say brokenhearted. Go by and see his unusual grave in the Avarua CICC church graveyard, complete with a bronze bust peering down at you wearing Sir Albert's own black spectacles.

A truly multi-dimensional man, Dr Tom Davis, leader of the Democratic Party, was the new Prime Minister. Before returning to the Cook Islands to enter politics he'd qualified as a doctor in New Zealand, become Chief Medical Officer to the islands, written a book titled *Doctor to the Islands*, studied in Australia, sailed a yacht to the US and studied at Harvard, and become an expert on space medicine with NASA.

In the next election in 1983, however, the Democratic Party was bundled out and another Henry took over as Prime Minister. Dr Davis had become Sir Thomas Davis during his period in power but in the 1983 election he even lost his seat in parliament. Unfortunately for the new leader, Geoffrey Henry, a cousin of Albert Henry, politics in the Cook Islands is a family affair and his family quickly turned against him. When another important Henry withdrew his support Geoffrey Henry soon found he'd lost his parliamentary majority. Parliament was dissolved, a new election was called and this time around the Democratic Party squeezed back in with Sir Thomas Davis once more Prime Minister. In his own electorate Sir Thomas' majority was just five votes in this second 1983 election.

In 1984, a split occurred in the governing Democratic party. As a result, they lost their majority, and the loyal Democrats started lobbying with the opposing Cook Islands Party (CIP). This led to the first coalition, with the Demos and CIP's facing off against the rebel Demos. Also in 1984, Geoffrey Henry came in again, this time as Deputy Prime Minister under Sir Thomas.

It was not to last for long. In 1985, just a couple of days before the South Pacific Forum convened in Rarotonga, Sir Thomas sacked Geoffrey Henry, and the Deputy Prime Ministership was taken over by Terepaii Maoate, the former deputy leader of the opposition under Geoffrey. This caused another split, resulting in another coalition, this time with loyalist Democrats and CIPs in

Top: Dancers at the Tiare Festival parade, Avarua, Rarotonga (NK)
Left: Boys beside the road display Aitutaki's major export crop (LB/C)
Right: The Banana Court Bar, Rarotonga – one of the best bars in the Pacific (TW)

alliance against a mixture of rebels from both parties.

In 1987, yet another split occurred. The entire cabinet was sacked by Parliament and Sir Thomas was booted out as Prime Minister. Then the Demo/CIP coalition elected all the same cabinet ministers back in again, with Dr Pupuke Robati, the former minister from the Northern Group island of Rakahanga, as Prime Minister. The Deputy Prime Minister, Terepaii Maoate, retained his seat.

In 1989 Geoffry Henry was again returned to power as Prime Minister after five years in opposition. However the CIP only managed to secure 12 out of the 24 contested seats.

Politics may be colourful but the Cook Islands are generally quite stable, despite all the ins and outs of the various individual characters. The government's biggest problem is simply managing the economy and trying to keep some sort of balance between the meagre exports and the avalanche of imports.

GEOGRAPHY

The Cook Islands have a total land area of just 241 square km – that's about a quarter of the area of the Australian Capital Territory or of Rhode Island (the smallest USA state). This inconspicuous land mass is scattered over about two million square km of sea, an area as large as western Europe. The islands are south of the equator, slightly east of the International Date Line and about midway

between American Samoa and Tahiti. Rarotonga is 1260 km from Tahiti and 3447 km from Auckland, New Zealand.

The 15 islands are conveniently divided into northern and southern groups, separated by as much as 1000 km of empty sea. The islands are:

Southern Group

island	land area (square km)	type
Rarotonga	67.2	high volcanic
Mangaia	51.8	raised atoll
Atiu	26.9	raised atoll
Mitiaro	22.3	raised atoll
Mauke	18.4	raised atoll
Aitutaki	18.1	high volcanic & lagoon atoll
Manuae*	6.2	coral lagoon atoll
Palmerston	2.0	coral lagoon atoll
Takutea*	1.2	low coral atoll

Northern Group

Penrhyn	9.8	coral lagoon atoll
Manihiki	9.8	coral lagoon atoll
Pukapuka	5.1	coral lagoon atoll
Rakahanga	4.1	coral lagoon atoll
Nassau	1.2	low coral atoll
Suwarrow*	0.4	coral lagoon atoll

* unpopulated

There are some clear differences between the two groups quite apart from their geographical separation. The southern islands are generally larger, more heavily populated, economically better off and more closely connected with the outside world. They're actually a continuation of the Austral Islands in the south of French Polynesia. They lie along the same north-west to south-east fracture in the earth's crust. The southern islands are also volcanic, mountainous islands while the northern islands are coral atolls. The southern islands make up about 90% of the total land area of the whole Cook Islands.

That simplistic definition of high volcanic islands in the south versus atolls in the north can be further refined. Only Rarotonga, which is the youngest island in the group, is a straightforward volcanic, mountainous island like Tahiti in French Polynesia. Aitutaki is mountainous, but also has a surrounding atoll reef like Bora Bora in French Polynesia.

Four of the southern group – Atiu, Mangaia, Mauke and Mitiaro – are raised atolls. They have been raised up from the ocean floor at some time in the past and their fringing reef has become a rocky coastal area known as a *makatea*, surrounding a central region of volcanic soil. In Atiu and Mangaia the *makatea* surrounds a hilly central plateau while Mauke and Mitiaro are virtually flat with a swampy central region. Two of the southern group are uninhabited and very small while Palmerston is a coral atoll like the northern group, and indeed is sometimes included with those islands.

All the northern group are coral atolls and most take the classic Pacific form with an outer reef encircling a lagoon and small islands dotting this reef. An atoll of this type is basically a submerged volcano – only the outer rim of the volcano breaks the surface of the sea and this is where the reef and islands are. The lagoon in the centre is the volcano crater. All the northern islands except Penrhyn rise from the Manihiki Plateau, an area of the ocean bottom 3000 metres deep. Penrhyn rises from west of this platform where the ocean is 5000 metres deep. The Penrhyn volcano is thus much 'higher' than the other northern islands. Nassau is unique in the northern group because it is simply a single island with an encircling reef – not a group of islands around a lagoon. All the northern atolls are very low – waves can wash right over them in hurricanes and you have to be very close in order to see them from a ship.

CLIMATE

Rarotonga, the largest and most important of the Cook Islands, is virtually directly south of Hawaii and about the same distance south of the equator as Hawaii is north. The climate is therefore very similar to that of Hawaii although the seasons are reversed: December is the middle of summer, August the middle of winter. July and August can be rather cool.

The Cooks have a pleasantly even climate year round with no excesses of temperature, humidity or rainfall although it can rain quite often. Rarotonga, with its high mountains, is particularly likely to be wet and although you'd have to be unlucky to suffer one of the rare week-long rainy periods an umbrella is not a bad thing to take with you. The wettest months are usually December through March when around 25 cm of rain can fall each month. These are also the hottest months although the seasonal variation is very slight.

Despite the relatively heavy annual rainfall some of the islands, particularly the atolls of the northern group, suffer from severe water shortages and great care must be taken to conserve water supplies.

Hurricanes usually come in the summer season from November to March. On average a mild hurricane will pass by two or three times a decade but extremely severe hurricanes are a much rarer occurrence, happening only about once in 20 years.

The last one was Hurricane Sally, which struck the Northern Group island of Suwarrow on 26 December 1986, moved southwards and made a loop or two before hitting Palmerston on 31 December, and then made a fair bee-line for Rarotonga, arriving with full force at Rarotonga on 1 January '87. Lots of material damage occurred, but no loss of life, and international relief efforts helped to put the island back together before long. Everybody on Rarotonga has drama-filled hurricane stories to tell!

FLORA & FAUNA

In common with most other Pacific islands the fauna is limited. The only native mammals are rats (which reach plague proportions on many islands) and bats. Pigs were introduced at some early stage, however. Today many of them run wild and cause a great deal of damage. There are many domestic pigs which are usually kept by the simple method of tying one leg to a coconut tree. Not unexpectedly they frequently escape. There are also a great number of dogs on Rarotonga and limited numbers of goats, horses and cattle.

Birds are more plentiful although the number of land birds is very limited and they have been considerably affected by the iniquitous mynah bird. Introduced from India, supposedly to eat wasps or hornets or something, the mynah found life in the Cook Islands so cushy that it didn't need to bother about doing what it was originally brought in for. Today the mynah is found in great numbers on most islands and has considerably reduced the number of native birds. In Rarotonga in particular you have to go up into the inland hills to find native birds.

Despite the limited number of birds there are some of great interest to bird-watchers including a surprising number of endemic birds – birds found only in the one localised area. Birds of particular

interest include the cave-dwelling Atiu swiftlet on the island of Atiu, the chattering kingfisher of Atiu and Mauke and the Mangaia kingfisher of Mangaia. For more information pick up a copy of the booklet *Guide to Cook Islands Birds* by D T Holyoak (Cook Islands Library & Museum, Rarotonga, 1980).

Of course there are many fish in the waters around the islands. Fortunately for divers, sharks are not a problem. The islands of the southern group generally have such shallow lagoons that sharks and other large fish are usually found only outside the reef. Outside the reef, however, the drop-offs are often very steep and there are wonderful opportunities for scuba divers. Some divers even see whales, particularly in September and October.

There are some other creatures you're likely to come across in the Cooks. Around Rarotonga, on the sandy lagoon bottom of Aitutaki and on other islands there are great numbers of sea slugs, also known as *bêche de mer* or in Maori as *pirau*. Certain varieties of these strange sausage-like creatures are a noted delicacy. Bright-blue starfish are also a common sight. On land as well as in the water the Cooks have a great number of crabs – ranging from amusing hermit crabs to large coconut crabs.

The island flora varies widely from island to island. The two most noticeable features are probably the coconut palm and the great variety of flowers which seem to grow with wild abandon almost everywhere. On the atolls of the northern group the soil is usually limited and infertile and there is little vegetation apart from the coconut palms. Rarotonga has a wide variety of vegetation. The damp, mountainous central part of the island is densely covered in a luxuriant jungle with ferns, creepers and towering trees.

The raised atoll islands of the southern group such as Mangaia or Atiu are particularly interesting for the sharp dividing line between the fertile central area with volcanic soil, the swampy transition zone between the fossil coral *makatea* and the central region and the wild vegetation on the *makatea* itself. Although the *makatea* is described as rocky and infertile it's actually covered with amazingly lush growth, although the actual range of vegetation that can survive in this inhospitable region is very limited.

GOVERNMENT

The Cook Islands have a Westminster parliamentary system of government like that of England, Australia or New Zealand. Of course with a population of 20,000 it's on a small scale and the Cook Islands Parliament inhabits an inconspicuous building beside the Rarotonga airport. It was originally built as a hostel for airport workers during the airport's construction in 1974 and later converted for use as the Parliament building. The Prime Minister has an office here and another one over the Post Office in Avarua.

The Parliament has two houses. The lower house or Legislative Assembly has 24 elected members. The upper house or House of Ariki represents the island chiefs but they have only advisory powers.

Away from Rarotonga each island has an appointed Chief Administrative Officer or CAO. This is a direct carryover from the Resident Agent of colonial times and indeed the CAO's house on each island is still known as The Residency. The CAO generally has more power than the elected Island Council.

ECONOMY

The Cook Islands' economy is far from balanced – exports are far lower than imports. The biggest factor in making up the shortfall is good old foreign aid, particularly from big-brother New Zealand. Considerable amounts of money are also sent back by Cook Islanders living abroad – remember there are more Cook Islanders living overseas than are actually in the Cooks.

Exports are almost totally dependent on New Zealand so if the Kiwis sneeze the Cook Islanders catch a cold. New Zealand is a small market and for the Cooks it has sometimes been a fickle one. The biggest export category is clothing and footwear which enjoys privileged entry into New Zealand. Next up comes fresh fruit and vegetables. Citrus fruit is the major agricultural export although pineapples (from Atiu), other tropical fruits such as bananas and papayas (pawpaw) and vegetables such as beans, tomatoes, capsicums (bell peppers) and zucchini (courgettes) are also exported. Much of this produce is air-freighted out; an important plus for tourism is that agriculture creates an additional demand for aircraft. The inevitable copra, produced throughout the Pacific, is another important export and there is also a continuing supply of pearl shell.

The most important money earner for the Cooks, however, is tourism. It's number one and growing faster than anything else. Other important money earners include the Cook Islands' beautiful and cleverly marketed postage stamps and the status of the islands as a tax haven.

For the casual visitor it's very hard to get any sort of handle on the economy of the Cooks, or more particularly of Rarotonga. On one hand the balance of trade is undoubtedly pretty horrific and the Cook Islanders live far beyond their means. On the other hand everybody is undeniably well fed. It's a popular joke that when *Merry Christmas Mr Lawrence* (a WW II prison camp drama starring David Bowie) was filmed in Rarotonga it proved impossible to find 500 people who looked thin enough to appear as prison camp extras. Extras had to be flown in from New Zealand.

In fact the excess of food is appalling – food simply drops on the ground and rots. The fat 'plop' of breadfruit landing on the road is a familiar sound to anybody strolling around Rarotonga. Avocadoes grow in such profusion that they are chiefly used as pig food. Exotic tropical fruits litter the ground around trees all over the island. It's a wasteful and saddening sight but, in part at least, it can't be blamed on the Cook Islanders – it's simply too difficult and too expensive to get this excess produce to market and the market (New Zealand) is too small to absorb it in any case.

What is surprising, given this agricultural excess, is how bloody expensive things are. If there's so much produce that it falls to the ground because it's not worth picking how come vegetables are five times more expensive than they are in Australia? Even oranges, the one really important export crop, are much more expensive. Why is the market in Avarua such a pale shadow of the colourful, packed, bustling markets of other countries? Why are the supermarkets packed with imported fruit juice from New Zealand when they produce excellent fruit juice right here in Rarotonga? It's true many of the supermarket shoppers are island visitors but not every local resident grows their own produce. And let's not even think about the ultimate obscenities: canned fish on a Pacific island.

Perhaps from the point of view of a western work ethic, living in Rarotonga is simply too easy. The climate and the soil is of a type where any stick shoved into the ground is a tree by next week and bearing fruit by the week after. Islanders comment how a couple of months work a year provides all the food they could possibly eat and the hardest work they have to do is getting their export produce to the airport on Saturday mornings. Yet the outside world beckons beyond this easy life; alcohol is a major problem with the younger people and the population drain to the bright lights of Auckland continues unabated.

Land Ownership

The Cook Islands' land ownership policy has a great influence on the islands' economy and its social patterns. A law makes it impossible for outsiders to own land in the Cooks by prohibiting anybody from selling or buying land. Land ownership is purely hereditary and land can only be leased to an outside party. As usual with any such arrangement it's a two-edged sword.

The plus side is that there has been no invasion by the outside world. No

international hotel groups have bought up the coastline of Rarotonga and international jet-setters haven't grabbed land all over the islands for holiday homes. But on the other hand there are no large and efficient agricultural operations which might have encouraged exports and helped solve the problems which lead to such an awesome proportion of Rarotonga's agricultural output simply rotting. Nor is anybody very keen on spending money or effort on improvements to land or buildings. Why bother? You can't sell it to anybody and if your children have all moved abroad there's nobody to even leave it to. There are a surprising number of derelict houses around the islands.

The land ownership policy has its amusing consequences as well. Because land is passed from generation to generation but never sold to outsiders people start to own curiously divided chunks of property. Many families seem to have a house by the coast, a citrus plantation somewhere else, a taro patch somewhere else again and the odd group of papaya trees dotted here and there. It can be a full time job commuting from one farmlet to another.

Today the houses you see around the islands are almost all cheaply made imitation-European-style with fibro walls and tin roofs. Very few of the old *kikau* houses with their roofs thatched with pandanus remain.

PEOPLE

In the 1986 census the resident population of the Cook Islands was 16,455, with another 1000 people visiting on census day, bringing the total to 17,455. There's at least that number again outside the Cook Islands, most of them in New Zealand where Cook Islanders have residence rights. The story of the Cook Islands' population is a story of continuing movement from the outer islands to Rarotonga and from there to New Zealand.

Over 90% of the population lives on the southern islands. None of the lightly populated atolls of the northern group have a four figure population. Population estimates are:

island	group	population
Rarotonga	southern	9678
Aitutaki	southern	2391
Mangaia	southern	1235
Atiu	southern	955
Pukapuka	northern	760
Mauke	southern	687
Manihiki	northern	508
Penrhyn	northern	496
Rakahanga	northern	283
Mitiaro	southern	272
Nassau	northern	118
Palmerston	northern	50
Suwarrow	northern	6

There are a number of unpopulated islands in both the northern and southern groups.

The population is over 90% Polynesian – closely related to the Maoris of New Zealand. Maoris and Cook Islanders even speak basically the same language and the Cook Islanders relate stories of how they set out to populate New Zealand from Rarotonga. There are small minorities of Europeans, principally New Zealanders, and Chinese.

There are often subtle differences between the islands, in some cases due to their isolation. The people of Pukapuka in the north, for example, are in some ways more closely related to Samoa than to the other islands of the group; geographically the northern Cook Islands are closer to Samoa than they are to the southern Cook Islands.

CULTURE

Visitors to the Cooks often only get a superficial impression of the place and are disappointed, upon seeing the close-cut lawns, the western-style clothing, the electricity and the New Zealand-type houses, that there is so little sign of Polynesian culture. Yet, right underneath this thin western veneer, layer upon layer of the old Cook Islands culture survives.

It's in the land system – how it's inherited, how it's managed, how it's leased but never sold. It's in the way people transact business. It's in the concept of time. Tradition survives intact in hospitality, in how to dance and make music and celebrate, in the wearing of flowers and in so many other day-to-day things.

Every native Cook Islander is part of some family clan, and each family clan is connected in some distinct way to the ancient *ariki* system of chiefs, sub-chiefs and landed gentry which has survived for centuries in an unbroken line. Rarotonga's six *ariki* clans are still based on the original land divisions from when the Maoris first came here.

Even today, when an *ariki* is installed, the ceremony takes place on an ancient family *marae*. The new *ariki* and all the attendants are dressed in the traditional ceremonial leaves and the ancient symbols of office – a spear, woven shoes, a feather-shell-tapa cloth headdress, a woven fan, a huge mother-of-pearl shell necklace and other emblems – are presented. You'll see these things in museums, but for Cook Islanders, they are not just museum pieces.

You'll see many graves of the ancestors beside modern houses. For many Cook Islanders, the spirits of the ancestors are an ever-present reality. The spirits are not feared as 'ghosts' are in some other cultures. It is simply a fact of life that they live here along with everything else.

Dance

Dancing in the Cook Islands is colourful, spectacular and popular. The Cook Islanders are reputed to be the best dancers in Polynesia, even better than the Tahitians say the connoisseurs. You'll get plenty of opportunity to see dancing as there are dances on all the time, particularly at the ubiquitous 'island nights'. Entry charges to see the dances are usually only two or three dollars if you arrive at an island night around 9 or 9.30 pm, after the buffet. Some of the nightclubs also host dance performances.

The dancing is often wonderfully suggestive and, hardly surprisingly, this caused some upset to the Victorian European visitors. You can almost sense William Wyatt Gill, the observant early missionary, raising his eyebrows as he reported that:

Respecting the *morality* of their dances, the less said the better; but the 'upaupa' dance, introduced from Tahiti, is obscene indeed.

Things haven't changed much!

The sensual nature of Cook Islands dance is rooted in its history, when dances were performed in honour of Tangaroa, god of fertility. This also explains the similarity in the dances of the Cook Islanders, Tahitians and Hawaiians, all of whom shared the same religion, taking

their god Tangaroa with them as they migrated from one island group to another.

If you go to the annual dance championships in Rarotonga the points which judges watch for will probably be outlined. They include the difficulty of the dance, the movements of the hands which must express the music, the facial expressions and the grace with which the dance is done. Male dances tend to be aggressive and energetic, female dances are often all languid suggestiveness and gyrating hips. It's a lot of fun. Don't concentrate solely on the dancers – the musicians are wonderful to watch and the audience often gets involved in a big way. Some of the fat mamas are simply superb and, despite their weight, can shake a hip as well as any young *vaine*. Take note of how it's done though; a feature of almost every island night is dragging an unsuspecting *papa'a* on stage to perform!

Of course western ideals of beauty have gained considerable ascendancy these days and it's only as they get older that some Polynesian women start to widen so dramatically. In the missionary period William Wyatt Gill wrote:

The greatest requisite of a Polynesian beauty is to be fat and as fair as their dusky skin will permit. To insure this, favourite children in good families, whether boys or girls, were regularly fattened and imprisoned till nightfall, when a little gentle exercise was permitted. If refractory, the guardian would even whip the culprit for not eating more, calling out 'Shall I not be put to shame to see you so slim in the dance?'

Another interesting thing to see is how much the traditional dance movements permeate even the modern 'western-style' dancing here. Go to the Banana Court or any other nightclub and you'll see disco, pop, rock-n-roll and even sometimes ballroom dancing spiced with hip-swaying, knee-knocking, and other classic island movements. Don't be afraid to join in and try it yourself, after you've seen how it's done – the locals will love it and you'll have a great time too!

Arts & Crafts

Although the arts and crafts of the Cook Islands today are only a shadow of their former importance they were once widespread and of high quality. The early missionaries, in their passion to obliterate all traces of heathenism, did a comprehensive job of destroying much of the old art forms but, fortunately, they also saved some of the best pieces, many of which can now be found in European museums.

There was no real connection between the southern high islands and the northern atolls in the pre-European period and the art of the small islands to the north is much more limited. Domestic equipment and tools, matting, and inlaid pearl shell on canoes and canoe paddles were about the extent of their work. In the south however, a variety of crafts developed with strong variations between the individual islands.

The Art of Tahiti by Terence Barrow (Thames & Hudson, London, 1979) is more accurately a guide to the art of Polynesia and includes an interesting chapter on the Cook Islands.

Wood Carving Figures of gods carved from wood were amongst the most widespread art forms and were particularly common on Rarotonga. These squat figures, variously described as fisherman's gods or as images of specifically named gods such as Tangaroa, are similar to the Tangaroa image which has become symbolic of the Cook Islands today. Staff gods with repetitive figures carved down a pole, war clubs and spears were other typical Rarotongan artefacts. The incredibly intricately carved mace gods, often from Mangaia, and the slab gods from Aitutaki, were other examples of wood carving which are no longer found today.

Ceremonial Adzes Mangaian ceremonial adzes were an important craft now found only in museums. At first they probably had an everyday use but with time they became purely ceremonial objects and more and more stylised in their design. Each element of these adzes was beautifully made – from the stone blade to the carefully carved wooden handle and the intricate sennit binding that lashed the blade to the handle. Ceremonial adze making probably died out about 50 years ago.

Buildings Houses and other buildings were made of natural materials which decayed rapidly so no ancient buildings survive to the present day and very few buildings of traditional construction remain on any of the southern islands. Wood carving was only rarely used in houses although some important buildings, including some of the first locally built mission churches, had carved and decorated wooden posts. Artistically impressive sennit lashing was, however, found on many buildings. Since nails were not available the wooden framework of a building was tied together with carefully bound sennit leaf. Each island or area had its own distinctive style for the plaiting of the sennit and this skill is still followed today. If you are on the island of Mangaia you can see fine sennit lashing on the roof beams of the CICC churches. The Rarotongan Resort Hotel on Rarotonga commissioned craftspeople to bind the beams of verandahs and walkways with sennit.

Other Woven fans, feathered head-dresses bound with sennit, woven belts and baskets, and wooden seats from Atiu were other artistic crafts of the pre-European period. Some of these crafts have survived but most are found only in museums.

RELIGION

Only a few people today know much about the pre-European religion of the Cook Islands, with its sophisticated system of 71 gods, each ruling a particular facet of reality, and its 12 heavens – seven below the sun, five above it, plus another dominion below the earth – each the dwelling place of particular gods and spirits. The early missionaries held 'pagan beliefs' in such utter contempt that they made virtually no effort to study, record or understand the native religion. They did, however, make great efforts to wipe it out and destroy any heathen images they came across. Fortunately some fine pieces of religious art were whisked away from the islands and are now prized pieces in European museums.

The Cook Islands today are over-whelmingly Christian – in fact people from Christian cultures who haven't been to church (weddings and funerals apart) for years suddenly find themselves going back to church for fun! The major local sect is the Cook Islands Christian Church or CICC. An offspring of those first British missionaries in 1821 it's a blend of Church of England, Baptist, Methodist and whatever else was going down at the time – Roman Catholicism definitely excepted. Today the CICC still attracts 60% of the faithful, in Rarotonga at least. The remaining 40% is squabbled over by the Roman Catholics, the Seventh Day Adventists, the Church of the Latter Day Saints (Mormons, looking as out of place in their white shirts and ties as ever), Assembly of God, Apostolic Revival Fellowship and various other sects. The Baha'is, also, have a small but avid following.

The CICC still has an overwhelming influence on local living habits and in many cases the pattern is exactly that established by those original British missionaries a century and a half ago. Rarotongan villages are still divided into four sections which take turns in looking after the village church and its minister. Each family in the congregation contributes a monthly sum into the church fund which goes towards church costs. The church minister is appointed for a five year period after which he moves to another church. He gets a small weekly stipend but in addition the village group responsible for that week also collects to provide him with a more reasonable weekly salary. The weekly contribution is read out during the Sunday service to the shame or pride of that week's responsible group!

This village responsibility has two sides for the church minister. He is responsible for far more than just his church: if the village teenagers are playing up or hanging around the local bars the blame is likely to be laid at the CICC minister's door! And if he doesn't do something about it then a pitifully low weekly contribution can be interpreted as a strong hint to get on with the job. In fact islanders say that they prefer to have a minister with no local connections – someone from an outer island, say. That

Tangaroa

way if they decide to kick him out by cutting the money supply he's not going to find it so easy to fall back on the food from his local gardens!

Visitors are more than welcome to attend a Sunday church service and it's a delightful event to visit. You're looked upon as a useful way of augmenting the collection and anyway there's nothing much else happening on a Sunday. The service is held mostly in Maori although there will be a token welcome in English and parts of the service may be translated into English as well. The islanders all dress in their Sunday best and the women all wear strikingly similar wide-brimmed hats. When you go, show respect by observing a few simple rules of dress: no shorts for men or women and no bare shoulders. The main CICC services all over the island are held at 10 am Sunday, with other services held on Sunday evenings and other evenings throughout the week.

The major attraction of a CICC service is the inspired hymn singing – the harmonies are superb and the volume lifts the roof! This wonderful singing has a pre-European origin. When the missionaries arrived they found the people were already singing praise to their gods, so they simply put Christian words to the existing songs. Thus the harmony, rhythm and basic structure of the music you hear has its roots in a time long before the arrival of Christianity. Of course you will also hear a familiar tune or two, but sung in a distinctively Cook Islands style!

Early Missionaries

Important figures in the early spread of Christianity through the islands included:

Aaron Buzacott Following in John Williams' footsteps Buzacott not only did most of the work in translating the Bible into Maori, he also composed most of the hymns in the CICC Maori hymn book. Buzacott also supervised the construction of the church in Avarua, Rarotonga and died in 1864 after 30 years' work in the Cook Islands. The story of his life and labours is told in *Mission Life in the Islands of the Pacific*.

William Gill Author of *Gems from the Coral Island* William Gill built the present CICC church at Arorangi, Rarotonga and also its predecessor, destroyed by a hurricane in 1846. He worked at Arorangi from 1839 to 1852 when he returned to England. His brother George Gill was the first resident missionary on Mangaia.

William Wyatt Gill Author of *From Darkness to Light in Polynesia* William Wyatt Gill was no relation to William Gill. He spent 20 years on Mangaia – see the Books section for more details.

Maretu Maretu's accounts (see the Books section) of the spread of Christianity are particularly interesting because they are by a Cook Islander rather than a European. A native of Rarotonga, Maretu later worked as a missionary on Mangaia, Manihiki and Rakahanga.

Papeiha Probably the most successful of the local mission workers Papeiha was brought from Raiatea in the Society Islands and introduced Christianity to Aitutaki in 1821 and to Rarotonga in 1823. He died in Rarotonga in 1867 having spent 46 years in the Cook Islands.

John Williams A pioneer mission worker in the Pacific he was instrumental in the spread of Christianity to the Cook Islands. He was killed (and eaten) on the Vanuatu island of Eromanga in 1839.

HOLIDAYS & FESTIVALS

There are lots of holidays in the Cook Islands and they're good opportunities to see dancing and other activities. The two major sports in the Cooks are rugby which is played with all-out passion from

May to August, and cricket, played over the summer months, particularly December to March.

In addition to the official annual holidays mentioned here, many other island-wide events continually pop up. 'Any excuse for a good time' seems to be the motto, and the locals exuberantly turn out to support all manner of marches, runs, walks, sports competitions, music/dance/art/cultural events, youth rallies, religious revivals, raffle drawings, international mobilisations for one cause or another – you name it! Don't be shy about attending any function – visitors are always welcome.

New Year's Day 1 January is a public holiday and there is horse racing at Muri Beach.

Cultural Festival Week In the third week of February, this week is marked by canoe races, *tivaivai* (quilt) competitions, and arts and crafts displays.

Island Dance Festival Week In the second week of April dance displays and competitions include the important individual Dancers of the Year Competition.

Anzac Day (public holiday) As in New Zealand and Australia 25 April is an annual memorial day for the soldiers of the two world wars, with a special parade and services.

Linmar's 15 km Road Race Taking place just before Easter, the Linmar's shop sponsors a 15 km foot race.

Good Friday & Easter Monday The two principal Easter days are both public holidays. On Easter Monday there is horse racing at Muri Beach.

Queen's Birthday As in New Zealand and Australia the Queen's 'official' birthday

is a public holiday, usually celebrated on the first Monday in June.

Constitution Celebration This 10-day festival starts on the Friday before 4 August and celebrates the 1965 declaration of independence with sporting activities, dances, musical performances, historical and cultural displays, and many other events. This is the major festival of the year.

Cook Islands Art Exhibition Week Second week in September. Visual arts exhibitions from local artists and sculptors.

Cook Islands Fashion Week Third week in October, featuring local fashion and accessories.

Gospel Day (public holiday) *Nuku* religious plays are performed to commemorate the arrival of Christianity to the Cook Islands, when missionary John Williams arrived on 26 October 1823. Every major church participates with Biblical dramatisation involving music, processions, colourful costumes, etc.

Flag Raising Day (public holiday) The raising of the British flag over Rarotonga on 27 October 1888 by Captain Bourke of the HMS *Hyacinth* is celebrated on 27 October, with traditional string band and drumming competitions.

All Souls Day (Turama) The Catholic community decorates graves with flowers and candles on 1 November.

Round Rarotonga Run This popular early November fun run circles the island on the coast road. The record for the 32 km distance is just over 98 minutes.

Tiare (floral) Festival Week In the third week in November tiare float parades and flower arrangement competitions are held.

Takitumu Day The first Saturday in December, visits are made to the 46 *marae* (historical religious meeting grounds) in Takitumu, the section of Rarotonga encompassing the villages of Titikaveka, Ngatangiia and Matavera. Takitumu has historically been the home of some of the most powerful Maori High Priests and sages.

Christmas Day (public holiday) 25 December is celebrated with church services.

Boxing Day 26 December is also a public holiday and there is horse racing at Muri Beach.

New Year's Eve The new year is welcomed with dancing and other entertainment.

LANGUAGE
The language of the Cook Islands is Cook Islands Maori or Rarotongan but English is very widely spoken, usually with a broad New Zealand accent, and you will have no trouble at all getting by with English.

Learning a few words and phrases of Maori can be fun; try the following:

yes	*ae*
no	*kare*
thank you or good	*meitaki*
man	*tane*
woman	*vaine*
goodbye	*aere ra*

kia orana – all purpose greeting, literally 'may you live'
kia manuia – good luck (a toast)
Maori – Polynesian person, the local language, anything local – *tiare Maori* means a local flower
Papa'a – westerner, also English language

If you want to learn some more Maori pick up a copy of *Say it in Rarotongan* (Mana Strickland, Pacific Publications, Sydney, 1979) which is widely available in the Cook Islands. Although there are minor variations between the islands the language is virtually the same everywhere. Cook Islands Maori is also very closely related to the Maori language of New Zealand and to the other eastern Polynesian languages including Hawaiian, Marquesan and Tahitian. A Cook Islander would have no trouble understanding someone speaking those languages. Cook Islands Maori, in its Rarotongan form, was first written down by the missionaries in the 1830s. Later they produced a Rarotongan version of the Bible.

Names
To our ears the Cook Islanders have some pretty strange given names. There's no differentiation between male or female names and they're often given to commemorate some event that happened around the time the name's recipient was born. Big brother just left your island to go off to school on another island? Well you might end up as 'Schooltrip'. The school was far away in Whangarei, New Zealand? You could be named 'Whangarei'. Big brother won a medal in the Commonwealth Games? You're 'Silver Medal'! But why would somebody be named 'Tipuni' or 'Teaspoon'? And why are there so many people named 'Unlucky'?

VISAS

For most nationalities no visa is required and a 31-day stay is granted on arrival. This can usually be extended at the immigration department in Avarua, next door to the airport. If you are intending to visit the northern islands (and not continue through to Samoa) it's wise to extend your permit before heading up as there are often delays. One long-stay visitor wrote that extending his families' visas in Aitutaki took forever. 'The immigration officer was always waiting for information from Rarotonga and we finally got our visas in order three days before we left the Cooks and three months after they had officially expired!'

The only requirements for visitors are the loosely policed 'prior booking' arrangement (see Accommodation) and the fact that your airline tickets out of the country are checked on arrival. Presumably if you intended to depart the Cook Islands by the infrequent shipping service through to Samoa you would have to do some fast talking at the airport and, most probably, provide proof of your financial stability.

If you want to stay longer than the initial 31 days you should have no problems so long as you can show you've got adequate finances and still have your vital ticket out. Each one-month extension costs NZ$25 and must be applied for 14 days before the expiry of your current permit. You're allowed three one-month extensions to take you to a total of four months. If you want to stay more than four months you're supposed to apply from abroad to either the Principal Immigration Officer, Department of Immigration in Rarotonga; to the Cook Islands Government Office in Auckland; or to a New Zealand diplomatic office.

The major problem with long term visits to the Cooks is finding a place to live. No land can be bought or sold and land or property for lease is hard to find, despite the many empty or even derelict houses on the islands. If you're persistent enough, you can usually find a house to rent by the week or the month.

MONEY

The Cook Islands use both Cook Islands and New Zealand currency, both valued exactly the same, which currently exchange at the following rates:

US$1	= NZ$1.60	NZ$1	= US$0.60
A$1	= NZ$1.25	NZ$1	= A$0.80
£1	= NZ$2.70	NZ$1	= £0.37
C$1	= NZ$1.35	NZ$1	= C$0.75

You get about 4% more for travellers' cheques than for cash. There are not many places you can change money – the Westpac Bank in Avarua, its branch bank in Arorangi, the post office in Aitutaki and some hotels. You're better off changing all your money in Rarotonga rather than hoping to be able to change money on the outer islands.

All prices in this book are quoted in NZ$

since the Cook Islands dollar is tied to, and valued the same as, the New Zealand dollar. New Zealand and Cook Islands paper money is used interchangeably – the Cook Islands issued its first bank notes ever in July 1987, in denominations of $3, $10 and $20. The $3 note is a rarity, only one other country has such a note. There is also a complete set of Cook Islands coins – 1c, 2c, 5c, 10c, 20c, 50c, $1, $2 and $5. Most of the coins are the same size and shape as the New Zealand coins (and Australian ones for that matter) so you can use New Zealand coins for pay phones or other such uses quite easily. The old huge $1 Tangaroa coin is now a collectors item – grab one if you get the chance – having been replaced by a smaller, wavy-edged $1 coin, still bearing Tangaroa's image. The $2 coin is also an oddity, it's triangular!

Cook Islands money, whether coins or paper bills, cannot be changed anywhere else in the world, so be sure to either spend it or change it back into New Zealand or other currency before you leave the country.

Ina & the Shark

Until 1987 the Cook Islands did not issue its own bank notes. New Zealand notes, which have exactly the same value as Cook Islands currency, were used instead. The series of notes issued in 1987 are mainly intended for collectors and would be difficult to exchange outside of the Cooks. The notes are $3, $10 and $20 and the three dollar note, with a traditional fishing canoe on the reverse, is definitely something of an oddity! On the $10 note gods of the Southern Cook Islands are illustrated while the $20 note shows a conch shell superimposed on a drum with a turtle shell in the background.

The obverse of the notes all have the same design based on a painting of the legend of Ina and the Shark by Rick Welland. The story is related in a song

Cook Islands
$3 banknote and the
original art by Rick Welland

from the island of Mangaia which tells how the beautiful Ina searched the seas for Tinirau, the god of the ocean. She called on the fish to help her in the search but they were too small to carry her so she rode on the back of a shark. As the journey progressed Ina became thirsty and cracked open a coconut on the shark's dorsal fin. Later she became thirsty again and cracked open another coconut, this time on the shark's head. This did not please the shark which shook her off but she was rescued by Tekea the Great, king of the sharks, who took her the rest of the way to Tinirau's floating island. To this day sharks have a lump on their head which is known as Ina's bump.

Credit Cards

Bankcard, the standard credit card in Australia and New Zealand, is readily accepted at most places in Rarotonga. Visa and Mastercard are also widely accepted; American Express and Diners Club are accepted at the better hotels and restaurants. Some places have signs indicating they accept all and sundry cards but when it comes to the crunch good old Bankcard is all they want to see.

COSTS

There's no way round it, the Cooks are expensive. Fortunately, while they are more expensive than Fiji they're not quite at the horrendous levels of Tahiti and French Polynesia. The New Zealand connection is both a factor for and against the steep costs. The Cook Islands are heavily dependent upon New Zealand for their imports so there's a healthy slug on top of New Zealand prices to cover the shipping costs. Shipping is a major element in the high prices of most Pacific islands. Additionally, and again like many other Pacific islands, there's a sad lack of self-sufficiency. It's a major disappointment to see the cans of mackerel and tuna in every trade store when the reef abounds with fish. Similarly, Rarotonga is extravagantly

fertile but, oranges and some other fruit apart, much fruit and produce is imported at high cost. Even eggs are imported from New Zealand although chickens run underfoot in every village.

The plus point about the Cook Islands' strong links to New Zealand is that for a number of years the New Zealand dollar has not been the world's strongest currency. So if the New Zealand dollar sinks relative to your home market currency then prices in the Cook Islands also translate into that much less.

Another factor which can help to cut costs is that there is some cheaper accommodation although camping out is frowned upon. Most importantly, nearly all accommodation offers opportunities for preparing your own food at a substantial saving to eating out. See the Accommodation and Food sections for details.

Many visitors to the Cooks come on all-inclusive package holidays. There are many brochures available on these tours and land costs vary widely depending on the place you stay and whether or not meals or further travel are included.

Tipping & Bargaining

Don't. Tipping doesn't exist in the Cook Islands and a price is a price, don't expect to get it lowered.

TOURIST INFORMATION
Tourist Office

If you want information on the Cook Islands you can write to the Cook Islands Tourist Authority, PO Box 14, Rarotonga, Cook Islands (tel 29-435, telex RG 62054).

Overseas Offices

In New Zealand there's the Cook Islands Government Office in the Auckland suburb of Parnell or contact the Cook Islands Tourist Authority representative, Travel Industry Services Ltd, PO Box 3647, Auckland (tel 79-4314, telex NZ 21419, fax (09) 37-1546).

In Australia contact the Cook Islands

Tourist Authority representative at Walshes World, GPO Box 51, Sydney, NSW 2001 (tel 232-7499, telex AA 70655, fax (02) 221-8297). The Cook Islands airline, Cook Islands International, also has information on the Cooks. In Sydney, it's at 50 King St (tel 268-1431), toll free (008) 251-442, telex AA 20143, fax 262-1117). They also have an office in Melbourne at 408 Bourke St (tel 668-1401, telex AA 30085) and general sales agents throughout the country. The Australian company Ansett Airlines manages and operates Cook Islands International so their offices can also provide information. Any Air New Zealand office should also be able to provide at least some information.

There's now a Cook Islands Tourist Authority representative in Hong Kong, too. It's Pacific Leisure, in the Tung Ming Building, 40 Des Voeux Rd Central, Box 2582, Hong Kong (tel 524-7076, cable Mypleasure, telex 73038 MYPLS HX).

GENERAL INFORMATION
Post

Postage stamps are a major source of revenue for the government. They produce some beautiful stamps and by limiting the supply and availability they've managed to make many of them valuable collectors' items. The Cook Islands' Philatelic Bureau was set up by an American entrepreneur, Finbar Kenney. He was entangled in the late Sir Albert Henry's fly-in-the-voters programme in 1978 but despite NZ$80,000 in fines and court costs he continued to manage the lucrative stamp trade. You'll find the Philatelic Bureau office directly opposite the post office in Avarua, offering a wide selection of stamps, coins and bills.

At the least, you can send some attractively stamped postcards home from the Cooks. Postage rates include:

	aerogrammes & postcards	air letters
Pacific	65c	70c
North America	70c	85c
Europe	75c	95c

You can receive mail c/o poste restante at the post office, where it is held for 30 days.

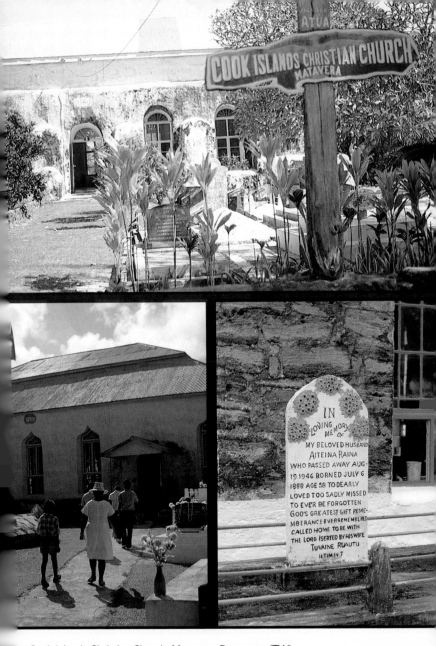

Top: Cook Islands Christian Church, Matavera, Rarotonga (TW)
Left: Sunday service at the Arorangi CICC church, Rarotonga (TW)
Right: Gravestone, Titikaveka CICC church, Rarotonga (TW)

Top: Which way to the beach in Mauke? (LB/C)
Left: Typical island transport, Arorangi, Rarotonga (TW)
Right: Island road, Atiu (TW)

Telephone

Rarotonga has a modern phone system. Big red pay phones are found in many hotels, bars, restaurants, etc and require a 10c coin for local calls. International collect calls can be made from any telephone; for other international calls, visit the Cable & Wireless office on Tutakimoa Rd behind Avarua, open 24 hours a day, seven days a week. International calls are always charged at the same rate – there is no cheaper time to call. Cable & Wireless also has public booths for telex and fax, and it's from here that international telegrams must be sent.

On the outer islands, phone systems, if they exist at all, are not so modern. In Aitutaki, for example, all calls must still be placed through an operator.

Electricity

Electricity is 240 volts, 50 cycle AC just like in Australia and New Zealand and the same three-pin plugs are used. US two-pin plugs can often be bent to fit although, of course, the voltage is different. In Rarotonga the supply is usually regular and quite dependable. On smaller islands it may be available only when the generator is running and will shut down sometime in the evening. On very small islands plan on packing your own generator if you want power.

Business Hours

Monday to Friday, 8 am to 4 pm is the usual business week and shops are also open on Saturday mornings from 8 am to 12 noon. Small local grocery stores often keep longer hours. The main Westpac Bank in Avarua, Rarotonga is open 9 am to 3 pm, Monday to Friday. The handful of other banks are usually open only 9 am to 12 noon.

Nearly everything is closed on Sunday – bars close at midnight on Saturday; even the two local airlines don't fly on Sundays. The only exceptions, again, are the small local groceries, some of which open for a couple of hours very early Sunday morning and for a couple of hours again in the evening. Even most restaurants are closed on Sunday, except for hotel restaurants, which serve all meals, seven days a week. Several of the larger hotels serve up special Sunday meals – brunches in the late morning, barbecues in late afternoon.

Time

The Cook Islands are east of the International Date Line. This is effectively one of the last places in the world; tomorrow starts later here than anywhere else. More precisely when it is 12 noon in the Cooks the time in other places (making no allowances for daylight saving and other seasonal variations) is:

Auckland, New Zealand	10 am next day
Sydney & Melbourne, Australia	8 am next day
San Francisco & Los Angeles, USA	3 pm
London, England	10 pm

Remember, however, that in common with many other places in the Pacific the Cook Islands also have Cook Islands Time, which means 'sometime, never, no hurry, no worries.'

The International Date Line

The early LMS missionaries generally came to the Cook Islands from Sydney, Australia and were unaware that they had crossed the International Date Line and should have turned the calendar back a day. This anomaly continued for 75 years until 1896 when Christmas was celebrated two days in a row and the Cooks came into line with the rest of the world. Or at least some of the Cooks came into line; it took a bit longer for the message to get to all the other islands and for it to be accepted. Accounts of visiting ships at that time indicate that considerable confusion existed for a while.

MEDIA
Newspapers & Magazines

Rarotonga has a daily newspaper, the

Cook Islands News. It provides a very brief summary of international events and a nearly equally brief coverage of local events. All in all it provides something between 30 and 60 seconds of reading time on an average day.

The *New Zealand Herald* arrives in Rarotonga on the same day it's published, three times a week according to flight schedules - at this writing, Monday nights, Thursday and Saturday mornings. Most other overseas papers and news magazines take a long time to get to the Cooks, so their news is somewhat dated by the time you receive it.

Search is a monthly journal published by the Rarotonga branch of the University of the South Pacific, with thought-provoking essays and articles on a wide variety of issues pertaining to the islands.

Radio & Television

The Cooks have two local radio stations, one AM frequency and the other FM frequency, the first FM station in the south Pacific. Apart from local programmes they also broadcast Radio Australia's overseas news service.

Television has yet to come to the Cooks - the topic of its advent remains under discussion year in and year out - but videos have hit the islands in a big way, with video rental shops popping up like mushrooms and more and more homes and hotels getting VCRs. All the video systems are VHS-PAL.

On Rarotonga, the only movie theatre currently in operation is the Empire Theatre in Avarua, where a censoring board meets weekly to judge whether the films scheduled for the week are fit to be shown. However, there is no censorship of video films and at least one local minister reports that the effects of these video films on the minds of the locals is quite noticeable.

HEALTH

The Cook Islands provide no unexpected health risks apart from putting on weight through overeating and inactivity! The water is drinkable and there are no risks from diseases of insanitation, unless you should happen to come at one of the highly unusual times when rainfall has been low,

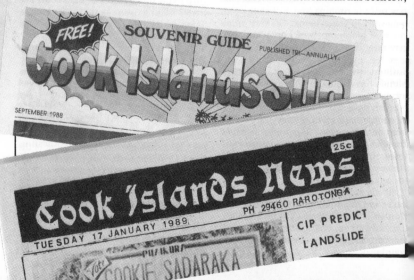

in which case you might want to boil your water before use.

As at any tropical beach locale, you should beware of the sun. Don't overdo exposure on the first days and wear a good sun screen to protect against sunburn.

Be careful not to cut or scratch yourself on coral – coral wounds seem to be particularly susceptible to infection, they can take a long time to heal and can be quite painful. If you do get cut on coral, be sure to clean the wound thoroughly, get all the coral out, and keep it clean and disinfected until it heals. You can treat the wound with mercurochrome or try the local cure – fresh lime juice. Cuts and scratches are prone to infection anywhere in the tropics, treat them with care.

Stomach upsets and diarrhoea are a common occurrence for travellers everywhere, simply due to changes in diet. For mild diarrhoea the best treatment is to simply do nothing and wait for your system to recover. The process can be speeded up by not eating, sticking to liquids like tea or flat soft drinks. Chewing papaya (pawpaw) seeds is a local natural remedy.

At certain times of year mosquitoes can be a real nuisance although they are not malarial. Bring repellent. Large centipedes can give a painful or irritating bite but they rarely come indoors. There are also large red and yellow wasps but they are easily spotted and easy to avoid. The tiny reddish-brown ants have an annoying but not dangerous sting.

In the sea and lagoon, you won't encounter sharks, but on very rare occasions someone finds a poisonous stonefish. Jellyfish also appear at certain times. If you're out reefwalking don't thrust your arm into deep tidepools, eels sometimes lurk there.

No vaccinations are required unless you're arriving from an infected area but it's always wise to keep your vaccinations and boosters up to date. In the remote islands medicine is often at a very basic level.

DANGERS & ANNOYANCES

The Cook Islands are probably safer than most places in the world, but a certain amount of precautionary common sense is still called for. In general, you will find the Cooks to be just as idyllic as the tourist brochures lead you to expect and the people some of the friendliest you will ever meet. As anywhere crime does exit but with normal minimal caution you should have no problems.

Theft

Theft is not a problem in the Cook Islands and you have to be very slack to get anything stolen. People routinely leave car windows down (risking inundation from a sudden tropical downpour) and I've never seen so many cars and motorcycles standing around with their keys left in the ignition. I imagine a mugging would be a major event and so long as you don't leave cash heaped on your bedside table there doesn't seem to be too much theft from hotel rooms either.

Despite all this Maureen and I both had something stolen in the Cooks and both losses, we discovered afterwards, were fairly typical Cook Islands thefts. On the second night we were in the Cooks I lost a running shoe (that's right, just one) from the verandah in front of our room. I saw the thief: he was dark-brown, had floppy ears, a long tail, four legs and would have said 'woof' if I'd managed to catch him and ask him why the hell he took it. I never found it. Right at the end of the trip Maureen lost her bikini bottom (that's right, just the bottom) off the clothesline. Afterwards we were told that shoe-stealing dogs and off-the-clothesline knicker nickers were notorious. So watch out.

Motorcycles are easy to hotwire and it's conceivable that someone could take off with yours. Always be sure to remember the license plate number.

Swimming

In the sheltered lagoons swimming could

hardly be safer but be very wary of the breaks in the surrounding reef. Currents are especially strong here as the lagoon waters sweep swiftly out to the open sea and often straight downwards due to the very steep drop-offs just off the reef. The island of Rarotonga has several such passages, notably at Ngatangiia, Avaavaroa, Papua and Rutaki, and they exist on other islands as well. Danger signs for swimmers are posted on shore but you should check the position of reef passages before swimming. Some unnecessary deaths have occurred. Venturing outside the reef should only be done if you are fully aware of the tidal flow and currents and then only with great care.

FILM & PHOTOGRAPHY

You can buy straightforward film – print film, Kodachrome 64, etc – at the two photo shops, the duty free shops and other outlets in Rarotonga. Finding unusual film – Ektachrome, black & white film – can sometimes be more difficult. And the prices, duty free or not, are very unexciting. Kodachrome 64 is approximately twice the price you pay at discount outlets in Australia. In other words bring your film with you!

On Rarotonga, you can get film developed at two places. Cocophotos (tel 20-555) is a professional photography shop and lab on the main road on the airport side of Avarua. Colour printing prices are approximately NZ$19 for 24 exposures, NZ$25 for 36. Same-day developing is available. Cocophotos also does slides, enlargements, photography jobs (weddings, etc) and offers free pick-up and delivery from any motel. Kis Photo in the Pharmacy in Avarua (tel 29-292) offers one-hour colour print processing at the same prices.

Developing standards are as high as anywhere in the world because they use the same modern equipment. Kodachrome slides have to be sent overseas for processing.

The Cook Islanders are generally quite happy to be photographed but the usual rule applies – it's polite to ask first. It's also worth bringing some high speed film with you. If you're photographing in the densely forested mountain country of Rarotonga or in the *makatea* of Atiu it can be surprisingly dark. Bring a flash if you plan to visit the caves in Atiu or Mangaia.

ACCOMMODATION

Although there is no visa requirement for most visitors to the Cooks there is one stipulation for all visitors – you must have pre-booked accommodation. This isn't quite as totalitarian as it sounds. For a start they don't say how long you have to book for – conceivably you could book for the first night only. Secondly there's nothing to stop you changing your mind as soon as you see the place you've booked into and to go looking elsewhere – some people do change their minds quite legitimately. And thirdly nobody really checks – you could easily walk out of the airport saying you'd booked into Hotel A or Z when you'd done nothing of the sort.

This rule is supposedly to stop people sleeping on beaches, camping out or staying with local people. The Cooks could indeed do with more cheap hostel accommodation or even a good campsite. At present camping is virtually impossible.

People staying longer term often rent houses locally. You can get quite a reasonable place for NZ$100 to NZ$150 a week. No doubt some people stay with locals although it probably doesn't happen much on Rarotonga. On outer islands where accommodation is very limited you will have to stay with local people. On some islands – such as Mangaia – this is organised, arranged and prices are firmly set. On others, where visitors are few and far between, arrangements are likely to be very informal. In such a case make certain that you do not take advantage of Polynesian hospitality, be sure to pay your way.

Rarotonga is far and away the major

attraction and it has far and away the most places to stay. There's a handful of places to stay on Aitutaki, a place or two at a few of the other islands but everything else is on Rarotonga. On Rarotonga there are two major hotels, some hostel-style accommodation and pretty much everything else is motel-style, closely related to the motels in New Zealand. This is no bad thing in one way – nearly every place has some sort of kitchen or cooking facilities.

On the other hand it's a disappointment that the accommodation makes so little reference to the Pacific. The average Rarotongan motel could easily be in Newcastle, Australia or Palmerston North, New Zealand. They're dull, dull, dull. The *Atiu Motel* on Atiu, which makes extensive use of local materials, could show most places in Rarotonga how things can be done with just a little imagination.

FOOD

Rarotonga has a surprising variety of good restaurants. Elsewhere in the islands the choice of places to eat is likely to be much more limited. Even on Rarotonga the scattered locations of the places to stay and the places to eat mean you're quite likely to be either a long way from restaurants or find that the conveniently located eating places are very limited.

Fortunately most accommodation, particularly on Rarotonga, has kitchen facilities so you can fix your own food and save some money along the way. The catch here is that much food is imported and is consequently expensive. There are a couple of ways of improving this situation. First of all look for local produce. There's little in the way of local packaged food apart from the expensive Frangi fruit juices and the terrible Vaiora soft drinks; virtually all other packaged food is imported (usually from New Zealand) and is very expensive. The price tags on anything from packaged cereal to yoghurt can be astonishing.

There are, however, plenty of locally grown fruits and vegetables. The trick is finding them – you're likely to do much better looking for them in local shops or even buying direct from the locals than from big supermarkets. Whereas locally grown vegetables can be very reasonably priced, in the supermarkets you often find the vegetables have come straight from New Zealand and cost several times the New Zealand or Australian prices. Bread is also baked locally on the larger islands and again is fairly reasonably priced.

The second way of economising is to bring some supplies with you. All food imports must be declared on arrival and although fresh produce may be confiscated you should have no problem with packaged goods. You can save some money by bringing your favourite breakfast cereal, rice, noodles, spaghetti, even packaged meals and the like.

Remember that just as costs on Rarotonga are much higher than in New Zealand, Australia or North America, costs are also much higher again on the outer islands than on Rarotonga. If you're going to the outer islands it's wise to bring some food supplies with you both for economy and variety. If you're going to a place with no formal accommodation it's only polite to supply as much food as you eat and some more besides.

Local Food

You won't find too much local food on the restaurant menus but at 'Island Night' buffets or at barbecues you'll often find interesting local dishes. An *umukai* is a traditional feast cooked in an underground oven: food is *kai*, underground is *umu*.

Some dishes you might come across include:

breadfruit – spherical fruit which grows on trees to grapefruit size or larger. They're so abundant that they fall and squash on the roads everywhere. Breadfruit is more like a vegetable than a fruit and can be cooked in various ways, including like French fries.

eke – octopus

ika mata – marinated fish with coconut cream

kumara – sweet potato

poke – pawpaw pudding

puaka – suckling pig

taro – all purpose tuber vegetable. The roots are prepared rather like potato; the leaves, known as *rukau*, can also be cooked and look and taste very much like spinach.

DRINK

The truly local drink is coconut water and for some reason Cook Islands coconuts are especially tasty.

Cook's Lager, the islands' own beer, is quite good as well as being the least expensive beer in the Cooks. It's been available since late '87 and you can tour the brewery in Avarua Monday to Friday 8 am to 4 pm, Saturday 8 am to 12 noon. The tour is followed by a free beer.

A wide variety of New Zealand beers are also available, Steinlager being the favourite, plus Fosters (Australian), San Miguel (Philippines), Heineken (Dutch), Hinano (Tahitian) and Viamo (Western Samoan). They cost around NZ$2 to NZ$3 a can in bars and are cheaper from shops.

Until independence Cook Islanders were strictly forbidden western alcohol which was, however, permitted to *papa'a*. Beer is a problem on the Cook Islands: far too much money gets spent on it and drunkenness is a social problem. Fortunately it's nowhere near as major a problem as it is in some countries in the Pacific, Papua New Guinea in particular.

The South Seas Distillery makes two delicious local liquors from pineapples grown on the island of Mangaia. Mangaia-Ara has the fresh pineapple taste, while Rum-Ara is rum-flavoured, made by ageing the pineapple liquor in an oak cask for one year. Both are strong (40% alcohol) and taste best mixed with pineapple or orange juice. You can visit the distillery in Mangaia, or the more accessible bottling plant and tasting room in Avarua, Rarotonga.

Imported liquors are available in the Cooks, but are heavily taxed and thus

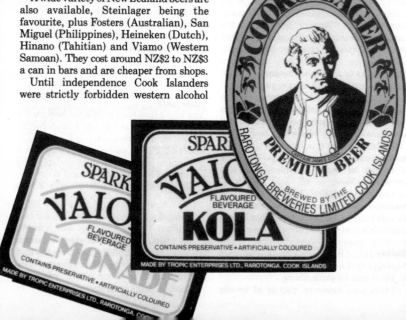

quite expensive. The widest selection is found at Cook Islands Liquor Supplies on the main road near Avatiu Harbour in Rarotonga.

The local soft drink bottling company is called Vaiora – they make cola, lemonade, orange and other fairly awful imitations. Apart from the drinks being flat the bottles are notable for having labels that always fall off.

Try the excellent coffee from Atiu and if you go to that island you should definitely try to go to a *tumunu* or bush beer-drinking session. *Tumunus* are also held on Mauke but although there is a bar named the Tumunu on Raro they are really only found on those two islands. The old ritual *kava* ceremonies, to which the *tumunu* is related, were completely stamped out by the missionaries and are no longer found in any form.

BOOKS & BOOKSHOPS

There have been a surprising number of books written about the Cooks or in which the Cooks make at least an appearance. Unfortunately some of the most interesting are out of print and you will have to search libraries or second-hand bookshops if you want to find them. There are a number of unusual books actually available in the Cook Islands – in Rarotonga try the Bounty Bookshop, Island Crafts, Cook Islands Trading Company and the Library & Museum. All have a selection of books you'd be lucky to find elsewhere. The University of the South Pacific, opposite the library, also has a wide selection of books for sale and all their titles can be bought cheaper here than anywhere else.

You can borrow books from the extensive Pacific Collection at the library by obtaining a Temporary Borrower's Card – see the Library section below.

History

Alphons M J Kloosterman's *Discoverers of the Cook Islands & the Names they Gave* (Cook Islands Library & Museum, Rarotonga, 1976) gives a brief history of each island, the early legends relating to that island and a record of its European contact. It makes interesting reading and there's an exhaustive listing of the early descriptions of the islands by European visitors.

The Cook Islands, 1820-1950 by Richard Gilson (Victoria University Press, Wellington, 1980) is a rather starchy and dry history of the Cooks. There is an introductory chapter on the pre-European history of the islands but basically it relates the story from soon after the first missionary contact up until just after WW II. It concentrates heavily on boring descriptions of the economics and politics of the Cook Islands since annexation by New Zealand. It's also almost exclusively a Rarotongan history; little mention is made of the other islands in the group.

The Gospel Comes to Rarotonga by Taira Rere (Rarotonga, 1980) is a concise, locally written account of the arrival of Christianity in the Cook Islands, particularly in Rarotonga. There are interesting thumbnail sketches of the various important participants in this chapter of the islands' history.

H E Maude's *Slavers in Paradise* (Australian National University, Canberra & Stanford University Press, Stanford, 1981) provides a readable yet detailed analysis of the Peruvian slave trade which wreaked havoc in Polynesia between 1862 and 1864. Some of the northern atolls were particularly badly hit by this cruel and inhumane trade. This book is available in the Cook Islands as a paperback from the University of the South Pacific (Suva, Fiji, 1986).

Cook Islands Politics: the inside story (Polynesian Press, Auckland, 1979) is an anthology of articles by 22 writers, representing many points of view, telling the story of the toppling of Prime Minister Sir Albert Henry from power: the historical background, the intrigues, corruption and bribery.

Missionaries' Accounts

The Reverend William Gill turned up in Rarotonga in 1839 and lived in the Cooks for the next 30 years. His book *Gems of the Coral Islands* (1858) is perceptive but heavily slanted towards the missionary view of life.

The Cooks had a second William Gill: William *Wyatt* Gill was no relation at all to the other William Gill (he was only 11 years old when the older Gill started his missionary career) but he lived on the island of Mangaia for 20 years from 1852 and wrote several important studies. *From Darkness to Light in Polynesia* was originally published in 1894 but has recently been reissued in a University of the South Pacific paperback (Samoa, 1984). *Cook Islands Customs* (University of the South Pacific, Suva, 1979) is a direct reprint of a fascinating illustrated manuscript originally published in 1892, telling of the customs of the Cook Islanders as the missionaries found them when they arrived.

Mission Life in the Islands of the Pacific (University of the South Pacific, Suva, Fiji, 1985) is another recently reissued missionary account. It traces the life and work of the Reverend Aaron Buzacott, who arrived in Rarotonga in 1828 and laboured as one of Rarotonga's foremost missionaries until his death in 1864. In Rarotonga his name is remembered in the Avarua CICC church which he constructed, the Maori Bible which he helped to translate and in the many hymns which bear his name in the CICC hymn book.

Amongst these reports on the Cook Islands by foreign-born missionaries there is also one interesting insider's point of view. The author, Maretu, was born in the Ngatangiia area of Rarotonga sometime around 1802. He was an older child when Europeans first visited Rarotonga in 1814 and a young man when the missionaries first arrived in 1823. Maretu later became a missionary himself and worked on several other islands in the group. In 1871

he sat down to write, in Rarotongan Maori, an account of the extraordinary events he had witnessed during his lifetime. Translated into English and extensively annotated, his illuminating work has been published as *Cannibals & Converts* (University of the South Pacific, 1983).

Residents' Accounts

A number of Cook Islands residents have gone into print with their tales of life in the South Pacific. Unfortunately very few of them are currently in print.

Robert Dean Frisbie's books *The Island of Desire* (1944) and *The Book of Puka-Puka* (1929) are classics of South Pacific life. Frisbie was born in the USA and ran a store on Pukapuka; his eldest daughter Johnny also wrote of the Cook Islands in *Miss Ulysses from Puka-Puka* (1948) and *The Frisbies of the South Seas* (1959). Frisbie's first book, *The Book of Puka-Puka*, subtitled 'A Lone Trader on a South Sea Atoll,' was a collection of articles he wrote for Atlantic Monthly and is available in paperback from Mutual Publishing, Honolulu, Hawaii. See the Pukapuka section of the Northern Group chapter for more about the colourful Frisbies.

One of the best known resident writers would have to be Tom Neale, who wrote of his life as the hermit of Suwarrow in *An Island to Oneself* (Holt, Rinehart & Winston, New York, 1966; Fontana Silver Fern, Auckland, 1975; and Avon paperback). Tom Neale lived by himself on the beautiful but totally isolated northern atoll of Suwarrow for a total of six years in two three-year spells in the late '50s and early '60s; his book recounts this period. He then returned to Suwarrow and lived there for most of the '70s until he was brought back to Rarotonga shortly before his death in 1977. Many Rarotongan residents have anecdotes to relate about Tom Neale or opinions of him and it seems that his book, which was actually ghost written, makes him out to be a much more reasonable fellow than he actually was. One person's opinion was that he was so cantankerous an uninhabited island was the only place for him. See the Suwarrow section for more details.

Isles of the Frigate Bird (Michael Joseph, London, 1975) and *The Lagoon is Lonely Now* (Millwood Press, Wellington, 1978) are both by Rarotongan resident Ronald Syme. The first book is mainly autobiographical and relates how the author came to the Cook Islands in the early '50s and eventually settled down. Before finally ending up on Rarotonga he spent some time travelling around the islands and also lived on Mangaia for a while. The second book is more anecdotal, relating legends, customs and incidents of island life. It becomes a little tiresome at times with its constant reiteration of how much better things were in the 'old days' and how much better things could be if progress wasn't forced down the islanders' throats. Nevertheless both books make interesting reading and a good introduction to life in the Cook Islands, particularly during the period of great changes in the years since WW II.

There are countless earlier accounts of life in the Cooks, few of them currently available. F J Moss, for example, wrote of the islands in 1888 in his book *Through Atolls & Islands*. Julian Dashwood (*Rakau* or 'wood' in Maori) was a long running islands character and wrote two books about the Cooks. *I Know an Island* was published in the 1930s and he followed that with a second book in the '60s published as *Today is Forever* in the USA and as *Island Paradise* in England. *Sisters in the Sun* by A S Helm and W H Percival (Robert Hale, London, 1973) tells of Suwarrow and Palmerston.

The Cook Islands' former Prime Minister, Sir Tom Davis, has also written a book of his time as a doctor on the islands, *Doctor to the Islands*.

Legends

Once you're in the Cooks you'll see numerous paperback books about the traditional legends of the various islands, many of them published by the University of the South Pacific's Institute of Pacific Studies. An excellent one is *Atiu Nui Maruarua* (University of the South Pacific, 1984), with stories of the island of Atiu in two languages, both Atiuan and English. The University of the South Pacific has many others on sale at its Rarotonga Centre, opposite the Library.

Travellers' Accounts & Guidebooks

Across the South Pacific by Iain Finlay and Trish Shepherd (Angus & Robertson, Sydney, 1981) is an account of a trans-Pacific jaunt by a family of four. The Cook Islands section is particularly interesting for its description of taking the Silk & Boyd ship the *Mataora* from Rarotonga through the northern group and across to Western Samoa. If you're considering island-hopping through the Cooks on a local freighter read this first!

The updated version of *How to Get Lost & Found in the Cook Islands* by John and Bobbye McDermott (Orafa, Honolulu, 1979, 2nd edition 1986) is another in the Air New Zealand funded series by a Hawaiian ex-adman. It's one of the better ones with an interesting concentration on the Cook's many colourful characters. The Cook Islands, you soon realise after reading a few books on them, are a pretty small pool. The same big fish keep popping up in every account!

If you want to know more about what types of islands there are, how they are formed and what lives in the sea around them then *Exploring Tropical Isles & Seas* by Frederic Martini (Prentice-Hall, Englewood Cliffs, New Jersey, 1984) makes interesting reading.

If you just want a souvenir of the Cooks *Rarotonga* by James Siers (Millwood Press, Wellington, 1977) has some pretty though at times rather dated photos. A newer book of excellent quality is *The Cook Islands: Images of Polynesia* (Cook Islands Typographical Services, 1988) by

Rick Welland, Robin Brill and Russell Bishop, three expatriates who have lived on Rarotonga for a number of years. Their collection of colour photographs of Rarotonga and other islands in the Southern Group are some of the best you'll see and the book gives an insight into the islands' culture, in both their modern and traditional aspects.

The same publisher also produced *A Hurricane Warning is Now in Force for Rarotonga* by Russell Bishop (1987), documenting the impact of Hurricane Sally on Rarotonga in 1987. Looking around at the island today, it's hard to imagine the devastation.

If you're travelling further afield in the Pacific look for the excellent *South Pacific Handbook* by David Stanley (Moon Publications, Chico, California, 1986). Lonely Planet also has a growing list of individual guidebooks for Pacific nations – see the information page in the back of this book.

Language
Say it in Rarotongan by Mana Strickland (Pacific Publications, Sydney, 1979) gives a good general introduction to the language of Rarotonga. *A Dictionary of the Maori Language of Rarotonga* by Stephen Savage (University of the South Pacific, 1980) is a more complete lexicon. A visit to the library in Avarua will turn up a number of other resources for tackling the language.

Library
Even if you're in the Cooks for only a short stay, you can get borrowing privileges at the library by obtaining a Temporary Borrower's Card. You pay a NZ$25 deposit which is refunded upon your departure plus a NZ$2 monthly library fee. This gives you access to the library's excellent Pacific Collection, which occupies an entire wall of the library, in addition to all the general circulation books. You may also be allowed access to the extensive collection of rare books, for use on the premises only, if you ask the librarian.

THINGS TO BUY
As important as what to buy in the Cooks is what not to buy. What not to buy is cheap tourist junk and there's lots of it. Tangaroa figures with spring-loaded, pop-up penises are about the most tasteless but there are plenty more where that came from. More insidious are the Cook Islands handicraft souvenirs that don't originate from the Cooks at all. A lot of the shell jewellery and wooden bowls were born in the Philippines! There are also plenty of New Zealand Maori items which the unscrupulous might try to pass off as Cook Islands Maori. In fact I'd be very suspicious of anything which could conceivably be made overseas – even supposedly indigenous items like Tangaroa figures. Fortunately the craft shops do seem to be remarkably honest and if you ask if a piece is local or made elsewhere you'll usually be given a straightforward answer.

Local arts and crafts include:

Tangaroa Figures
Tangaroa is the squat, ugly but well-endowed figure you find on the Cook Islands' one dollar coin. The God of Fertility he's become the symbol of the Cooks but it's been a long term rehabilitation because the early missionaries, in their zeal to wipe out all traces of heathenism, did a thorough job of destroying idols wherever they found them. Poor old Tangaroa, along with the rest of the old gods, was banned. When they did start to recarve Tangaroa figures they were often neuter, but now they're fully endowed once again. You can get Tangaroa figures ranging from key ring figures a couple of cm high up to huge ones standing a metre or more high and just about requiring a crane to move them. A figure about 25 cm high will cost around NZ$35.

Hats

The beautiful hats which all the women wear to church on Sundays are a Cook Islands speciality. These *rito* hats are woven of fine, bleached pandanus leaves and the best ones come from the islands of Rakahanga and Penrhyn. They cost from about NZ$50 so they're not cheap, but they're even more expensive in Tahiti.

Baskets

Some good quality basket work is still done but look out for plastic carton strapping and other man-made materials creeping into use.

Shell Jewellery

There's a lot of shell jewellery produced and also larger items like shell lamps. Some of this work is imported, principally from the Philippines, but some fine shell work is produced locally. Before you rush off to buy shells remember that something has to be evicted to provide the shell and conservationists are worried about some species being collected to extinction.

Tivaivai

These colourful and intricately sewn applique works are traditionally made as burial shrouds but are also used as bedspreads or simply as wall hangings. They're very rarely seen for sale; the Atiu Fibre Arts Studio on the island of Atiu has them, but they cost several hundred dollars due to the enormous amount of time required to make them.

Other Souvenirs

There are a multitude of other inexpensive things you can buy as souvenirs of the Cooks. Pure coconut oils and soaps come either in their natural state or scented with local flowers including tiare maori (gardenia), frangipani, starfruit flower and jasmine. The Perfume Factory in Rarotonga sells quality perfumes made from these same local flowers for about NZ$10 a bottle, for both men and women.

Colourful *pareus* come in many styles and thicknesses; original tie-dyed ones of very thin material, costing about NZ$17, are the most popular and the best for the hot climate. You can also find a multitude of T-shirts in the shops around Rarotonga.

Traditional tapa cloth, made of pounded bark, is hard to find nowadays, but they still make it on Atiu at the Atiu Fibre Arts Studio. The Studio's Rarotonga connection is the Colonial Craft House in Matavera village.

Woven pandanus products such as mats, purses and fans are now in short supply on Rarotonga, since the pandanus which used to grow on this island has mostly died off, but you can probably find something if you look around in the arts and crafts shops. On most of the other islands of the southern group, all the traditional pandanus items are still made for everyday use. (This could change on the island of Atiu, though – imported pineapples brought an infestation of mealybugs which have threatened to kill off the pandanus on the island and at present Atiu is importing its pandanus from Mitiaro.) If you visit the outer islands, you can find pandanus products everywhere.

Carved wooden drums are a Polynesian specialty; if you don't find one you like in the crafts houses, see Exham, who operates Exham's Tours on Rarotonga; he is a woodcarver in his spare time and makes beautiful drums and statues. Ukuleles, made of wood and coconut shells, are another good souvenir, although it's not easy to find one to buy since most people just make their own. The Cook Islands Cultural Village in Arorangi village, Rarotonga, sells them and is an excellent source of woodcarvings (including drums), woven items and other traditional crafts.

A kg or two of Atiu Island Coffee is another good souvenir – it's won awards at international competitions. Mangaia-Ara and Rum-Ara, liquors made from the fresh pineapples of the island of Mangaia, are also a popular souvenir and can be bought at the South Seas Distillery tasting room on the traffic circle in Avarua, Rarotonga.

Rarotonga has a number of resident artists and their paintings and other artwork are on sale, often at very reasonable prices. See the Rarotonga chapter for more details.

WHAT TO BRING
The Cook Islands' balanced and moderate climate makes clothing choice a breeze – you rarely need anything warmer than a short-sleeve shirt or T-shirt but nor do you often find it too hot for comfort, the northern atolls apart. Remember, however, that these islands are relatively strait-laced and dress accordingly. Swimming gear is strictly for the beach and even on the beach going topless is frowned upon. Find an isolated beach before considering nudity – this is certainly not the Maldives if you're looking for an overall tan.

Bring an old pair of running shoes or sneakers for walking on the reefs. There are some things you'd rather not step on and coral cuts take a long time to heal. You'll also need those runners if you intend to go climbing or walking on Rarotonga or walking across the razor-sharp makatea on Atiu or Mangaia. Bring a torch (flashlight) if you're going to Atiu or Mangaia; it's essential equipment for exploring the caves. The Cook Islands are, of course, wonderful for snorkelling and

you can either bring your own equipment with you or rent or buy it on Rarotonga.

The Cook Islands are a major supplier of clothes to New Zealand so there's a pretty good choice of clothes locally, although prices tend to be high. Clothing apart, most western consumable commodities are readily available but, again, quite expensive. Better to bring a spare tube of toothpaste or another spool of film rather than have to buy it locally. Don't forget sun screen or suntan lotion although these are readily available. You may find you prefer the age-old local favourite: pure coconut oil, available everywhere. It does wonders for both skin and hair and smells delicious, whether you get it plain or scented with local flowers. Mauke Miracle Oil, a little more expensive, contains herbs which act as a natural sun screen.

The Cooks are a duty free port and there are a number of duty free shops in Avarua but the quantities they deal with are small so the prices, while a pretty good deal for Kiwis, will hardly be competitive with discount dealers in the USA, Europe or even Australia.

If you're planning to travel further afield, particularly if you travel deck class on the inter-island ships to the islands of the northern atolls, come prepared. You'll probably want a sleeping bag and some sort of foam mat to lay out on the deck. Cooking equipment and, of course, food supplies can also be useful.

Occasionally a cruise ship might call on the Cooks, with great luck you might find a passenger-carrying freighter, and some yachts pass through (although the Cooks are nowhere near as popular for yachties as Tahiti, Fiji or Tonga). Basically, however, getting to the Cooks means flying and Rarotonga has the only international airport. Yachties can enter the Cooks at a couple of other islands.

Flying is easy from New Zealand, Tahiti, Samoa, Fiji and Hawaii, fairly easy from Australia, Canada and the mainland USA, not so easy from elsewhere. Visitors from North America have to come via Honolulu, Tahiti or Fiji. Air New Zealand flights from Christchurch, Wellington, Brisbane, Melbourne, Sydney, Tokyo and Singapore all have to transfer at Auckland; Cook Islands International flights from Brisbane, Canberra, Melbourne and Perth all transfer at Sydney. Airlines that fly to the Cooks are Air New Zealand, Polynesian Airlines, Hawaiian Airlines, Air Rarotonga and Cook Islands International.

You know you're heading for somewhere pretty special when you fly out of Sydney on a plane that forms the national airline of two countries. Landing in Apia, Western Samoa, en route, the side with 'Polynesian Airlines' faced the terminal building; when we got to Raro the aircraft faced the other way so that all the locals could see that we had flown with 'Cook Islands International'.

Robert Stephenson, Australia

AIR
From New Zealand
Air New Zealand has two direct flights each week from Auckland and one weekly flight Auckland/Nadi (Fiji)/Rarotonga/ Papeete (Tahiti) and the reverse. The regular one-way economy fare Auckland to Rarotonga is NZ$724 (double for return). Epic excursion return fares from Auckland range from NZ$878 in the low season to NZ$1078 in the high season. To get the low fare you have to travel both directions in low seasons – usually January through April. The regular economy fare from Auckland to Los Angeles with stopovers in the Pacific is NZ$2275 one way, this is no bargain compared to Circle Pacific fares.

Air Rarotonga also has one weekly flight Auckland to Rarotonga and the reverse, priced at NZ$638 one-way, double for return, with the same price all year round. This flight has connections with Wellington and Christchurch, transferring at Auckland. The special Discovery Fare is NZ$799 return during low seasons (January through April, June, July, and 15 September to 8 December), NZ$950 the rest of the year.

Also ask travel agents in New Zealand about package tours to the Cooks – they frequently offer some great deals.

From Australia
Air New Zealand has connections from Australia with fares from Melbourne of A$934 in the low season, A$1121 in the high season. From Sydney the equivalent fares are A$849 and A$986. These are advance purchase fares which must be booked 21 days in advance. There's an aircraft change in Auckland and you must either make careful plans to choose a good connection or spend some time in Auckland. The regular economy fare from Sydney to Los Angeles with unlimited Pacific stopovers (including the Cook Islands) is A$2065 one way, from Melbourne it's A$2125. This is no bargain when you compare it to Circle Pacific fares detailed below.

In late '86 Cook Islands International started a weekly direct flight from Sydney to Rarotonga and return. Fares are the

45

same as with Air New Zealand and the flight takes about 11 hours, with two stops along the way (Noumea and Apia) but no change of aircraft. Connections are also available from Brisbane, Canberra, Melbourne and Perth, transferring at Sydney.

In Australia, too, package tours are often available that offer big savings over purchasing your airfares and accommodation separately. Ask travel agents for details.

From North America

Hawaiian Airlines has a flight to the Cooks from the west coast via Honolulu. Advance purchase fares (14 days in advance) are US$750 round-trip during low season, April through November.

Air New Zealand has service to Rarotonga on a flight departing from Los Angeles, going Los Angeles/Papeete (Tahiti)/ Rarotonga/Nadi (Fiji)/Honolulu/ Los Angeles, or the other way around. This is an excellent way to be able to stop off and visit a couple of other islands at no extra cost – it's a six-month ticket with unlimited stopovers, priced at US$850 from April through November (14-day advance purchase necessary).

You can also make a stopover in the Cooks on a trans-Pacific ticket with several airlines at no extra cost. Many people are taking this chance to see the Cooks, on their way to or from somewhere else. See Circle Pacific Fares and Other Pacific Fares, in the separate sections following.

From Other Pacific Destinations

Air New Zealand has weekly Auckland/ Nadi/Rarotonga/Papeete (and the reverse) flights. Connecting through Auckland, they have service from many other parts of the world.

Polynesian Airlines has a weekly flight Apia (Western Samoa)/Pago Pago (American Samoa)/Rarotonga and return.

Hawaiian Airlines offers the largest variety of flights, with transfers in Honolulu from Guam, Seoul, Taipei (Taiwan), and Tokyo, in addition to many American cities and even Anchorage, Alaska. Once you're in Honolulu, it's a direct six-hour flight to Rarotonga. Other Hawaiian Air flights provide service from Tonga, Pago Pago (American Samoa), Apia (Western Samoa), and Papeete.

Great bargains are often available on flights between Rarotonga and Western Samoa – a Flexi Fare flight costs around NZ$275 return. Ask at travel agents to see what they're offering. Frequently, upon discovering how inexpensive the fares are, visitors to Rarotonga will take a jaunt over to Western Samoa, just because it's a good opportunity to do so.

Circle Pacific Fares

Many more travellers are slotting in the Cooks on a trans-Pacific jaunt, often because of the attractive Circle Pacific tickets. Circle Pacific fares are an extension of the popular Round The World tickets which allow you to combine the routes of two airlines and stop pretty much wherever you choose. Air New Zealand combines with Cathay Pacific, Korean Airlines, Malaysian Airlines, Singapore Airlines or Thai International to offer a NZ$3060 (economy class) Circle Pacific Fare from New Zealand. From Australia the same ticket is A$2240 ex-Sydney or A$2390 ex-Melbourne.

From North America the official Circle Pacific fares are US$2020 or C$2599 and they can originate from Vancouver, San Francisco or Los Angeles. You can fly Air New Zealand through the South Pacific (including Rarotonga) to Australia and return with Thai International, Singapore Airlines or Cathay Pacific through the North Pacific. Shop around as Circle Pacific fares are sometimes discounted several hundred dollars; they must be purchased 21 days in advance. Using one of these tickets you could fly Los Angeles/ Papeete/Rarotonga/Nadi/ Auckland/ Sydney/Los Angeles. Usually four stopovers are included free but there is an extra cost for additional stopovers.

Other Pacific Fares

Air New Zealand also combine with Polynesian Airlines for a Circle Epic fare which allows you to loop out from Auckland to Tonga, Apia, Rarotonga and back to Auckland for NZ$1275.

Or you can get a Polypass for A$999 (US$799) which is valid for 28 days and allows you to fly anywhere on the Polynesian Airlines/Cook Islands International route network during that period. Polynesian fly from Sydney and Auckland to numerous Pacific Islands including Rarotonga, Western and American Samoa, Tahiti, Tonga and Fiji. Contact Ansett Airlines for more details.

Departure Tax

There's a NZ$20 departure tax when you fly out of Rarotonga; for children aged two to 12 it's NZ$10 (children under two are exempt).

Flying to the Cooks

Aviation in the Cook Islands has had quite an interesting history. During WW II, airstrips were built on Penrhyn, Aitutaki and Rarotonga and in 1945 a DC3 service operated every two weeks on a Fiji/Tonga/Western Samoa/Aitutaki/Rarotonga route. This service by New Zealand National Airways Corporation was dropped in 1952 but Tasman Empire Airways Limited had meanwhile started a monthly Solent flying boat service on the 'Coral Route' from Auckland to Papeete via Fiji and Aitutaki. See the Aitutaki section for more details on this route.

The Solent service was increased to once every two weeks and continued until 1960. For a time there were no flights at all to the Cooks apart from infrequent New Zealand Air Force flights. In 1963 Polynesian Airways started a service from Apia in Western Samoa to Rarotonga but this was stopped in 1966 due to new regulations banning small aircraft making such long-distance flights over water. Once again the Cook Islands were left without international connections and it was not until the new airport was opened in the early '70s and big jets could fly into Rarotonga that flights resumed.

YACHTS

The Cook Islands are not a major Pacific yachting destination like French Polynesia, Tonga or Fiji. Nevertheless a steady trickle of yachts do pass through the islands. Official entry points are Penrhyn in the northern group and Aitutaki and Rarotonga in the southern group. Many yachties only visit the uninhabited atoll of Suwarrow in the northern group – illegally if they haven't already officially entered the country. Yachties are liable for the departure tax just like people who arrive by air.

There are basically just two ways of getting from island to island around the Cooks (if you don't own your own yacht). In the southern group you can fly with Air Rarotonga or Cook Islandair or you can take the inter-island freight ships of Silk & Boyd Lines. If you want to go to the northern islands you've got no choice – uncomfortable freighters are all there is on offer! There are airstrips on a couple of the northern islands but the distances are so great that the cost of flying to them in the small aircraft used around the southern islands would be prohibitive.

Rarotonga to Mangaia NZ$100 (AR); Rarotonga to Mitiaro NZ$99 (CI); Atiu to Mauke NZ$68 (CI); Atiu to Mitiaro NZ$58 (CI); Mauke to Mitiaro NZ$58 (CI). Children ages four to 11 (CI) or four to 14 (AR) fly at half fare. The chart illustrates the possible routes.

Air Routes

AIR

Cook Islandair (CI) has Air New Zealand as its majority owner and operates an eight-seater Britten-Norman Islander aircraft plus a 20-seater Twin Otter. Air Rarotonga (AR) is privately owned and operates a 10-seater Beechcraft, a 15-seater Heron and a four-seater Cessna 172 for charters. Between them they fly to Aitutaki (both airlines), Atiu (both), Mauke (both), Mitiaro (CI) and Mangaia (AR). One-way fares (double for return) include Rarotonga to Aitutaki NZ$99 (CI) or NZ$110 (AR); Rarotonga to Mauke NZ$99 (CI) or NZ$110 (AR); Rarotonga to Atiu NZ$87 (CI) or NZ$100 (AR);

Cook Islandair offers a special 'Early Bird' discount of NZ$20 off the normal price if you pay seven days in advance; this discount is available only if you purchase your ticket locally and applies to all flights except the short ones between Atiu, Mauke and Mitiaro.

Neither airline flies anywhere on Sunday. The rest of the week Air Rarotonga flies to Aitutaki twice daily, to Atiu three times a week, to Mangaia four times a week and to Mauke twice a week. Cook Islandair flies to Aitutaki twice daily and to Atiu, Mauke and Mitiaro twice a week. The Cook Islandair flights between Atiu and Mauke, between Atiu and Mitiaro, and between Mauke and Mitiaro

Top: Cook Islandair flight (TW)
Bottom: Flying over the lagoon, Aitutaki (TW)

Top: Loading inter-island ships at Avatiu Harbour, Rarotonga (TW)
Left: On board the wreck of the *Yankee*, Avarua, Rarotonga (TW)
Right: Silk & Boyd freighter *Manuvai*, at the dock in Rarotonga but now wrecked
on the reef at Nassau (TW)

all go once a week, with connections from each of these islands through to Rarotonga on those days.

Another option is to charter a plane through Air Rarotonga, but of course this works out to be more expensive than going on the scheduled flights. You can charter a plane to any licensed airport in the Cook Islands, including the islands of the northern group, and even internationally. The standard charter plane is a Beechcraft Baron 58, accommodating up to five passengers (plus one pilot); larger aircraft are available subject to schedule commitments. The normal charter fare includes the pilot, but if you have a pilot's licence, you can bring in your logbook and see about flying the plane yourself if you wish. Ask at Air Rarotonga for details.

In Rarotonga, you'll find the Cook Islandair office at the Rarotonga International Airport. The Air Rarotonga office is further south along the main road. The airlines' addresses are:

Air Rarotonga PO Box 79, Rarotonga, Cook Islands (tel 22-888, telex 62036, fax 20 979)
Cook Islandair PO Box 65, Rarotonga, Cook Islands (tel 26-304, telex AIR NZ 2541, attn Cook Islandair)

Inter-Island Tours

Several worthwhile tours to outer islands in the Southern Group are operated by Stars Travel (tel 23-669 or 23-683), in Avarua. These packages make an easy way to visit some of the outer islands even if you only have a limited time available.

The Island Combination Tour, departing three times each week, allows you to visit the islands of Atiu, Mauke and Mitiaro all in seven days. Prices start at NZ$436 per person, double occupancy, and include return air fare, all transfers, accommodation and some meals. Three separate plans are offered, allowing flexibility on how much time you spend on which islands and the level of accommodations you wish to choose.

Stars Travel also offers separate two-night packages to Aitutaki (NZ$217), Atiu (NZ$211), Mitiaro (NZ$217) and Mauke (NZ$211) and day tours of Aitutaki (NZ$210). Prices are minimum rates, per person, double occupancy, and can be higher if you opt for more deluxe accommodation.

All of these tours come out cheaper than what you can do for yourself by booking your flights and accommodation separately. Ask to see Stars Travel's printed brochure, spelling out all the various options and prices.

Flying in the Cooks

If you haven't flown on small local carriers like Air Rarotonga and Cook Islandair you've got quite a treat in store. For a start they don't just weigh your baggage, they weigh you as well. Secondly they usually have to arrange the passengers for the best weight distribution – on Air Raro's Beechcraft this means putting the heavies up front. I made one flight where two super-heavies at the front had real difficulty getting their belts round their middles. I usually seemed to be right at the back!

It's out on the outer islands, however, that you get the real feel for island flying. At the airstrips all and sundry turn out to see the planes come and go and to welcome and farewell travellers. Usually they simply drive their trucks out and park them around the aircraft to load and unload. Departures are tearful occasions and the passengers usually leave loaded down with colourful and fragrant *eis*. In fact some flights depart looking like aerial florist's shops and the perfume inside can be quite overpowering!

SEA

Shipping services have had a colourful history in the Cooks: companies have come and gone, ships have run onto reefs, fortunes have been made but more often lost. Despite the increasing use of air services shipping is still of vital importance to the islands. The northern islands can only be served by ship and throughout the islands ships are necessary to bring in commodities and export produce.

Shipping in the islands has two major

problems to face. First of all there are simply too few people and they're too widely scattered to be easily and economically serviced. From the ship owners' point of view shipping between the islands is only feasible with a government subsidy. From the islanders' point of view it's difficult to produce export crops if you can't be certain a ship will be coming by at the appropriate time to collect them.

The second problem is that the islands generally have terrible harbours. The south sea image of drifting through a wide passage in the reef into the clear sheltered waters of the lagoon doesn't seem to apply to the Cooks. In the northern atolls the reef passages are generally too narrow or shallow to allow large ships to enter. In the southern volcanic islands the passages through the fringing reefs are usually too small to let a ship enter and dock. Even Rarotonga's main harbour Avatiu is too small for large ships – or even too many small ones. All this means that ships have to anchor outside the reef and transfer passengers and freight to shore by lighters. At some of the islands even getting the lighters through the narrow reef passages is a considerable feat. Unless conditions are ideal it's not even possible to anchor offshore at some of the Cook Islands and freighters have to be under way constantly, even while loading and unloading.

The Cook Islands' shipping service is usually operated by the one-ship company of Silk & Boyd. Don Silk and Bob Boyd turned up in Rarotonga on their way across the Pacific from New Zealand on their yacht. Their Pacific cruise ended right there when they bought a recently wrecked ketch and found themselves in the shipping business. In mid-89 the Silk & Boyd shipping operation was in limbo as their single ship had been wrecked in late '88. See the Nassau section in the Northern Group chapter for the full details.

At this writing, shipping is being handled by Stars Travel in Avarua, using provisional vessels. Presumably Silk & Boyd will have another ship in operation before too long but the schedule and fare details given below are based on their operations prior to the accident. If you're planning a voyage, check it out with Silk & Boyd (tel 22-442) or with Stars Travel (tel 23-669 or 23-683).

If you plan to explore the outer islands by ship you need to be flexible and hardy. Schedules are hard to pinpoint and unlikely to be kept to. The Silk & Boyd office is beside the Avatiu harbour in Avarua and office hours are Monday to Friday from 8 am to 4 pm.

Generally speaking, the schedule is planned in two-month cycles, with two voyages to the Southern Group and one to the Northern Group occurring within the two-month period. Voyages to the Southern Group take from two to five days; to the Northern Group, it's about three weeks. Along the way schedules are quite likely to change – weather, breakdowns, loading difficulties or unexpected demands can all put a kink in the plans.

At each island visited, the ship stays just long enough to discharge and take on cargo. Travellers thus get the chance to spend a few hours visiting each island before taking off again. Outside of Rarotonga, only the northernmost island of Penrhyn has a wharf; at all the others, you have to go ashore by lighter or barge.

On board the ships, conditions are cramped and primitive: these are not luxury cruise ships. They're also small and the seas in this region are often rough. If you're at all prone to seasickness you'll definitely spend time hanging your head over the side. There are two classes of accommodation on board: cabin class and deck class. Cabin class means you get a cabin – or at least a bunk in a cabin. In deck class you're out on the open deck with everybody else. If it's hot and still it's much more comfortable on deck. If it's pouring with rain you'll wish you were in a cabin. Food in cabin class (cabin class passengers are provided with all meals) is usually pretty reasonable, so long as you're not seasick. In deck class you provide your own food.

Fortunately the trips are usually not too long and many of the islands are only a day's travel apart. Few are more than two or three days apart. In the southern group, fares for a single hop start at NZ$37 for deck class, NZ$75 for cabin class and go up to NZ$95 and NZ$250 respectively if you have to go to five or six islands before reaching your destination. A Rarotonga out-to-one-island and return trip costs NZ$55 and NZ$115 respectively.

Fares are not so simple in the northern group – it depends on where you go and what route you take. Some sample fares include:

	deck	cabin
Rarotonga/Rakahanga	NZ$100.00	NZ$304.75
Rarotonga/Palmerston	NZ$ 40.40	NZ$110.95
Aitutaki/Penrhyn	NZ$ 89.00	NZ$208.60
Aitutaki/Manihiki	NZ$ 75.60	NZ$252.90
Rarotonga/Pukapuka	NZ$105.90	NZ$353.60
complete Northern Group	NZ$306.00	NZ$938.00

The Silk & Boyd office address is PO Box 131, Rarotonga, Cook Islands – telex RG 62042 Traders, fax 22-462, cable SilkBoyd or tel 22-442.

Why They Don't Run to Schedule
In Aitutaki we met a group of marine geologists from Fiji, a woman off to Manihiki to research musical instruments and other associated artefacts and a man off on a loop around the northern islands. Supposedly two days out from Rarotonga towards Manihiki, the ship was already four days behind schedule.

Day one was lost at Mauke when it was too rough and they had to wait for conditions to improve before unloading. Day two was lost because although the ship was not supposed to be going to Aitutaki in the first place it had been diverted there because of the marine geologists and all their equipment. Then because of the day lost at Mauke the ship arrived at Aitutaki on a Sunday instead of a Saturday. Since no

work gets done on a Sunday they couldn't unload and another day was lost. On Sunday night a ferocious wind blew up (some yachties told us the next morning they recorded wind speeds of 50 knots) and continued all day Monday – so again there was no unloading. The marine geologists spent the day climbing hills to see if they could spot the ship, with their equipment, offshore. It had moved round to the other side of the island to shelter from the wind.

On Tuesday we flew back to Rarotonga, leaving them all wondering whether they would get their gear off that day and if the ship would be continuing north that night.

LOCAL TRANSPORT

On Rarotonga there's a bus service, lots of taxis, lots of rental cars and rental motorcycles and pushbikes. On Aitutaki there are a handful of taxis, lots of rental motorcycles and bicycles. On Atiu the sole place to stay has a number of motorcycles to rent. Elsewhere you can walk.

The
Southern
Islands

Introduction

Rarotonga and Aitutaki are the most important southern islands and 99% of visitors to the Cook Islands get no further than these two islands. A trickle do continue to the other islands of the southern group, fewer still to the northern group.

The southern group of islands are larger in terms of both size and population than the northern islands. These volcanic islands are also economically better off than the coral atolls of the northern group.

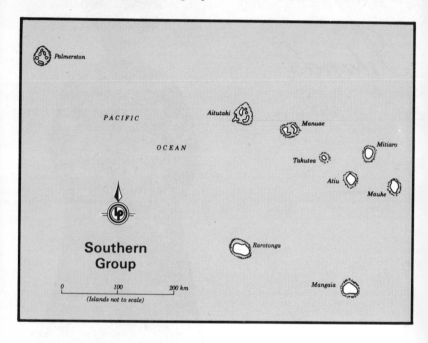

Raratonga

Population: 9678
Area: 67.2 square km

Rarotonga is not only the major island and population centre of the Cook Islands it's also, like Tahiti in French Polynesia, virtually synonymous with the whole island chain. Nobody goes to the Cook Islands – they go to Rarotonga. Many people do not even realise there is anywhere else to go.

The island is extravagantly beautiful – it's spectacularly mountainous and lushly green. The interior is rugged, virtually unpopulated and untouched. The narrow valleys and steep hills are simply too precipitous and overgrown for easy settlement. In contrast the coastal region is fertile, evenly populated and as neat, clean and 'pretty' as some sort of South Pacific Switzerland. You almost feel somebody zips round the island every morning making sure the roads have all been swept clean and the flowers all neatly arranged and watered. Fringing this whole arcadian vision is an almost continuous, clean, white beach with clear, shallow waters and, marked by those ever-crashing waves, the outer reef.

History

Numerous legends touch upon the early existence of Rarotonga which was clearly one of the best known and most important of the Polynesian islands. It is also said to be the island, or one of the islands, from which the Maori people set off on their great canoe voyage to settle New Zealand. Rarotongans believe the reef passage at Ngatangiia was the starting point.

Surprisingly, considering this historic importance and also that it is the largest and most populous of the Cook Islands, Rarotonga was one of the later islands to be 'discovered' by Europeans. The first discovery can probably be credited to the mutineers on the *Bounty*, who happened upon Rarotonga after they had returned to Tahiti and were searching for a remote island where they could hide from the British Navy. This was probably some time in late 1789, but, and this is hardly surprising, the mutineers didn't have much to say about their important discovery.

In any case the mutineers did not set foot upon Rarotonga; nor did the crew of Captain Theodore Walker's *Endeavour* who sighted the island in 1813. Their suggestion that the island might have sandalwood – a valuable commodity – led to the next visitor. Philip Goodenough, captain of the *Cumberland*, showed up in 1814 and spent three months on Rarotonga; three less than harmonious and peaceful months. Unable to find any sandalwood the crew of the *Cumberland* decided to take back *nono* wood instead. This was an unsuccessful gamble as *nono* wood turned out to be of negligible value.

During their stay at Ngatangiia the crew managed to get themselves involved in a number of local squabbles which resulted in the deaths of a number of the crew, including Goodenough's female companion, and, of course, numerous Rarotongans. Eventually the *Cumberland* left Rarotonga in some haste, but two local women and a man were taken with them and left at their next stop, Aitutaki. William Gill later described the *Cumberland's* visit to Rarotonga as a 'continued series of rapine, cruelty, vice and bloodshed.' Understandably, Goodenough did not go into great detail about his adventures so Rarotonga remained comparatively unknown. In the following years a number of vessels visited Rarotonga but none stayed for more than short periods.

In 1821 Papeiha, the Polynesian missionary or 'teacher' from Raiatea in

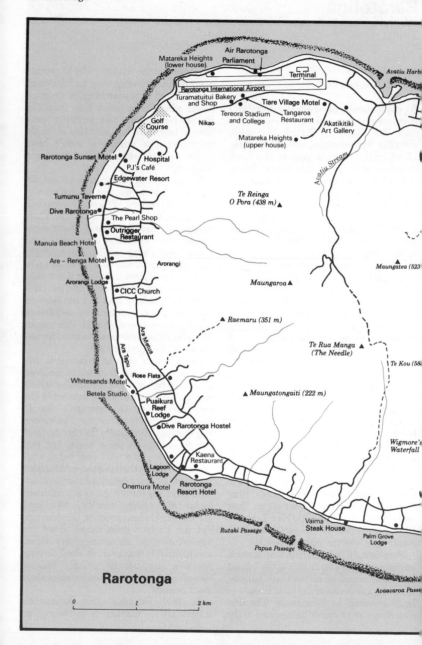

Rarotonga

0   1   2 km

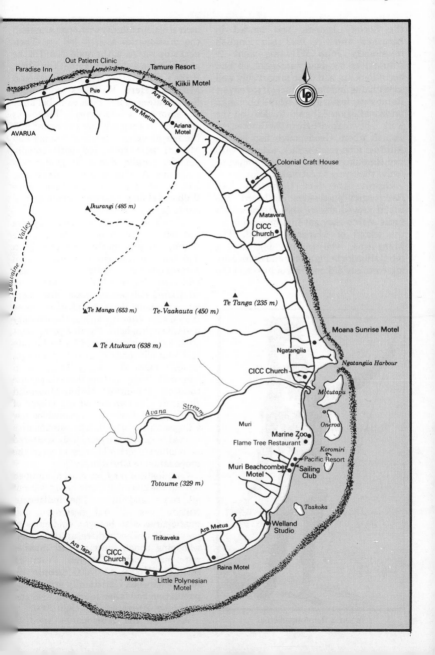

the Society Islands, was landed in Aitutaki and in 1823 the English missionary John Williams went to Aitutaki to see how successful he had been. Papeiha had done remarkably well so Williams and Papeiha set off to convert Rarotonga, leaving two other Polynesian missionaries on Aitutaki to carry on the work. They took with them the Rarotongan women whom Goodenough had left on Aitutaki nine years earlier, together with two Rarotongan men who had somehow found their way to Aitutaki by canoe.

Despite the fact that they had Rarotongan passengers on board, the island proved elusive and after a week's futile search they gave up and made for the island of Mangaia instead. The Mangaians, who to this day have a reputation for being a dour and unfriendly lot, certainly did not rush out to greet the

Tepou, a Rarotongan chief

arrival of Christianity with open arms and the missionaries soon sailed on. Their next stop was Atiu, the main island of the group known as Nga Pu Toru ('The Three Roots') which also includes Mauke and Mitiaro. Here Williams convinced Rongomatane, a notorious cannibal king, to embrace Christianity. This was achieved in a remarkably short time and the neighbouring islands of Mauke and Mitiaro were converted with equally amazing rapidity due to Rongomatane's assistance. As a finale Rongomatane, who had never been to Rarotonga, gave Williams sailing directions which turned out to be spot on.

As he had been on Aitutaki, Papeiha was left on the island to convince the islanders to give up their earlier religion and take on the new one. And, as on Aitutaki, he succeeded with thoroughness and surprising speed. Four months later additional Polynesian missionaries were landed to assist Papeiha and in little more than a year after his arrival Christianity had taken firm hold. The first permanent *papa'a* missionaries were Charles Pitman and John Williams who came to Rarotonga in 1827, followed a year later by Aaron Buzacott. Between them these three men translated the entire Bible into Maori and Buzacott also established the village of Arorangi which was to be a model for new villages on the island. The missionaries wished to gather the previously scattered population together in order to speed the propagation of Christianity.

Cannibalism may have been stamped out but the arrival of Christianity was not all peace and light. The indigenous culture was all but destroyed and missionaries also brought epidemics of previously unknown diseases: dysentery whooping cough, mumps and measles were just some of them. From an estimated 6000 to 7000 people on Rarotonga when Christianity arrived the population had fallen to 2800 in 1848 and in another 20 years to less than 2000.

Although the missionaries tried t

exclude other Europeans from settling more and more whalers and traders visited the island. In 1850-51 more than 20 trading ships and 60 whalers paused at Rarotonga and Buzacott's wife lamented that men of 'some wealth and little religious principle' were settling on the island. The Rarotongans had been firmly warned to beware of the French, however, who had taken over Tahiti in 1843. The dangers of Papism were a major worry for the London Missionary Society!

In 1865 the Rarotongan *ariki*, frightened by rumours of French expansionary intent, requested British protection for the first time. This request was turned down but in the following years the missionaries' once absolute power declined as more Europeans came to the island and trade grew. Finally in 1888 a British protectorate was formally declared over the southern islands and Rarotonga became the unofficial capital of the group.

What to do with the islands next was a subject of some controversy but eventually in 1901 they were annexed to newly independent New Zealand and the close relationship between the two countries that continues to this day was established.

Geology

Rarotonga is the only straightforward, high volcanic island on the Tahiti model in the Cook Islands. The inland area is mountainous with steep valleys, razorback ridges and swift-flowing streams. Most of this area is covered with dense jungle. Rarotonga is the youngest of the Cook Islands: the volcanic activity which thrust it above sea level occurred more recently than on any of the other islands. The major mountains of the island are the remains of the outer rim of the cone. The cone is open on the north side and Maungatea rises in the very centre.

The narrow coastal plain with its swampy area close to the hills is somewhat akin to the raised, outer coral fringe or *nakatea* of several other islands in the southern group. On Rarotonga the plains are far more fertile than on islands like Mitiaro, Atiu, Mangaia or Mauke.

The lagoon within Rarotonga's outer reef is narrow around most of the island but it widens out around the south side where the beaches are also best. Muri Lagoon, fringed by three sand cays and one volcanic islet or *motu*, is the widest part of the lagoon although even here it is very shallow. There are few natural passages through the reef and the main harbour at Avatiu has been artificially enlarged. Yachts also anchor at Avarua and at Ngatangiia.

Orientation

Finding your way around Rarotonga is admirably easy – there's a coastal road around the edge and a lot of mountains in the middle. Basically it's that simple. A number of roads run inland from the coast but if you want to get all the way into the middle, or cross the island from one side to the other, you have to do it on foot.

AVARUA

Avarua, the capital of the Cook Islands and the main town, lies in the middle of the north coast stretch, a couple of km to the east of the airport. It's a sleepy, little port, very much the image of a south seas trading centre. Avarua doesn't demand a lot of your time but it does have a small, interesting museum and library, a fine old church, a couple of interesting shipwrecks and one of the best bars in the Pacific.

Orientation

Finding your way around Avarua is no problem – there's really only one road and that is right along the waterfront. Starting from the western (airport) end of town some local landmarks include the main harbour of Avatiu, then the shops, bank, petrol station and so on along the inland side of the road. There's a grassy strip along the coast side where you find the bus shelter and the small open market.

Beyond the major Cook Islands Trading Company shop you come to the Tourist Office, the Banana Court Bar and then the roundabout by the post office just across from the small Avarua harbour.

Then there are shops, restaurants and the Empire Cinema just across the small bridge as you continue out of town, past the Cook Islands Christian Church (CICC) with its distinctive surrounding graveyard. If you turn off and go down past the church a short distance, you come to the Library and Museum, the small University of the South Pacific centre and, a little further on, the Takamoa Mission and College.

Information

Tourist Office The Cook Islands Tourist Authority (tel 29-435) has an office right in the middle of Avarua. They have the usual sort of tourist office information including copies of *What's On in the Cook Islands*, an excellent annually produced information-and-adverts booklet guide to Rarotonga and Aitutaki. There's also a good bulletin board with info on everything from Rarotonga nightspots to inter-island shipping services and flights. The office is open Monday to Friday from 8 am to 4 pm, Saturday from 9 am to 12 noon.

Airline Offices Air New Zealand (tel 26-300) and Cook Islandair (tel 26-304) share an office at the international terminal at the airport. Air Rarotonga (tel 22-888) is a half km or so further down the road. Other airlines are Polynesian Airlines (tel 20-845) and Hawaiian Airlines (tel 21-210), both with offices at the international terminal.

Shipping Office The Silk & Boyd office (tel 22-442) is right by the Avatiu Harbour.

Post The Central Post Office is just off the main road in Avarua. It's open 8 am to 4 pm on weekdays, not at all on weekends. Poste Restante is handled at the very first counter; they will receive and hold mail

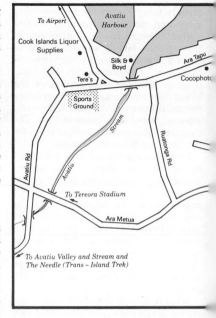

To Avatiu Valley and Stream and The Needle (Trans – Island Trek)

for you for 30 days. With the relative infrequency of flights to the Cook Islands it depends when letters are mailed how long they take to get in and out.

The Cook Islands' stamps are collector's items – lots of letters go out with far more stamps on them than are strictly necessary. Right across the road from the post office there's the Philatelic Bureau if you want mint copies; they also have mint sets of Cook Islands coins and the $3, $10 and $20 notes.

Telephone, Telegrams, Telex & Fax All international telephone, telegram, telex and fax services are handled at the Cable & Wireless office on Tutakimoa Rd – turn inland at Cook's Corner and go straight ahead a couple of blocks. You can make an international collect phone call from any phone on the island, but if you want to pay for the call yourself, you have to come in and place it here. Public booths are available

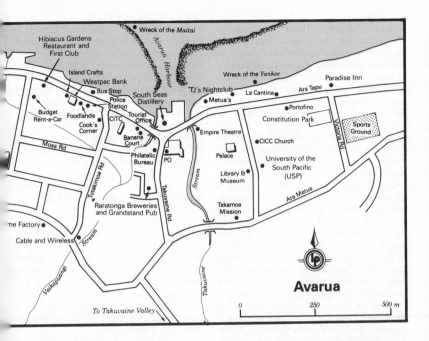

Avarua

for telex and fax. Cable & Wireless is open 24 hours, seven days a week.

Emergencies Rarotonga has an Outpatient Clinic on the main road just east of Avarua. The hospital is on a hill up behind the golf course, west of the airport. You can go to either one. Emergency phone numbers are:

Police – 999
Ambulance & Hospital – 998
Fire – 996

Banks In Avarua the main Westpac Bank is open 9 am to 3 pm on weekdays. It also has a branch bank in Arorangi village, open 9 am to 12 noon. You can change travellers' cheques and major currencies in cash at either one. The ANZ bank also has an office in Avarua (in the big white three-storey building between the police station and the Foodland supermarket) where you can change New Zealand travellers' cheques. When they move into their larger offices upstairs, they plan to start changing all major currencies.

Travellers' cheques and major currencies in cash can also be changed at larger stores and hotels, but you'll get a better rate of exchange at the bank.

Bookshops The Bounty Bookshop in the building between Foodland and the Police Station has a reasonably good selection of books and magazines. They also have a small selection of books on the Cook Islands and other Pacific destinations. You'll find interesting titles you may not even have heard of elsewhere although the choice is small. Several other places also have books on the Cooks and other places in the South Pacific. Try the Cook Islands Trading Company, Island Crafts, and in particular the Rarotonga Library & Museum; between them you'll find a surprising variety of titles. In addition to the books that the museum has for sale, you can have access to the library's entire Pacific Collection by simply signing up for a Temporary Borrower's Card. There's a refundable deposit and a borrowing charge. Right across the road from the Library & Museum the University of the South Pacific Centre sells the wide selection of books published by USP, at prices better than you'll find anywhere else.

The Survey Department office behind the Central Post Office has topographical maps of the Cook Islands. There are excellent maps of Rarotonga and Aitutaki and they may have maps of equally good quality for some other islands. If not they can provide photocopies of smaller scale maps. Also check at the Bounty Bookshop or Pacific Supplies, beside Cocophotos on the main road heading out towards the airport, as they sometimes have the odd map which the Survey Department hasn't.

Right on the corner of the post office building on the main road in the Internal Affairs Office, the Conservation Officer has a leaflet (50c) with maps of several good walking routes around the island, published by the Cook Islands Conservation Service.

Cinema The Empire Cinema shows films nightly except Sunday, with double-feature films changing every couple of days. The shows begin at 7.30 pm and prices are cheap: NZ$2 for adults, half price for children, a few cents more if you choose to sit upstairs.

Duty Free There are a number of duty free shops around Avarua with a reasonable selection of all the regular Japanese goodies, French perfumes and so on. Compared to New Zealand the prices may not be too bad but Rarotonga isn't Singapore or Hong Kong. Don't make duty free shopping a major reason for coming to the Cooks.

Film & Photography The only professional-

quality photo lab in the Cook Islands is Cocophotos (tel 20-555), on the main road on the airport side of Avarua. They offer every type of photographic service – film, developing, enlargements, passport photos, studio work and assignments to cover special events. They also offer same-day developing, if needed, and free pick-up of film from any hotel.

One-hour developing of basic colour prints is also offered at Kis Photo (tel 29-292) in the Pharmacy in Avarua, which also sells film. Prices for colour print developing are the same at either shop: NZ$18.65 for 24 prints, NZ$24.75 for 36 prints.

Laundry Snowbird Laundromat (tel 21-952), in the Empire Theatre building in Avarua, has a few washers and dryers. Prices are NZ$3 per washload, including soap and softener, NZ$1.20 to dry. If you want to just drop it off and pick it up later, wash-dry-fold is NZ$7.50 per load. It's open 8 am to 5 pm Monday to Friday, Saturday 8 am to 3 pm.

There's another Snowbird Laundromat in Arorangi village (tel 20-952); the sign is easy to see on the main road.

Island Activities

The first issue of the new *Cook Islands Sun* tourist paper led with the story – 'Cook Islands - Fast Lane or Sleepy Haven?' The answer is it can be either. Rarotonga has no major world-class sights or things you *must do* although to miss seeing a dance performance and a visit to the Cultural Village would be a shame. Simply relaxing and enjoying the scenery, climate and lack of rush or pressure is very easy. New arrivals, realising how small the island is, often wonder if there will be enough to do. In fact there's plenty of activity, *if* you want it.

Snorkelling & Diving Snorkelling in the lagoon is wonderful, with lots of colourful coral and tropical fish. The lagoon is shallow all the way around but the south side, from the Rarotongan Hotel to Muri Lagoon, is the best. Snorkelling gear is available at many motels, from Dive Rarotonga and from the Sailing Club on Muri Lagoon.

Scuba diving is good off the reef. There's coral, canyons, caves and tunnels and the reef drop-off goes from 20 to 30 metres right down to 4000 metres! Most diving is done at three to 30 metres where visibility is 30 to 60 metres depending on weather and wind conditions. For the novice diver, the sheltered lagoon makes an excellent practising ground.

Dive Rarotonga (tel 21-873) in Arorangi village operate daily diving trips and has gear for sale or hire and fills tanks. The diving trips last about three hours and with one tank they cost NZ$35 or if you need gear as well they are NZ$40. Diving instruction is available from Greg Wilson at Cook Islands Divers (tel 22-483). Scuba diving prices in the Cook Islands are among the lowest in the world.

Deep Sea Fishing & Cruises Deep sea fishing is excellent right off the reef and with the steep drop-off there's no long distance to travel out to the fishing grounds. World-class catches are made of many Pacific fishes, including tuna, mahimahi, wahoo, barracuda, sailfish and marlin. Try the *Seacat* (tel 22-153), the *Seafari* (tel 20-328), or Pacific Marine Charters (tel 21-237). Rates are around NZ$70 for a four-hour excursion.

Reef Walking Walking on the reef flat to see the colourful coral, crabs, shells, starfish and other creatures is always fascinating but make sure you wear strong shoes as the coral is very sharp and coral cuts can take a long time to heal. An old pair of running shoes is much better than thongs. Listen for the clicking sounds made by tiny hermit crabs as they clamber and fall across the rocks. Walk gently, try not to damage the coral, and if you turn anything over to see what is beneath remember to turn it back again.

Sports Tennis courts are available at the Rarotongan and Edgewater hotels. There are many other public tennis courts dotted around the island which you can use for free. Ask at the Tourist Office or your hotel. The Edgewater hotel has squash courts and you can usually find a volleyball game going on at the sandy net on the beach at the Rarotongan hotel. There's a nine-hole golf course just south of the airport and lawn bowling is held in Avarua most Saturdays and there's an annual tournament.

The Hash House Harriers meet every Monday at 5.30 pm for a fun run somewhere around the island. Phone David Lobb (tel 22-000) during business hours to find out where, or check with the Tourist Office. In the Cooks the Hash House Harriers have a couple of other branches – Hash House Harriers Hussies and Offspring!

For indoor sports, Cap't Andy's Pub (tel 21-024), opposite the Rarotongan Hotel, has cards, darts, billiards, table tennis, backgammon and other board games, plus outdoor croquet and a giant chessboard with foot-high chessmen. It's open every day until 6 pm.

For windsurfing, sailing, kayaking and snorkelling head for the Sailing Club on Muri Lagoon. Check with the Tourist Office for details on horseriding and the many other sports enjoyed on the island.

Visit an Artist Rick Welland, Edwin ('Edwin the Painter') Shorter, Clare Higham and Jillian Sobiesky all have studios where you can see their work. The Akatikitiki Gallery (tel 20-686) has an interesting collection of local artists' paintings, wood sculptures, ceramics, airbrush and block-printed clothing. It's on the Ara Metua just west of Avarua and you'll often find local artists at work there. Don't forget the Women's Craft Federation, to one side of the Banana Court in Avarua, and the Colonial Craft House, in Matavera village.

Seven-in-One Coconut Tree

Just to the east of the traffic roundabout, you'll see a group of seven tall coconut trees growing up in a perfect circle. Tradition has it that they are really all one tree! Supposedly in the distant past an amazing coconut with seven sprouts was found on the island of Takutea, near Atiu, and brought here to be planted. The locals absolutely *swear* it is true, and the tree has become a famous landmark.

Wreck of the Maitai

Directly offshore from the centre of Avarua is the wreck of the SS *Maitai*, a 3393 ton Union Steam Ship vessel which used to trade between the Cook Islands and Tahiti. She ran on to the reef, fortunately without loss of life, on 24 December 1916. Her cargo included a number of Model T Fords. All that remains today is her rusted boiler, just off the edge of the fringing reef. In the '50s a couple of enterprising New Zealanders brought up one of the ship's bronze propellers.

Wreck of the Yankee

On 24 July 1964 the brig *Yankee* broke her mooring line in a gale and ran onto the reef at the eastern end of Avarua. All that remains today is her rusting hull, high and dry on the beach. This much photographed hulk was equally well recorded during her heyday as she was once operated by the *National Geographic* magazine and appeared in numerous articles in the 1950s.

The *Yankee* had a long and interesting history before her ignominious end. The 30 metre (97 foot), 117 ton, steel-hulled vessel was originally built in 1912 in Germany but was taken by the British as a war prize after WW I. She served as the North Sea pilot vessel *Duhnen* until she was bought by Irving and Electra Johnson in 1946. Overhauled and re-rigged as a brigantine in Devonshire she carried 723 square metres (7775 square feet) of sail when fully rigged and circled the world no less than seven times before finally being

sold to Miami-based Windjammer Cruises in 1957. Earlier that year she had visited the Cooks with the Johnsons and she returned with her new owners in 1961.

On her third visit in 1964 she was in sorry condition and, say the pundits, her crew was too busy partying on with Rarotongan bar-girls to handle the storm when it blew up. At that time there was no regular air service to the Cook Islands and it took a long time to ship her irate American passengers out. You can see some mementoes from the *Yankee* in the museum, just up the road from her rusting remains. Over the years storms have pushed her further and further up the reef until now the remains are all the way up on the beach.

Church

The CICC church in Avarua is a fine, old, white painted building made of coral, from very much the same mould as other CICC churches in the Cooks. It was built in 1853 when Aaron Buzacott was the resident missionary. The interesting graveyard around the church is worth a leisurely browse. At the front you'll find a monument to the pioneering Polynesian 'teacher' Papeiha. Just to the left (as you face the church) is the grave of Albert Henry, the first prime minister of the independent Cook Islands – you can't miss it, it's the one with a life-size bronze bust wearing a pair of spectacles! Other well-known people buried here include author Robert Dean Frisbie.

You're welcome to attend services; see the Religion section in the Facts about the Country chapter for details. The main service of the week, as at all six of Rarotonga's CICCs, is Sunday at 10 am.

Palace

Across the road from the church is the ruin of Taputapuatea, the palace of Makea Takau. She was the 'Queen of Rarotonga' in 1888 when the London Missionary Society withdrew to the sidelines and the British government officially took control

Top: Muri Lagoon *motus* (islets) and the south-east coast of Rarotonga (TW)
Bottom: Sunset at Arorangi, Rarotonga (TW)

Top: Parliament House, Rarotonga (TW)
Left: Tangaroa carving (TW)
Right: Palace ruins, Avarua, Rarotonga (TW)

Avarua Church

of the Cook Islands (or at least the southern group), forestalling any possibility of a French takeover from Tahiti. The palace, once a grand edifice, was destroyed in the hurricane of 1942 and never rebuilt.

This whole area where the church and palace were built was once the location of the largest and most sacred *marae* (religious meeting ground) on Rarotonga. The missionaries wanted to take over and replace the pre-existing powers. Today nothing remains of the old *marae*.

Library & Museum

The small library with its friendly staff has a collection of rare books and literature on the Pacific locked away which, if you enquire, you may be able to inspect and read – but only on the premises. There's also an extensive Pacific Collection, as well as other general interest books.

The little museum has an interesting collection of ancient and modern artefacts – basketry, weaving, musical instruments, wooden statues of various old gods, adzes,

shell fishhooks, spears, tools and other historical items, even a beautiful old outrigger canoe and one of the original missionaries' printing presses. There are also exhibits from other Pacific islands and the New Zealand Maori. There's no admission charge but a donation is appreciated. The opening hours for both the library and museum are Monday to Friday 9 am to 4.30 pm, Tuesday and Thursday evenings 7 to 8.30 pm, Saturday 8.30 to 11.30 am.

University

The University of the South Pacific, based in Fiji, has its Cook Islands Centre in the building directly opposite the library. The centre was established in Rarotonga in 1975 and moved into this building a few years later. Most classes are taught externally from the main campus. A wide selection of books on the Cook Islands and other parts of the Pacific, all published by the university, are on sale in the office. The monthly *Search* journal is also published here. If you're planning a lengthy stay in the Cooks, you might want to ask here about classes for learning the Cook Islands Maori language.

Takamoa Mission

Just down beyond the Library & Museum is the Takamoa Mission House built in 1842. One of the earliest mission compounds on the island, it is in its original condition and still in use. It was established to train locals for the ministry and from here missionaries were sent out to many parts of the Pacific. Today, it still educates CICC ministers for work in all of the Cook Islands; those wishing to do international missionary work must study further in New Zealand.

Constitution Park

Just inland from the Paradise Inn, on Victoria Rd, is Constitution Park, where many local gatherings, events and celebrations take place.

Rarotonga Breweries

Founded in 1987 Rarotonga Breweries produces the Cook Islands' own beer – Cook's Lager. Free brewery tours are operated during business hours (Monday to Friday 8 am to 4 pm, Saturday 8 am to 12 noon) and finish with a glass of beer upstairs at the Grandstand Bar. To get to the brewery take the road in front of the post office, turn on the first right turn where you see the sign and continue to the large two-storey warehouse-style building.

South Seas Distillery

For a taste of real Cook Islands liquor, made from fresh pineapples grown on the island of Mangaia, stop by the bottling plant/tasting room of the South Seas Distillery, just off the traffic circle by the Avarua harbour, any day during business hours. The two strong (40%) drinks, Mangaia-Ara and Rum-Ara, tasting like pineapple and rum respectively, are especially delicious mixed with fresh pineapple or orange juice.

The Perfume Factory

Another business making use of local products is The Perfume Factory, easy to spot on the Ara Metua road just behind town heading west. Here you can buy perfumes and colognes, scented with local flowers; pure coconut oil scented with frangipani, starfruit, jasmine or plain; handmade coconut oil soap; and also many imported French and other perfumes, lotions and shampoos, all at discount prices. This business has been enormously successful since its opening in 1981 and has now begun to export its products. It's open 8 am to 5 pm Monday to Saturday, closed Sunday.

Places to Stay

Normally in our guidebooks we categorise accommodation by price and then, if necessary, sub-categorise it by location. This policy doesn't work so well with Rarotonga where the places to stay are simply dotted round the coast road.

In general, though, to help you break down what's available, here are a few basic guidelines. Rarotonga now has two huge resort hotels, mostly catering to the international package-tour trade: the Rarotongan and the Edgewater. On the other end of the scale, four places offer basic shared accommodation for the student/backpacker: Dive Rarotonga Hostel, Matareka Heights, Tiare Village and the Arorangi Lodge. Rose Flats is another inexpensive place to stay, for those on a rock-bottom budget. It's even less expensive than the hostels and you get your own private flat; the Are-Renga and the Onemura are also private and come out about the same price as the hostels provided you have two to share the cost.

Most other places fall somewhere in between, they're small to medium size, medium budget, usually quiet and relaxed, with very friendly service.

If you're looking for the most beautiful beach on the island, choose one of the two motels right on Muri Beach. The beaches along the south and west sides of the island are all good for swimming – but not those on the north and east sides, where the reef is too close to shore, making the beaches rocky and the lagoon too narrow. If you want to see the sunset from your hotel then of course it's the west side of the island for you.

Almost every place to stay shares one basic similarity with its competitors: they nearly all offer some sort of kitchen or cooking facilities. This is great if you have kids or are trying to economise since you can prepare your own food at some financial saving over eating out. Since accommodation and restaurants both tend to be scattered it's also a considerable convenience – if you don't feel like eating out in the same place every meal of your stay.

The list that follows simply works its way round the island in a counterclockwise direction from the airport. Each hotel is followed by its km distance from the centre of town, first in a counterclockwise then a clockwise direction, and then its price category – bottom, middle and top. The airport terminal is 2.5 km from the town centre, counterclockwise; the total distance around the island is 32.5 km. The prices listed here *include* a 10% government tax.

It's a good idea to make your reservations early – many hotels are booked up months in advance.

Tiare Village Motel (tel 23-466 or 23-477, telex RG 62067, fax RG 20-969), (3 km, 29.5 km, bottom end). This backpackers' haven is in a rather remote location, on the Ara Metua back road out behind the airport. You'll probably like the place best if you plan to rent a motorcycle or other transportation, as you are off the bus line here and it's a long walk into town.

Accommodation include one three-bedroom house and three bungalows, each sleeping four people, all self-contained with shared kitchen and bathroom facilities. Each bedroom sleeps two, with twin or double beds and prices are NZ$13 per person, children under five free. Fresh

fruits and vegetables are in abundance here, which you are welcome to eat, and the place is famous for its hospitality. Bring a mosquito coil as you are inland here.

Matareka Heights Guest House (tel 23-670, telex RG 62050), (4 and 5 km, 28.5 and 27.5 km, bottom end). This is another place with shared facilities, in two separate houses in different locations.

The upper house is on the steep hill overlooking the airport – not bad if you have a motorcycle or car, but quite inconvenient otherwise. Nevertheless, it's pleasantly quiet up here, with spacious well-maintained grounds and a big three-bedroom house, each bedroom having three twin beds and its own separate bathroom, plus a large communal kitchen. Bring mosquito coils.

The lower house is right on the main coastal road, near the end of the airport runway and across the road from the radar station and the beach. It's a duplex-style house, sleeping six altogether, with one shared kitchen serving both sides. There's no sign here – look for the house with the long wooden decks.

At both houses, prices are NZ$12 per person to share a room, NZ$15 per person for a couple in a private room, NZ$25 for a single person in a private room. Several travellers have written to say what a great place this is and how friendly Hugh and Joanna Baker, the owners, are.

Rarotongan Sunset Motel (tel 28-028, telex RG 62074, fax 28-026), (6 km, 26.5 km, middle). The first real motel you come to on the coastal road when moving round the island counterclockwise is the Sunset Motel which opened in mid-86. It has 20 self-contained units with the usual motel-style mod cons including well-equipped kitchen facilities. There's a guest laundry, freshwater pool and a video unit in every room with daily in-house videos. Twelve of the rooms can be interconnected. Prices are NZ$66 (single or double) or NZ$77 for the nine beachfront units. Extra people cost NZ$16.50 each but children under two are free.

Edgewater Resort (tel 25-435, telex RG 62059 EDGEW, fax 25-475), (7 km, 25.5 km, middle). the Edgewater has 173 rooms making it the biggest resort in the Cook Islands. It's a mixture of resort hotel and the motel-style accommodation found at most places on Rarotonga. There's a bar, restaurant and various entertainment facilities but there are also cooking facilities in all the rooms. The rooms are quite straightforward with the three different categories differing mainly in their views (garden, partial beach view or beachfront) and furnishings. Singles/doubles/triples start at NZ$67/76/85 and go up to NZ$80/90/101 and NZ$91/102/117. Extra people cost NZ$11; children ages five to 12 are NZ$5; infants free. If you come on a package tour, as many guests do, prices are cheaper.

There's a freshwater swimming pool and the resort is right on the beach although it's not one of the best stretches of beach. There are four tennis courts and four squash courts, cars, motorcycles and pushbikes for hire, plus a travel desk where you can book a variety of activities including tours, dives and scenic flights.

Manuia Beach Hotel (tel 22-461, telex RG 62060, fax 25-611), (8 km, 24.5 km, top end). Next up is the 20-room Manuia Beach Hotel, another comfortable and well-kept place right on the beach, completely renovated since its former days as the Beach Motel. The lagoon here is very shallow and the coral is not so good but it's OK for splashing around and lackadaisical snorkelling. The white sandy beach is just fine and also offers excellent sunsets. You can always swim in the beachfront freshwater pool.

The thatched-roof, open-air, sand-floor *Right-On-The-Beach Restaurant & Bar* is popular with guests as well as outsiders. Wednesday evenings the big Island Night banquet and dance performance is held; the Sunday evening barbecue also attracts a crowd.

All 20 rooms have mini-bar, tea and coffee-making facilities, but not a full kitchen. Single/double rooms are NZ$165 garden or NZ$192.50 for the beachfront units, NZ$22 for each extra person, children under 12 free. Most of the guests here come on some sort of an airline package holiday, making the room rate less expensive.

Are-Renga Motel (tel 20-050), (8.5 km, 24 km, bottom end). There are 23 units in this very straightforward motel on the inland side of the road through Arorangi. Rooms cost just NZ$23/29/43 for singles/doubles/triples, children aged five to 12 NZ$5.50, infants free. Although they're not the latest thing all the rooms are comfortable little apartments, with separate bedroom, kitchen and sitting room. Laundry facilities are available. If you're looking for a low priced motel you may well find them ideal.

Arorangi Lodge (tel 27-379, telex RG 62034), (8.5 km, 24 km, bottom end). On the beach side of the road just a little further into Arorangi there are eight well-equipped and well-kept units. High season rates are NZ$38.50/49.50 for singles/doubles plus NZ$6 for each extra person; NZ$5.50 for children ages two to 12. Off-season rates are about NZ$15 less. You can also ask for the special share rate of NZ$12 per person, so this is another place worth considering if you're economising.

Whitesands Motel (tel 25-789), (11 km, 21.5 km, bottom end). On the beach side of the road at the far end of Arorangi there are six units with kitchen facilities, facing right onto a nice beach with coconut trees scattered about the lawn. Prices are NZ$40/46/59 for singles/doubles/triples but unfortunately they're not very well kept or equipped; you'll do better elsewhere.

Rose Flats (11 km, 21.5 km, bottom end), (tel 27-777). On the Ara Metua, about 400 metres off the coast road at the southern end of Arorangi, these seven small apartment flats are very straightforward but also low priced at NZ$10/20 for singles/doubles, with a NZ$50 weekly rate available.

Puaikura Reef Lodge (tel 23-537, telex RG 62045, fax 21-537), (11 km, 21.5 km, middle) has 12 modern and well-equipped units. They each have a kitchen and eating area and the family units are wonderful if you're with children as the main sleeping area has a concertina door which you can slide across to shut off the living area (where the kids can sleep). There are also some studio units. Singles or doubles are NZ$70, extra people cost NZ$15 each, NZ$10 if they're kids under 10. There's a swimming pool, with a barbecue off to one side. The only drawback is that it's very close to the main road although after dark there's very little traffic. The beach, narrow but pleasant and with good swimming, is only a few steps away on the other side of the road.

Dive Rarotonga Hostel (tel 21-873, telex RG 62046), (11.5 km, 21 km, bottom end). Just off the coast road and just beyond the Puaikura Reef Lodge this is the back-packing travellers' centre for Rarotonga. There are six twin rooms, one double room and two single rooms, all priced at NZ$13 per person; you can specify a preference for single or shared accommodation. The toilets and shower are shared and there's a large communal kitchen with utensils and equipment, a comfortable lounge area and yard. The hostel is inconspicuous, with no sign; to find it, turn inland at the building marked 'Kavera Bus Stop' and look for the first two-storey house on your right. Dive Rarotonga, the diving organisers who run the hostel and who handle all

bookings, are on the main road near the Edgewater Motel in Arorangi. They will arrange airport transfers for NZ$2.

Lagoon Lodge (tel 22-020, telex RG 62076, fax 28-026 attn LL), (12 km, 20.5 km, middle) is next along the coastal road from the Puaikura Reef, just across the road from the beach. At NZ$77/82.50 for singles/doubles (plus NZ$16.50 for each extra person or NZ$11 for each extra child) it's also just a bit more expensive. The advantage is that it stretches back from rather than along the road so there's less traffic noise and it's safer for children; the grounds and bungalows are also much more spacious. There are 14 bungalows plus a tennis court, trampoline, barbecue and small pool.

In addition to six studio units, several of the bungalows are larger one or two bedroom units – very spacious with a kitchen and living room area, a large verandah and virtually your own private garden. If you've got kids these larger rooms are amongst the best on the island. The larger rooms are NZ$99 for two or three, the extra charge for a fourth person is NZ$16.50 (adult) or NZ$11 (child). There's also a weekly rate of NZ$423.50 for stays of two weeks or more.

Onemura Motel (tel 24-770), (12 km, 20.5 km, bottom end). This simple duplex-style place has two self-contained studio units right on the main road across from the beach. Each unit sleeps two people; they can also be interconnected to accommodate a group of four. Prices are NZ$25/30 for singles/doubles, with discounts for long-term stays.

Rarotongan Resort Hotel (tel 25-800, telex RG 62003, fax 25-799), (12.5 km, 20 km, top end). This 151-room resort is the only 'international standard' hotel in the Cook Islands. It has everything including a seven-day-a-week shop; tennis courts; a swimming pool; a choice of bars, coffee shops and restaurants; its own beach; a travel centre; and on-the-spot car, motorcycle and pushbike rental. There's also a business centre with telex, secretarial, photo-copying and fax facilities and even a conference centre although the idea of conferring in the Cooks is a little strange!

The Rarotongan underwent major renovations and upgrading in mid-86 with a major emphasis on giving the hotel a real island feel by using many local craftsmen and acting as a display centre for the best of Polynesian craftsmanship. There are four standards of rooms: standard, superior, deluxe and suites. The differences are principally whether you face the garden or the beach and some variation in equipment levels. Counting up through the grades: singles or doubles are NZ$160/182/204/259, triples NZ$176/198/220/275. There is no extra charge for children under 16 if they occupy the same room as their parents.

The vast majority of visitors to the Rarotongan are on package deals so these 'rack rates' bear little reality to what people are actually paying. People staying here are more likely to be on a fairly short visit to the Cooks, perhaps part of a quick zip around several Pacific destinations. If you want all mod cons, the feeling of being in a real resort hotel and so on then this could be your place. On the other hand it doesn't have the kitchen facilities and easy living space of the more family oriented motel-style places so if you're here on a longer family vacation you might not find it so convenient.

Even if you are not staying at the Rarotongan, you can still come to partake of the many activities. 'Island Night' buffets and dance performances take place two evenings a week – if you don't want the buffet you can come around 9 pm and pay a cover charge of NZ$3 to see the dancing, featuring some of the best troupes on the island. The resort beach has kayaks, outrigger canoes, snorkel-and-masks, volleyball, badminton, windsurfers (at NZ$8 per hour – lessons NZ$15 per hour) and so on. A sign announces that all 'furniture and equipment for hotel guests only,' but no one seems to check. An activities list at the front desk describes the various events being held each day.

Palm Grove Lodge (tel 20-002, telex RG 62067 Chamber, attn Palm, or telex RG 62076 Lagoon, attn Palm, fax 20-969 Cookschamber), (16 km, 16.5 km, middle). This very pleasant place has eight bungalows (two family units plus six new studios) set in a large garden with a fine stretch of beach right across the road. The family units have a separate bedroom and sleep up to four people; the studios sleep up to three. All have fully equipped kitchens and a verandah in front and there's a small swimming pool. It's a nice place to stay at NZ$80/88 for singles/doubles, NZ$15 for each extra person; children under 12 stay for free.

Moana Sands Resort (tel 26-189, telex RG 62044), (20 km, 12.5 km, middle). Brand new in mid-86 Moana Sands has a two-storey block of rooms, 12 in all, facing directly onto the beach, each with a verandah. The rooms are well equipped, have fridges, tea/coffee making facilities, toaster and electric frypan and cost NZ$99 for singles, NZ$110 for doubles or twins, NZ$132 for triples, NZ$16.50 for ages 12 and under. Six of the rooms are interconnecting. Apart from your own limited cooking facilities there is a restaurant and bar at the motel. The staff are very friendly and there are daytime and evening activities and events including picnics, barbecues, legend nights, hikes, fishing, pony riding, tours and so on. Nice beach, too, with kayaks, canoes, snorkelling, volleyball and other things to keep you busy.

Little Polynesian (tel 24-280, telex RG 62065 Rarmark), (20 km, 12.5 km, middle). Only a short distance from the Moana Sands and also right on the same nice stretch of beach this longer-established place has nine rooms, all with full kitchen facilities. Two of the rooms are family units with a separate bedroom area. One room is a totally separate 'honeymoon' unit – standing alone, presumably so the occupants can make more noise! There's a swimming pool and single or double rooms cost NZ$82.50, NZ$11 for extra people (children under two free). There are motorcycles for hire, boats and a trampoline, and daily fresh fruit in season.

Raina Motel (tel 20-197, telex RG 62026), (20.5 km, 12 km, middle). This curious looking three-storey place with no sign, built in a modernistic concrete style, is just across the road from the beach. Two family units downstairs have separate bedrooms for two, each sleeping up to seven people. The upstairs units are smaller, without the separate bedroom, but have the same lounge area, kitchen facilities and so on. Prices are NZ$88 for singles or doubles, NZ$11 for each extra person, kids under two free. Good snorkelling here.

Muri Beachcomber (tel 21-022, telex RG 62055 Muribch), (23 km, 9.5 km, middle). This popular beachfront place is pleasantly sited on Muri Lagoon, Rarotonga's most beautiful stretch of beach, next door to the Sailing Club. There are 10 regular doubles plus a couple of larger family units with separate bedrooms. Rooms cost NZ$77/91 for singles/doubles plus NZ$16.50 for each additional person. There's a swimming pool, children's pool, barbecue area and laundry facilities. The whole place is very modern, well kept and well run. Booking in advance is generally a must.

For groups, a nice, large house next door to the hotel is rented out for stays of a minimum of one week, usually longer, at a rate of NZ$36 per person per night, or NZ$203 for a group of up to seven adults, whichever price comes out lower.

Pacific Resort (tel 20-427, telex RG 62041 PRMBRG), (23.5 km, 9 km, top end). One

of Raro's newest and nicest places to stay is on Muri Beach, the loveliest beach on the island. The 32 rooms all have self-contained kitchens, one or two bedrooms, sitting rooms, private verandahs and good views of the beach, garden, pond and swimming pool. Garden rooms are NZ$110 single/double; family units NZ$110 for up to five people. It's NZ$16.50 for each extra person in a room, with children under 12 free. Four beachfront 'executive/honeymoon' suites, complete with waterbed and complimentary champagne, go for NZ$132. Interconnecting suites are available. All guests have free use of the watersports equipment at the Sailing Club next door. The resort's intimate *Barefoot Restaurant/Bar*, right on the sand, is a popular place with a lovely view.

Sunrise Beach Motel (tel 20-417, telex RG 62064 attn Sunrise, fax 21-085), (25 km, 7.5 km, middle). This is a newish place just beyond Ngatangiia Harbour with eight small, modern bungalow units right on the beach, most with an ocean view. All are self-contained with kitchen, bath and private verandah. A tiny swimming pool, barbecue and laundry complete the facilities. The lagoon here is very narrow so swimming is not so good, especially for children, but it's not too far to walk back to sheltered Muri Lagoon. Singles/doubles/triples are NZ$61/66/77, additional people NZ$11.

Ariana Motel (tel 20-521, telex RG 62000 CWPGRAM), (29 km, 3.5 km, middle). Situated 200 (uphill) metres off the main road the Ariana Motel has a lush, green garden with a wonderful mountainous backdrop, fruit trees ripe for the picking, and a peaceful, quiet atmosphere. The nine self-contained bungalows each have a fully-equipped kitchen, separate bedroom and a private balcony. Most sleep three persons – other, larger ones sleep six. There's a pool, barbecue area and a self-service laundry. Rates are NZ$44/50 for singles/doubles, NZ$11 for each extra person, children under five free. Video machines, pushbikes and motorcycles are available for hire.

Kii Kii Motel (tel 21-937, telex RG 62008), (29.5 km, 3 km, middle). The 20 room Kii Kii is on the beachfront (although the beach here is not good for swimming) and also has a beachfront swimming pool. Prices for the spacious, self-contained studio units vary from NZ$52/66 single/double for the cheapest rooms through NZ$65/81 up to NZ$69/86 single/double for the seaview units. A couple of smaller 'budget rooms' cost NZ$41/51. Extra adults are NZ$16.50, children under 12 NZ$13.

Tamure Resort Hotel (tel 22-415), (30 km, 2.5 km, middle). On the eastern edge of Avarua this 35-room waterfront hotel is best known for its 'Island Night' entertainment, at least two nights per week. Otherwise, however, it's no great shakes as a place to stay. In particular the garden areas are overgrown or worn bare, the pool is cloudy and the garden furniture mildewed. It's on the waterfront but the beach here is not good for swimming. Singles/doubles/triples are NZ$50/66/83, children under 12 free.

Paradise Inn (tel 20-544, telex RG 62026 attn Paradise), (31.5 km, 1 km, middle). This pleasant seafront inn is the closest hotel to the centre of Avarua, just a short walk on the main road. It was one of Avarua's liveliest dance halls until early 1985, opening again as a 15-room motel in April '86. Although the beach is rocky and shallow here, not good for swimming, the amenities are good, with a large and attractive lounge area, video movies, board games, library, informal bar and a barbecue area on the seaside patio. Plus the place is virtually covered in passionfruit vines! Most of the rooms are townhouse-style and spacious, with a double bed in the ample sleeping loft and sitting room/

kitchen/bath areas downstairs. Prices for these are NZ$52/59/73 single/double/triple. There's also a family unit, sleeping five, for NZ$82.50, and two budget single rooms for NZ$41.

Renting a House One of the best deals, especially if you're staying on the island for a while, is to rent a house by the week. A fully equipped two-bedroom house sleeping four or five people usually costs around NZ$100 to NZ$150 per week. The challenge is to find one – quite a few people around the island have them available for rent but only occasionally are they advertised in the *Cook Islands News*. If you ask around, though, you can probably turn up something.

The owners of the Kii Kii Motel, the Onemura Motel, Matareka Heights and the Rose Flats are good people to ask for a start. There's also a house out behind Vaima Rentals which is sometimes available (tel 22-222). The Tourist Authority can refer you to a couple of agencies that handle rental houses.

Places to Eat

The widest choice of eating places is found in Avarua although there is also a scattering of places right around the island. Some of the accommodation has restaurant facilities although many visitors opt to fix their own food for at least some meals. The majority of places to stay have some sort of cooking facilities. See the Places to Stay section and the introductory Food section.

One pleasant surprise with Rarotongan eating is the quality of the local ingredients. Of course a lot of the raw materials (steaks for example) arrive frozen or airfreighted from New Zealand but the locally grown vegetables are excellent. Tomatoes, for example, may not look as technically perfect as you get used to in the USA or Australia but they're certainly tasty.

Avarua If you want cheap snacks or take-away food Avarua is where you'll find it. Along the waterfront the *burger vans* have burgers, meat pies and other take-away food of the lowest order. They're cheap but little more; their major strong points are their handy location and long hours. At least one van will stay open all night long on Friday night.

Foodland, the major supermarket, has a take-away section where you can get a variety of fairly reasonable pastries, plus sandwiches, meat pies, cold drinks and ice cream. There's also the *Frosty Boy*, an open-air ice cream stand in the Cook Islands Trading Company car park.

The *Hacienda Restaurant* (tel 22-345) in Cook's Corner is a casual place for inexpensive snacks and light meals. A separate bar and beer garden are off to one side.

Just beyond the roundabout in Brownes' Arcade there's *Metua's* (tel 20-850), pleasantly situated on the waterfront although rather hidden away. It's a good budget place for all meals as well as light snacks, has a bar and features live music for listening or dancing on Friday and Saturday nights from 8 to 11 pm.

Avarua also has a number of more expensive restaurants. Not far past Metua's the Mexican restaurant *La Cantina* (tel 29-900) has quite good food and I certainly had no complaints about the enchiladas which were a meal in themselves. A simple meal of a big taco, enchilada or empanada with rice and salad is NZ$7.50, other main courses range from NZ$13 to NZ$17. There's a bar adjoining and a curious mix of Mexican and South Pacific decor, with colourful serapes, sombreros and bullfight paintings on the walls, woven pandanus mats on the floor. Open for lunch and dinner daily except Sunday.

Across the road is *Portofino* (tel 26-480) where the accent is nautical, the food Italian. It's all carried off with some flair and ability. In fact this place is reputed to be about the best on the island and is so popular in the evening that reservations

are becoming a must. There's a bar, a surprisingly extensive (and reasonably priced) winelist, starters at NZ$7, good pastas at NZ$7 to NZ$13, main courses at NZ$18 to NZ$24. The fresh fish of the day is usually very good and so are the desserts. We certainly had no complaints, but it's no problem to spend NZ$80 to NZ$100 for two with a drink beforehand and coffee afterwards. They also have excellent pizzas both to eat-in and take-away; average prices are NZ$8 (small), NZ$11 (medium) and NZ$18 (large). Open for lunch and dinner daily except Sunday.

On the airport side of Avarua *Hibiscus Gardens* (tel 20-823 or 20-824) is a pleasant restaurant-bar-cafe with a moderately-fancy indoor restaurant plus a garden cafe and bar out under the gigantic Golden Shower tree to one side. There's quite a variety on the bar-cafe menu, with snacks and light meals priced around NZ$5 to NZ$8. The cafe menu is also available at the indoor restaurant, plus some more fancy dishes, but it still comes out being less expensive than most of Raro's fancy places – maybe around NZ$25 for a three-course meal – and you can dress up or come as you are. Late in the evening there's a lot of back-and-forth to the First Club disco out the back; the rest of the time it's quite peaceful. Open Monday to Saturday, 11 am to midnight.

Just before the airport *Romiad's Curry House* (tel 20-419) is a tiny place offering delicious beef, chicken, lamb or vegetarian curry meals at NZ$7.50 for lunch, NZ$12.50 for dinner. Other snacks, such as tasty fish & chips, are also available. Open for breakfast and lunch every day except Sunday, for dinner on Thursday, Friday and Saturday only. There's another Romiad's right at the airport.

Around the Island If you want to eat cheaply you've got a choice between what's available in Avarua or doing your own cooking. The more scattered places are generally more expensive and they can be difficult to get to at night unless you've got your own wheels (unless you manage to catch the Rarotongan Hotel's Jeepney bus, operating once an hour in the evening – see Buses). Most of them get around this by offering to pick you up and take you home after your meal. If you're phoning for reservations (a wise idea) you can check the collection and delivery situation at the same time. Some of the Avarua restaurants also offer transport.

Behind the airport on the Ara Metua, which at this point is a surfaced road, the *Tangaroa Restaurant* (tel 20-017) is a pleasant Chinese restaurant with a cocktail bar and lots of red and gold, lanterns and fans in the decor. There's a basic menu featuring all the standard Chinese dishes, which are well prepared, and the ingredients (particularly the vegetables!) are fresh. A complete dinner for two, from appetiser and soup through to dessert comes to about NZ$45. There's also a lunchtime combo for NZ$8.50. Open for lunch Monday to Friday from 11.30 am to 2 pm, dinner Monday to Saturday from 6 to 10.30 pm. Free transport is provided for the dinner hours – just phone ahead.

Also behind the airport, near the college, the *Turamatuitui Bakery & Shop* makes and sells all kinds of wonderful breads, rolls and cakes. The cheese bread and the brown wholegrain bread are both wonderful.

Out near the Edgewater Resort in Arorangi, *PJ's Cafe* (tel 20-367), with an indoor restaurant and a take-away counter, is the one place you can go for late-night dining, aside from the burger vans in Avarua – it's open Monday to Thursday from 10 am to midnight, and all weekend long, from 10 am Friday to 2 am Saturday night and on Sundays from 11 am to 10 pm. The take-away counter has Chinese fast-food, which can be eaten at the the picnic tables out in front; inside, where there's a small piano bar with music on weekends, there's an 'Island Food' dinner served Wednesday to Friday for NZ$15, a Chinese menu with main courses for NZ$13, plus fish & chips (NZ$10.50), hamburgers and the like. Plans are in the works for a charcoal grill (steaks and seafood) and dancing in the evenings.

The *Reef Restaurant & Bar* at the Edgewater Resort (tel 25-435) was built in late 1988 and is one of the biggest on the island. There's a weekly schedule of 'Island Night' buffets, barbecues and other buffets, all with entertainment and after-dinner dancing nightly. Open for all meals, every day.

The *Tumunu Bar & Restaurant* (tel 20-501), next to the Edgewater, has a pleasant outside barbecue area, an indoor restaurant with lots of attractive Polynesian touches and a popular bar with a cocktail list that includes a 'Long Slow Screw', an 'Orgasm' and a 'Multiple Orgasm' – it makes a 'Tangaroa' sound positively innocuous! Seafood and steaks are the specialty here, with a big Fisherman's Platter at NZ$21 for one, NZ$32 for two. All up, dinner for two might come to about NZ$75, with soup, dessert and a bottle of wine. You'll feel right at home whether you dress up or go casual. There's a friendly darts competition once a week, with a carton of beer for a prize, and a barbecue night every Sunday. The bar is open from 4 pm to 12 midnight and dinner is served from 6.30 to 9.30 pm weekdays, until 9 pm Saturday and to 8.30 pm on Sundays.

Directly opposite the entrance to the Manuia Beach Hotel in Arorangi the *Outrigger Restaurant* (tel 27-378) is a small, relaxed place with moderately expensive but often very good food. Seafood is the specialty, with the Fisherman's Platter and the Surf & Turf steak-seafood combo (both at NZ$21.50) the most popular items on the menu. A variety of seafood delicacies (seafood crepe, crabsticks, oysters, mussels, sashimi, etc) are served either as appetisers for NZ$8 or as a main course for NZ$16. Open Monday to Saturday from 6.30 to 10 pm; transport available.

The *Kaena Restaurant* (tel 25-433), 50 metres north of the Rarotongan Hotel, again specialises in seafood. Put together a meal for two including all the house specialties – seafood chowder, fish of the day and a delicious banana crepe for dessert – and your bill will come to about NZ$50. There's quite a wine, beer and bar list. The pleasant covered-garden-style dining patio off to one side doesn't look like much from the outside, but it's very attractive inside, especially at night, with lots of plants all around. Open 6 to 11 pm, Monday to Saturday.

The Rarotongan Resort Hotel (tel 25-800) has several restaurants including *Brandi's*, the fanciest (and also the most expensive!) restaurant on the island. Most items on the menu include seafood or steak, prepared in a variety of unusual ways, with a heavy accent on French sauces. A dinner for two with appetiser, soup, main course, dessert and a special coffee easily comes to NZ$100 – a bottle of wine will add another NZ$18 to NZ$70. Open for dinner from 7 to 11 pm every night except Tuesday. Downstairs, the *Whitesands Restaurant* is not as fancy or

expensive and has a lot less atmosphere; the basic seafood menu is adequate, but nothing special, and dinner will still cost about NZ$70 for two, more if you have wine. 'Island Night' buffets and performances take place here twice a week. The *Mana Terrace*, down by the swimming pool, serves breakfast and lunch daily and has an excellent Sunday brunch from noon to 3 pm followed by a poolside barbecue from 6.30 to 9 pm.

Only a couple of km beyond the Rarotongan Resort the *Vaima Restaurant & Bar* (tel 26-123) bills itself as a steakhouse although it actually has a fairly varied menu. In addition to the daily blackboard specials, there are fresh lagoon fish of the day, surf & turf combos and, of course, steak, all deliciously prepared and attractively served. A meal for two may come to about NZ$90, more if you have cocktails or wine. The extensive winelist has items ranging all the way from NZ$16 for New Zealand or Australian wines up to a bottle of French champagne at just under NZ$100. Most enjoyable is the live Polynesian string band performing every evening, with some of the local mamas and papas really crowing out some joyful tunes accompanied by their ukuleles and guitars. This is the kind of music everybody sings around the backyard on a Sunday afternoon while enjoying a few beers with the family and friends. The decor is pleasantly Polynesian, with lots of bamboo and Gauguin prints about. Open for dinner 6.30 to 10 pm, Monday to Saturday. Transport available.

Right on the island's most beautiful stretch of beach, the Pacific Resort's *Barefoot Restaurant & Bar* (tel 20-427) has a great view of the *motus* just across Muri lagoon. It's a very small place, with a wall of windows, open every day from 7 am to 9.30 pm for dining, until about 11 pm for drinks. Dinner reservations are a must, because it's always full. There's a small but quality selection on the daily blackboard menu, with inexpensive sandwiches or more exotic fare for lunch and a changing dinner menu with starters at NZ\$4, main courses NZ\$15 and desserts at NZ\$3.50. You might choose poached fish in white wine sauce, a big steak, apple pie or a banana split.

Finally, just past Muri Beach, the *Flame Tree* (tel 25-123) is one of Raro's newest and highest-quality restaurants, run by the owners of *Portofino's*. It has one of the most exciting menus on the island, with a truly international menu from India, Thailand, China, Japan, Vietnam, Sri Lanka and even West Africa. There are plenty of vegetarian dishes available, plus seafood, steaks, lamb and other meats. Appetisers are NZ\$6 to NZ\$9, main dishes mostly around NZ\$20, salads NZ\$5 and desserts NZ\$5.50. The classy dining room and bar, plus an outdoor dining patio, are all beautifully done. It's open for dinner Tuesday to Saturday, 6.30 to 9.30 pm; reservations recommended.

Island Dining

It's indicative of the scale of the Cook Islands that the tourist office's giveaway booklet boasts that you could stay *10 days* in the Cook Islands and not have to eat at the same restaurant twice! Surprisingly, however, dining out in Rarotonga can be a real pleasure so long as you're willing to spend the money to eat well.

In the last edition of this book we asked, 'So where's the best place if you have just one meal on Raro?,' and were able to answer the question with not one choice, but *three*. This time around, even that is hard to do. With the increasing development of tourism on the island, with the many top-quality restaurants in competition for the customers, and with the high quality of the fresh ingredients to start out with, quite a few come out tops, even by international standards. Portofino's, the Flame Tree, the Vaima and even Metua's all stand out in my mind as favourites, but all for different reasons. It's the rare place that doesn't serve delicious food. In the end, I'll just say the same thing as before – I'd be quite happy to try them all again!

Shopping

Best bargains on groceries are found at the *Foodland* supermarket in Avarua. If you have a lot of food shopping to do, it can be worth taking a trip in to town to do it here. Packaged and imported food is cheaper here than at the tiny local grocery shops dotted around the island; for produce, you're better off to shop elsewhere, even at the tiny local shops, where local produce is sold. Also check out the market near the traffic circle on the ocean side for a good selection and prices.

A wide selection and good prices on international alcoholic beverages are found at the government-run Cook Islands Liquor Supplies (tel 28-380) on the airport side of Avarua. It's open Monday to Friday from 9 am to 4.30 pm and Saturday from 8 am to 12 noon.

Entertainment

Island Nights Cook Islands dancing is reputed to be the best in Polynesia, superior even to the better known dancing of Tahiti. There are plenty of chances to see it at the 'Island Nights' that seem to be on virtually every night of the week. Although the prices hotels quote for their entertainment include meals you can usually get in for the price of a drink or just a small cover charge if you only want to watch.

The *Rarotongan, Edgewater, Tamure* and *Manuia Beach* hotels all hold Island Nights at least once or twice a week. They also hold barbecues and buffets which may include dancing and Polynesian bands. Sunday, when most restaurants are closed, is the big day for hotel barbecues and brunches. The *Banana Court* and the *Big Orange* hold weekly dance performances with the same bands.

The tourist office (tel 29-435) has complete up-to-date information on times and locations for all the Island Nights, dance performances, barbecues, brunches and so on. You can stop by their office in Avarua and pick up a printed weekly schedule any day during normal business hours.

Pubs, Bars & Discos The *Banana Court*

Bar (tel 27-362) on the main street in Avarua is undoubtedly the best known drinking hole in the Cook Islands, indeed it's one of the best known in the whole South Pacific. There's a disco on Monday and Tuesday and a live band from Wednesday to Saturday. On Friday it stays open late, well into Saturday but on Saturday it shuts at midnight and on church-going Sunday the Banana Court closes down completely. It's a hard-drinking locale but relatively peaceful for all that. The band is quite good and their music is much better than the schmaltz played at so many Rarotongan places. And the audience really gets going. With a combination of western and local music, hips sway and legs quiver like they never do back home! It's great fun.

If you want to kick on till even later then head down the road to the *First Club* (tel 21-110), a modern disco with flashing lights. It's behind the Hibiscus Restaurant and there's usually a crowd walking over there when the Banana Court finally shuts its doors.

TJ's Nightclub (tel 20-576), on Avarua's waterfront just past the Empire Theatre, is a popular larger disco which attracts a mostly younger crowd – it's about the most swinging place on the island for the 18-to-25 age group out for a good time.

A number of other similar nightclub/discos are dotted around the island. In Arorangi village, there's the *Big Orange* and *Club Tropicana*. *Purple Rain* is further along, in Kavera, not far from the Rarotongan Hotel.

The *Grandstand Pub*, upstairs at Rarotonga Breweries in Avarua, is a quieter place to go for a beer, a game of darts or billiards, or to see a show (usually sport) on the big-screen video. On weekend nights, a Polynesian string band gets the whole house rocking and singing along.

Metua's, in Brownes' Arcade on Avarua's waterfront, has an atmospheric and enjoyable bar where you can sit under the stars, gaze out to sea and, on Friday and Saturday nights, listen and dance to live music.

Also in Avarua, the outdoor bar at the *Hibiscus Gardens Restaurant* is another pleasant place. Late in the evening, there's a lot of back-and-forth to the nearby First Club disco; the rest of the time it's pretty peaceful.

Tere's, the outdoor bar opposite the Avatiu harbour, catches the offshore breezes and is pleasant and cool under a high pandanus-thatched roof.

At the Edgewater Resort, the *Reef Bar*, to one side of the restaurant, is a good place to come for the almost nightly entertainment of one kind or another. Nearby, the bar at the *Tumunu* is also popular and there's entertainment and a weekly barbecue too.

The *Right-on-the-Beach Bar* at the Manuia Beach Hotel is attractively tropical, right on the beach, just like the name says, with a pandanus roof and sandy floor. The poolside bar at the *Rarotongan Hotel* is another pleasant tropical-style place.

Other Let's not forget Piri Puruto III who zips up coconut trees, demonstrates traditional firemaking and other aspects of traditional Maori culture and gives a generally delightful and entertaining show most weekday afternoons at various locations around the island. A timetable for his shows, plus photographs and international letters of acclaim, are posted at the bus stop opposite the police station in Avarua. The cost of seeing 'The Master of Disaster' in action is NZ$7.50 for adults, NZ$3 for children.

The Master also puts on a weekly 'Piri's Fan Club Picnic' with a traditional *umu*, a feast cooked in an underground stone oven. You pick the three kinds of leaves to use for spicing the food. Cost is NZ$22, which includes free pick-up at your hotel. Piri is also a taxi driver, masseur and all-round colourful island character.

Things to Buy

There are numerous shops around Avarua selling island crafts – they vary from the truly dreadful to the very good. Island Crafts have an excellent selection and employ their own craftspeople who work on woodcarving and shell jewellery. The Cook Islands Women's Craft Federation, on the right-hand corner of the building housing the Banana Court Bar, is the place to look for rito hats and other women's crafts; they have an excellent selection. Local arts and crafts are also sold at the Cook Islands Cultural Village in Arorangi and at the Colonial Craft House in Matavera.

There are a number of boutiques, such as Joyce Peyroux, selling locally manufactured clothing, most of which is exported to New Zealand.

Getting There & Away

See the introductory Getting There & Away chapter for information on getting to or from Rarotonga from overseas and the Getting Around chapter for inter-island flights and shipping services within the Cooks. Airline offices are covered in the Information section.

Outer Island Tours There's more to the Cook Islands than just Rarotonga and even with only one day to spare it's possible to visit another island. Air Rarotonga (tel 22-888) and Cook Islandair (tel 26-304) both operate day trips to Aitutaki. The cost is about NZ$225 for adults, half price for children ages two to 12, and includes a snorkelling cruise of the big Aitutaki lagoon, lunch and some free time to explore. Day trips to Atiu are also planned.

Stars Travel in Avarua (tel 23-669 or 23-683) also offers Aitutaki day tours, plus a variety of two-night packages to Aitutaki, Atiu, Mauke and Mitiaro and a seven-night Island Combination tour including visits to Atiu, Mitiaro and Mauke. See the Getting Around chapter for details.

Getting Around

Airport Transport There are taxis and buses at the airport to meet incoming flights. If you opt for bus transport you're very efficiently organised into parties going in various directions, funnelled into waiting buses and shot off – all for a fare of NZ$5 per person. If you've prepaid (as well as prebooked) your accommodation it's probable you'll find your transport from the airport is included.

If on the other hand you're a real shoestringer and think NZ$5 per person is pretty outrageous for travelling five km to, say, Arorangi (it is) you can get together a group and check the taxis (say NZ$1 a km for the whole taxi) or even wait for the hourly public bus (NZ$2 to anywhere). Unfortunately some flights come in at ungodly hours when the public bus doesn't operate.

Bus There's an island bus service which departs hourly on the hour from the bus stop opposite the police station in the centre of Avarua. It runs right round the coast road in both directions. You can flag the bus down anywhere along its route and the fare is a flat NZ$2. It's a good way of doing a complete circuit of the island and getting an initial feel for the place. The first departure is at 6 am, the last at 4 pm on weekdays. On Saturdays departures are 7 am to 12 noon. On Sunday, plan to walk or take a taxi. The service seems to run pretty much on time so you can work out relevant arrival times around the island, 10 minutes past the hour in Arorangi for example.

Don't be surprised if you're made to get off the bus at the end of the line in Avarua and pay your NZ$2 again if you want to continue on in the same direction when the bus takes off again! The buses don't always do this, but they might.

The Rarotongan Hotel operates a 'Jeepney' bus service Monday to Saturday evenings, leaving the hotel every hour or the hour from 5 to 10 pm and making a complete circle of the island. Fare is NZ$2.50.

Taxi Taxis are radio-controlled so you can phone for them. They're unmetered but fares are usually around NZ$1 a km. A lot of the taxis are small Japanese minivans and they'll often pick up a couple more passengers going your way and offer you a lower fare. During the daytime, when buses are running, many taxi vans charge a fare of NZ$2 per person, the same as the buses.

Rent-a-Car Before you can rent a car or motorcycle you must obtain a local driving licence from the police station in Avarua. It's a straightforward operation taking only a few minutes and costing NZ$2. Even an international permit is not good enough for the Cooks and if your home licence does not include motorcycles you'll have to pay another NZ$2 and take a practical test. This seems to consist of riding down the road from the police station, round the roundabout outside the Banana Court and back again without falling off. You can come to get your licence anytime – the police station is always open – but you must come in the daytime if you need to take the motorcycle test.

You don't need anything very big in Rarotonga – the furthest place you can possibly drive to is half an hour away so the tiny Subaru minicars which are one of the most popular rental vehicles are quite adequate. Subaru seems to have a stranglehold on the Cook Islands car market – every other vehicle is either a Subaru minicar or a Subaru minivan. It's worth phoning around to check the rates as every company seems to have some sort of special rate going. At one extreme there's Budget, the big brother of Cook Islands rent-a-cars, with Subaru 700s and M70s, Daihatsu Micras and Suzukis at NZ$45 a day, Suzuki Sierra jeeps at NZ$55, Subaru Leone sedans and Suzuki minivans at NZ$55 and luxury Nissan Laurels at NZ$99. They sometimes have long weekend, three-days-for-the-price-of-two deals.

Locally-owned TPA is cheaper with older Honda Civics and Datsun 1200s at NZ$38 a day, Nissan Sunnys and Marches at NZ$48. Rental Cars in Avarua is another lower-priced company, also locally owned. The other companies' prices fall somewhere in between. Both Budget and Avis have offices at the airport.

The main Rarotonga companies are:

Ace Rent-a-Car (tel 21-902) – Muri
Avis (tel 22-833) – Rarotonga airport
Budget Rent-a-Car (tel 20-888) – Avarua
Rental Cars (tel 24-442) – Avarua
TPA Rentals (tel 20-611) – Arorangi

There are few surprises for drivers on Raro. The driving is reasonably sane (except late on Friday and Saturday, the two nights when there's heavy drinking) and there's no reason to go fast as there's not far to go wherever you're going. The speed limit is 40 km/h (25 mph) in town, 50 km/h (30 mph) out of town. You drive on the left – like in New Zealand, Australia, Japan and much of the Pacific and South-East Asia.

Be cautious and pay attention to all pedestrians on or near the roadway. Unlike in many parts of the world, where pedestrians keep their wits about them and take precautions not to get hit, in Rarotonga it's the other way around: pedestrians casually wander onto and across the roadway and it's the *driver* who must watch out. Children in particular should be watched for but you should also beware of adults, families, bicyclists, slow motorcycle riders, dogs, pigs and even coconut crabs. This is an especially good reason *never* to drive fast.

Another thing to watch out for is potholes, a notorious problem on Raro. You can be driving down a perfectly fine stretch of road and suddenly find yourself crashing and bumping along on a section full of deep holes. Potholes seem to appear overnight, especially after rain. A major road resurfacing programme is supposed to be completed during 1989. If you're on two wheels watch out for loose stones on some stretches of road.

There are two rental car rules: don't leave windows open, not because of the risk of theft but because of the chances of an unexpected tropical downpour leaving the car awash; and don't park under coconut palms, because a falling coconut can positively flatten a Subaru 600.

Rent-a-Motorcycle or Bicycle There are lots of motorcycles to hire – usually Yamaha or Honda 50 cc or 80 cc 'step throughs' with automatic clutches; they're very easy to ride. Many places rent them, but it doesn't hurt to phone around a bit to find the best deal. Lowest rates are about NZ$10 per day, but only a couple of places are that cheap and often their motorcycles are all taken; NZ$12 to NZ$15 per day is more common. Almost every hotel seems to have a few to rent, but their rates may be up to NZ$20 per day. Most places offer discounts for weekly rentals.

Some of the lower-priced agencies include:

M&T Rentals (tel 21-055) – NZ$10 a day, NZ$70 a week
TPA Rentals (tel 20-610 or 20-611) – NZ$10 a day, NZ$70 a week
Rental Cars (CI) Ltd (tel 24-442) – NZ$12 a day, NZ$72 a week
Odds & Ends (tel 27-595) – single-seaters for NZ$12 a day, NZ$70 a week; two-seaters for NZ$15 a day, NZ$80 a week; NZ$30 refundable deposit
Vaima Rentals (tel 22-222) – NZ$15 a day, NZ$90 a week
Road Runner Rentals (tel 21-144) – 80 cc for NZ$15 a day, NZ$90 a week; 100 cc for NZ$20 a day, NZ$120 a week

Bicycles are equally readily available and generally cost about NZ$7 a day. Many of the above agencies also rent pushbikes. Again the island is compact enough and

the traffic is light enough to make riding a pleasure.

Hitchhiking Hitchhiking is not the custom in the Cooks and it's quite likely that you'll never see anyone do it. However, it's not illegal, only rather cheeky, and if you do put your thumb out you'll probably get a ride in short order. Even if you're just walking down the road looking behind you like you need a ride, some friendly soul will often pull over and offer you a lift.

Tours There are a variety of tour operators on Rarotonga. Probably the best known

Top: South coast scene, Rarotonga (TW)
Left: The Needle (Te Rua Manga), cross-island trek, Rarotonga (TW)
Right: Cricket in the tropics, Rarotonga (TW)

Top: Ascending the final face of Raemaru, Rarotonga (TW)
Left: The Needle from Raemaru (TW)
Right: Bushwalking on Rarotonga (DC/CITA)

and certainly the most often recommended, is Exham Wichman who operates daily tours from Arorangi. His Life Style Tour (NZ$20) takes you along the inland roads to see crops and plantations and explains the land ownership system and continues with a visit to the CICC church and Exham's home. The Historical Tour (NZ$23) includes visits to a number of significant historical sites ranging from ancient to modern times and Exham's explanations will teach you as much about the history and background of this island and its people as you could learn by studying half a library of books. The tour ends with a lunch at Exham's home that is a veritable all-you-can-eat feast of authentic local foods, prepared by Exham's wife Maria, who must be one of the best cooks on the island. Make a reservation directly with Exham (tel 21-180) and he will pick you up and deliver you back to your hotel free of charge.

Two other companies – Union Citco (tel 21-780) and Tipani Tours (tel 22-792) – also operate tours. Union Citco, a travel agency based in Avarua, offers a circle island tour (NZ$16) or, if you're feeling energetic, an across-the-island trek (NZ$15). Tipani has a round-the-island tour (NZ$15), a historical tour (NZ$15) and also a traditional Polynesian lunch which, if you take it along with the tour, brings the tour price to NZ$25.

Air Rarotonga operate flightseeing tours of Rarotonga – if two people turn up, each with NZ$35 in hand (half price for children under 12), they'll send you up right away if there's a plane and pilot available. You get about 20 minutes of Rarotonga from above and a good chance to work out exactly where those mountain trails go and where the good diving spots are. To schedule your trip in advance, or for a free pick-up and delivery back to your hotel, call Air Raro directly (tel 22-888) or book through most hotels or travel agents.

AROUND THE ISLAND

Most island attractions are on or close to the coastal road that encircles Rarotonga. The coast road, a wide, well-surfaced route, is paralleled by a second road which is slightly inland.

This second road, the *Ara Metua*, follows the path of an ancient Rarotongan road which was originally built of coral blocks around 1050 AD. It was known as the 'Great Road of Toi,' although who, exactly, Toi was has been lost in history. Only traces of the old road remain in an original state as most of it was surfaced or built over during WW II.

Prior to the arrival of missionaries the Rarotongans were scattered inland around the plantations and gardens they tended. The missionaries moved them down to the coast and concentrated them in villages to make them easier to control. if you hire a motorcycle and go around the island on the inland road, the Ara Metua, you'll see another side to the island – swamp taro fields, white goats and black pigs grazing in pawpaw patches, citrus groves, men on ancient tractors or even digging out entire fields with a shovel, graves of the ancestors, off to one side of the houses. Everywhere you go, when you wave to the people, they wave back to you.

The following description moves around the island counterclockwise and km distances from the centre of Avarua are indicated. The island is divided up into regions. Puaikura Betela includes Arorangi on the west coast; the south-east part including Titikaveka, Ngatangiia and Matavera is known as Takitumu.

Airport (2.5 km)

The Rarotonga International Airport was officially opened in 1974 and tourism in the Cooks really started at that time. Artist Jillian Sobiesky (tel 21-079) may have an art gallery near the Air Rarotonga terminal, if she has managed to move out of her old gallery in Muri. She does beautiful paintings of local scenes and flowers, and they're not too expensive.

Behind the airport, on the Ara Metua road, is the Tereora Stadium, where many of Rarotonga's big events are held. It was constructed in 1985 for the South Pacific Mini Games, the first international stadium to be built in the Cook Islands. Beside it is Tereora College.

Cemetery (2.5 km)
Opposite the airport terminal is a small graveyard known locally as the 'brickyard'. A controversial Australian cancer-cure specialist Milan Brych (pronounced 'brick') set himself up in Rarotonga after being chucked out of Australia. When his patron, Cook Islands Prime Minister Sir Albert Henry, was run out of office in 1978, Brych was soon run out of the country as well - he's now in the USA. Cancer patients who died despite his treatment are buried in the graveyard.

Tom Neale, the hermit of Suwarrow atoll, is also buried opposite the airport. He died in 1977 and his grave is in the front corner of the Retired Servicemen's Association cemetery, entered through the gates with the 'Lest We Forget' sign.

Parliament (3.5 km)
The Cook Islands Parliament is just across from the Air Rarotonga terminal. The building was erected in 1973-74 as a hostel for the New Zealand workers that came to work on the construction of the airport. The Prime Minister's and other ministers' offices are in the former bedrooms, with a few walls rearranged.

Parliament meets February to March and July to September and so long as you're properly dressed you can watch proceedings from the public gallery. Hours are 1 to 5 pm Monday, Tuesday and Thursday, 9 am to 1 pm Wednesday and Friday. If you happen to wander in when Parliament is not in session, one of the staff will give you a short tour of the building.

Golf Course (5.5 km)
The Rarotonga Golf Club (tel 27-360)

welcomes visitors to play on its nine-hole course. A round (or two to make it 18) costs NZ$5 green fee and you can also rent a set of clubs for NZ$10 a half day. The golf course is open Monday to Friday from 8 am to 3.30 pm; Saturday is for members only and it's closed on Sunday.

Black Rock (6.5 km)
Just beyond the golf course and down on the beach is Black Rock, where Papeiha is supposed to have swum ashore, clasping the Bible over his head. Actually he was rowed ashore in a small boat! This is also the legendary departure point from where the spirits of the dead are supposed to commence their voyage back to the legendary homeland of Hawaiiki. If you follow the road up behind the hospital there are good views (see the Walking & Climbing section).

Arorangi (8 km)
Just south of the airport, this was the first missionary-built village and was conceived of as a model village for all the others on the island. There are a number of popular places to stay in Arorangi and a couple of popular restaurants. Along the road there are numerous small shops.

The main place of interest in Arorangi is the 1849 CICC church - a large white building which still has an important role to play in village life. The missionary Papeiha, the first to preach the Christian gospel in Rarotonga, is buried here, right in the centre front of the church; a huge monument to him has been raised by his many descendants.

Just to the left of the church is the old Tinomana Palace, built for the last local ruler by the British. The name of the palace is *Au Maru,* meaning 'the Peace brought by Christianity.'

Interestingly, Tinomana, the chief who first accepted the message of Christianity from Papeiha, is not buried in the church graveyard although he is honoured by a memorial plaque inside the church. He later became Papeiha's father-in-law when the missionary married one of his daughters and he gave the land that the church is built upon, but he is buried on the hill behind Arorangi, near his old *marae*. Did he have second thoughts about his adopted religion? If you go on one of Exham's Historical Tours, he may take you to see where Tinomana is buried.

The Clare Higham Art Studio (tel 20-238) is in Arorangi in a brown A-frame house right on the beach, just beside the Edgewater Resort's tennis courts. Although she is now in her 70s her watercolours and line-and-wash depictions of local Rarotongan scenes and flowers are much appreciated both in Rarotonga and New Zealand. Prices are in the NZ$40 to NZ$100 range. You'll find the friendly artist here from April to November, the rest of the year she lives in Mt Maunganui, New Zealand.

Arorangi is also the home of Vaikanoa, the only 24 hour petrol station and grocery shop on Rarotonga, near the Outrigger Restaurant. Rising up behind Arorangi is the flat-topped peak of Raemaru. See the Walking & Climbing section which follows for details of the climb.

Cultural Village (7 km)
The Cook Islands Cultural Village on Arorangi's back road is a delightful experience. The village open around 9.30 am Monday to Friday and the village tour visits old-style thatched huts with demonstrations of coconut frond weaving, coconut husking, traditional firemaking and cooking, ancient fishing techniques, history, woodcarving and more. Following your tour there's a feast of traditional foods and your tours hosts and the people from the various huts all get together for a wonderful show of traditional music, dance and chants, lasting until about 1.30 pm.

At NZ$28 for adults, NZ$14 for children five to 14, it's not cheap, but you'll learn more about traditional Cook Islands culture in one day than you probably will for the rest of your stay. Call in advance

(tel 21-314) to arrange free transport from your hotel.

The Pearl Shop (8 km)
The Pearl Shop (tel 21-901) in Arorangi has a fascinating collection of natural (not cultured) pearls from the Northern Group islands of Manihiki and Penrhyn. The shop also has pearls from other parts of the world including black and white cultured pearls, many from French Polynesia, and huge shiny mother-of-pearl shells of the black lip variety. The shop is open 10 am to 5 pm Monday to Friday, 10 am to 1 pm Saturday.

Betela Studio (10 km)
Edwin Shorter, known as 'Edwin the Painter,' is an eccentric artist born in 1902 who paints mostly in a Gauguinesque style but also does surrealist paintings, portraits and sculpture. His paintings in the Betela Studio are priced from about NZ$185 up to NZ$6000. When you approach the doorway, you'll see a hand-painted sign on the door stating that your visit must result in your buying a painting, or else a NZ$7 souvenir card! The Betela Studio (tel 25-733) is open Monday to Friday afternoons from 2.30 to 5.30 pm and by appointment.

South Coast (from 12 km)
The south coast of Rarotonga from the Rarotongan Resort right round to the Muri Lagoon has the best beach and swimming. The reef is much further out and the sea bottom is relatively free from rocks and sandier than the other beaches. There are lots of good places to stop for a swim, particularly from around the 16 to 20 km mark.

The southern end of the trans-island trek is at about 14.5 km, immediately before the Papua Stream. See the Walking & Climbing section for details. At 16.5 km you can pull off the road beside the beach and park: the beach is very fine here. Just across the road is a sign to the Duncan Bertram Memorial Garden which is half a km off the coast road, on the Ara Metua. It's just a pleasant garden where a resident has spent some time cultivating orchids and other local flowers.

Titikaveka (19 km)
There's another picturesque CICC church at Titikaveka with some interesting old headstones in the graveyard.

Muri Lagoon (22 to 25 km)
The reef is further out from the shore on the south side of the island and the Muri Lagoon has the best stretch of beach on the island. The water, though still shallow, has a sandy bottom dotted with countless sea slugs. Out towards the reef are four small islands or *motus*: Taakoka, Koromiri, Oneroa and Motutapu. Taakoka is volcanic, the other islets are sand cays.

The beach by the Pacific Resort, on the coast side of Koromiri, is particularly popular and at low tide you can easily wade out from the sailing club. Countless hermit crabs scuttle around in the forested undergrowth while offshore on

the reef is the rusted hulk of a Japanese tuna fishing boat, the *Iwakuni Maru No 1*, which washed up onto the reef in the early '60s. You can wade out to the wreck; the hull has now broken in two and debris litters the reef.

Sea slugs are an oriental delicacy and many people around Muri find their lagoon's abundant sea slug population delicious. Expatriate Rarotongans in New Zealand say that they absolutely crave them when they are away! The slug's internals look rather like spaghetti and around here a reference to eating spaghetti probably means sea slug rather than pasta. Sea slugs are best cooked with butter, garlic and spices but the locals are equally happy to eat them raw, even picking one up in the lagoon, tearing the skin open and squeezing the guts out.

Welland Studio (22 km)
Rick Welland is a personable Californian who has successfully made the seemingly impossible transition from Los Angeles to the Cook Islands. It's hard to imagine two places more diametrically opposed but

Taakoka motu, Muri Lagoon, Rarotonga

he's been here for 25 years so he must have managed the change. His paintings capture the people and scenery of Polynesia perfectly. The 'Ina and the Shark' artwork on all the Cook Islands dollar notes is based on a painting by Welland; the original painting is now on display at the Westpac Bank in downtown Avarua. Welland's watercolours are generally in the NZ$80 to NZ$120 bracket. The artist's studio (tel 23-666), in a small chalet in front of his house, is usually open during the daytime and you're welcome to drop in for a look.

Rarotonga Sailing Club (23 km)

The Sailing Club on Muri Lagoon welcomes visitors and has a bar and snack bar upstairs, with a small billiard table and a gorgeous view of the lagoon from the 2nd floor verandah. You can hire sailboats, windsurfers, kayaks, Indian and outrigger canoes, rowboats and snorkelling equipment, at hourly or daily rates from the Aqua Sports desk downstairs. Windsurfing lessons, novice scuba dives in the lagoon, guided reef walks and lagoon cruises in a glass-bottomed boat

are also available. The club (tel 27-350) is open Monday to Saturday from 9 am to 6 pm; it's often open in the evening as well, when it acts as a sort of social club for the locals to come in, have a beer, play billiards and socialise.

It's rumoured that the bones of Captain Goodenough's female companion were buried near the clubhouse. She was killed and eaten in 1814 while the *Cumberland* was at Rarotonga – see the Rarotonga History section.

Rarotonga Marine Park (24 km)

The Marine Park and Coral Garden (tel 22-450) has a large circular tank with a collection of the corals and tropical fish found in the waters around Rarotonga. The tiny animal zoo has a very small collection of native animals, including flying foxes or fruit bats. There are lots of turtles here and educational exhibits on sharks and other animals. It's open Tuesday to Saturday from 10 am to 4.30 pm; admission is NZ$4 for adults, half price for children. Telephone first before you come out, to see if it's open – the schedule sometimes changes and it's been closed down and reopened several times.

Ngatangiia Harbour (25 km)

Just north of Motutapu, the northern-most of the four Muri Lagoon islands, is the comparatively wide and deep reef passage into Ngatangiia Harbour. It's a popular mooring spot for visiting yachts. This is also the legendary departure point for the seven Maori canoes which set off around 1350 AD on the great voyage which resulted in the Maori settlement of New Zealand. Just across from the big white CICC church, a circle of seven stones commemorates this event, beside a historical plaque. On the point of land to your left as you gaze out through the harbour passage is the large well-preserved *marae* where the mariners were given their blessing for the journey and where human sacrifices were made to the gods.

Matavera (27.5 km)
The CICC church at Ngatangiia isn't one of the prettiest on the island but the one at Matavera makes up for that. The scenery inland of the stretch of road before Avarua is particularly fine.

Colonial Craft House (28.5 km)
Built in 1854 and recently restored the Colonial Craft House is one of the oldest colonial homes on the island. It now houses various shops offering local crafts and products from Rarotonga and the outer islands, including soaps, perfumes, jams and dried fruits, weavings and more. Out on the verandah, fresh fruit juices, Atiu coffee, homemade fruit breads and scones, and local fruit jams are all sold at the same low price of 50c. The Craft House (tel 21-238) is open Monday to Friday from 9 am to 4.30 pm, Saturday from 10 am to 2 pm.

Arai-Te-Tonga (30 km)
Just before you arrive back in Avarua a small sign points off the road to the most important *marae* site on the island. Marae were the religious ceremonial gathering places of pre-Christian Polynesian society; the *koutu*, similar in appearance, were political meeting grounds where *ariki*, the great chiefs of pre-missionary Rarotonga, held court. Ceremonial offerings to the ancient gods were also collected here before being placed upon the *marae*.

A great *marae* is on your right as you go down this road towards the Ara Metua back road. Beside the Ara Metua is a stone marked *koutu* site; if you walk down the Ara Metua to your left you'll see on your right yet another ceremonial ground. This whole area was a gathering place and the remains of the *marae*, the *koutu* and other meeting grounds are still here. Arai-Te-Tonga has the remains of an oblong platform four metres long that was at one time over two metres high. At one end stands the 'investiture pillar,' a square basalt column two metres high which

extends an equal distance down into the ground. Don't walk on the *marae*; it's still a sacred site.

Turn left (north-west) along the Ara Metua for about 100 metres and another sign indicates a stretch of still relatively original road. At one time, perhaps as long as 1500 years ago, the Ara Metua was composed of coral and lava rock along its entire length.

Inland Drives
Two inland drives on the north side of the island give you an opportunity to see the lush fertile valleys of Rarotonga, with mountains towering above on every side. Both go along streams and both are in areas historically populated by the Rarotongan people before the missionaries came.

The drive along Avatiu Stream begins at Avatiu Harbour – just turn inland at the harbour and keep going straight ahead. The road extends about 3.5 km inland; at the end of the road is the beginning of the Cross-Island Trek, which must be continued on foot past this point.

The other drive is up into the Takuvaine Valley, reached by going inland on the road past the post office in Avarua and continuing inland. You pass the ruins of the old Happy Valley Disco, one of Raro's favourite nightspots until it was destroyed in 1987 by Hurricane Sally. The homes and the agricultural lands have been repaired and restored and it's a wonderfully peaceful place. The Takuvaine road goes inland for about two km; a walking track extends inland and upwards to the Te Kou mountain.

WALKING & CLIMBING
You don't have to get very far into the interior of Rarotonga to realise the population is almost entirely concentrated along the narrow coastal fringe. The mountainous interior is virtually deserted and can be reached only by walking tracks and trails.

The Cook Islands Conservation Service

(see the Information section above) puts out a leaflet titled *A Guide to Walks & Climbs* with brief details on a number of interesting walks, some of which are covered in greater detail here. The trail details are very sketchy and the situation is not helped by the little used and indistinct trails. The valley walks are easy strolls suitable even for older people or young children and the scaling of the hill behind the hospital is also easy and short, although a bit steep, but most of the other walks are hard work, often involving difficult scrambling over rocky sections. Apart from the cross island track by the Needle most of the walks are a cross between scaling Everest and hacking your way through the Amazon jungle. Often the views aren't that good either – all you can see is the jungle right in front of your nose.

The interior of Rarotonga is surprisingly mountainous with some steep slopes and sheer drops. It's wise to keep an eye out for these drops as you can stumble across them quite suddenly. Although the trails are often difficult to follow Rarotonga is too small for you to get really lost. You can generally see where you're going or where you've come from. Anyway, following any stream will bring you back down to a coast road.

Walking will generally be easier if you follow the ridges rather than trying to beat your way across the often heavily overgrown slopes. Rarotonga has no wild animals, snakes or poisonous insects (except for centipedes, wasps and annoying red ants) but it's wise to wear some sort of leg or ankle protection as you can easily get badly scratched forcing your way through thick brush. Wear running shoes not thongs as the trails can often be quite muddy and slippery. Carry some drinking water too; hiking in Rarotonga can be thirsty work. Walking times quoted are for a round trip from the nearest road access point and do not allow for getting lost – which on most trails is a distinct possibility.

Organised Walks The popular trans-island trek is regularly organised through local travel agents. Pa, a big friendly, dreadlocked fellow, leads a not-too-difficult trek each Monday, Wednesday and Friday at 10 am. Cost is NZ$20 for adults, NZ$10 for children under 12, call 21-079 for details.

Trans-Island Trek (3 to 4 hours)
The trek across the island via 413 metre Te Rua Manga (The Needle) is the most popular walk on the island. It can also be

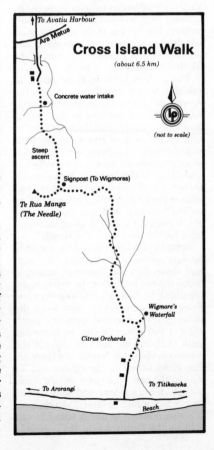

Cross Island Walk
(about 6.5 km)

(not to scale)

To Avatiu Harbour
Ara Metua
Concrete water intake
Steep ascent
Signpost (To Wigmores)
Te Rua Manga (The Needle)
Wigmore's Waterfall
Citrus Orchards
To Arorangi
To Titikaveka
Beach

done as a shorter walk from the north to the Needle and back again rather than continuing all the way to the south coast. Tour companies take parties on this walk. There are several places on this walk that get extremely slippery when there's been wet weather.

The road to the starting point runs south from Avatiu Harbour – it's the road running round the back of the airport. The turn-off from this road, which is actually the Ara Metua, is indicated with a sign 'To the Needle'. You can continue easily for about 2.5 km past the power station but then the road begins to deteriorate badly. Unless you're on a motorcycle you're best walking the last km to the starting point which is by a concrete water intake. A sign announces that you're at the start of the Te Rua Manga walking track.

The path is fairly level for about 10 minutes, then it drops down, crosses the Avatiu stream and then climbs steeply and steadily all the way to the Needle, about a 45-minute walk. If it wasn't for the tangled stairway of tree roots the path would be very slippery in the wet (which it often is). This makes the climb easy but also tiring. At the first sight of the Needle there's a convenient rock to sit on and admire the view. A little further on a sign to 'The Waterfall' indicates the way to the south coast; it's only a short diversion from here to the base of the Needle.

Actually climbing the Needle is strictly for very serious rock climbers – it's high and sheer. You can, however, scramble round the north side to a sheer drop and a breathtaking view from its western edge. From here you can look back down the valley you've ascended from the north coast or look across north-west to the flat peak of Raemaru. You can also see the south coast from the Needle and there are fine views across to Maungatea and Te Kou to the east. Take care on this climb though, there's a long and unprotected drop which would be fatal if you slipped. It's also possible to climb round in the split on the southern side of the Needle

but the view is no better and it's a considerably trickier climb.

Retrace your steps to the waterfall sign from where the south coast track drops slightly then climbs to a small peak that gives you get the best view of the Needle you're going to find. From here the track drops slowly down to the south coast, frequently crossing streams and eventually winding back and forth countless times across the Papua Stream. Despite the helpful tree roots this long descent can be annoyingly slippery.

Eventually you get back on to the flat coastal strip right beside the beautiful Wigmore's Waterfall. If you're hot, sweaty and muddy by this time the pool under the fall is a real delight. The sign near the pool warning that the stream is a drinking water supply and that hikers should keep out of it does not apply to the pool as the water intake point is above the waterfall.

From here you're on a vehicle track which brings you back to the coast road in about 15 minutes – passing through coconut and papaya plantations and fields of taro, beans and tomatoes.

Maungatea (3 to 4 hours)
Maungatea (523 metres) is the peak behind that impressively sheer cliff face directly overlooking Avarua. I did not find this climb particularly interesting and I'm not even sure if I got to the top as it is thickly overgrown and hard to see.

The entry road leads off the Ara Metua and ends just before two houses. You can leave a vehicle and walk straight on in the direction of the road through a small citrus grove and pick up the trail at the other side. The trail crosses the stream a couple of times and then starts to wind up the hill. If it has been raining the trail can be very muddy because of the many pigs around. Island pigs are kept by the simple method of tying a rope from a tree to a front leg. They're fed mainly on coconuts and you'll probably see some pigs – and certainly lots of coconut husks – in this area. Pigs seem to escape fairly regularly

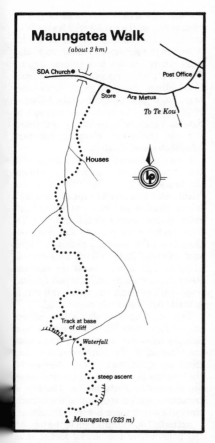

Maungatea Walk

(about 2 km)

SDA Church●

Post Office ●

● Store   Ara Metua

To Te Kou

Houses

Track at base
of cliff

Waterfall

steep ascent

▲ *Maungatea (523 m)*

the other side. It's very steep but there are plenty of roots and branches to hang onto. Take care, many of them are dead and rotten and break away if you put any weight on them.

Eventually you reach the top of the ridge, also a sheer rock face but facing the Takuvaine Valley. Here your troubles really start because there's no trail at all – you just have to push your way up through the ferns, bracken and bush. The ridge is a real knife edge but if you leave it and drop down on the west side it's much too steep and overgrown to get through. Occasionally you get glimpses of Avarua and the north coast at your feet. Looking over the valley from the ridge you have fine views of Ikurangi and Te Manga but mostly you just see dense bush. Whether you're getting close to the top is hard to tell. Perhaps it would be easier to try and hit the ridge top further up towards the summit but without knowing where you're going it's hard to tell.

Coming back down is pleasantly fast, you just slither down the steep slope, grabbing roots and branches as you go.

Te Kou (5 hours)

Te Kou (588 metres) is more or less in the centre of the island and is interesting because there is a crater at the top, indicating Rarotonga's volcanic origins. You can leave a vehicle on the road just before a small group of houses. A track leads off to the left (east) across the river – if you get to the large rectangular water tank you've gone too far. Follow the track until another leads off it to the left (east) and take the left track – don't take the first small foot trail, wait until you get to a wider track (big enough for a small jeep, although it soon becomes narrower).

You soon come out into a valley of taro patches which you have to make your way through by any route you can find. At the far end of the taro patches look for the trail on the right (west) side of the Takuvaine Valley. You progress through a dense patch of bush, wading through the river

so you'll also come across loose ones as well.

The trail starts to climb more steeply and as it does it becomes rather drier, eventually reaching the base of the sheer rock face of Maungatea Bluff. At times the trail seems to simply disappear but all you have to do is keep moving uphill and you'll reach the rock face. Follow the trail at the foot of the face round to the left (east) and eventually you'll meet a small waterfall trickling down the middle. Cross the stream and start climbing the hill on

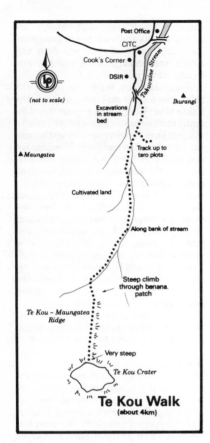

Te Kou Walk
(about 4km)

the west side of the valley for about five to 10 minutes until a rivulet trickles into the stream on the east side. This is the track! Abandon the stream and climb up to the ridge where the track is evident again. This is a typical Rarotongan hand over hand climb, hanging on to roots and branches to haul yourself up the hillside. Half way up the trail goes through a banana patch but eventually you come out on the ridge running between Maungatea and Te Kou.

If you go down the ridge slightly you come to a fallen tree; you can climb out on the trunk and get a fine view across to Maungatea and down to the north coast. It's worth marking where you reached the ridge so that when you descend from Te Kou you know the point to dive down off the ridge to the stream. The ridge is a real knife edge and there's a fairly distinct trail along it. This is not always the case on Rarotongan walking trails, in fact finding a soft drink can half way up this ridge trail actually felt pleasantly reassuring!

The climb up the ridge is fairly steep but not dangerous. There are even ropes to help the hiker on the steepest parts. From the summit, ie the northern crater rim, there are magnificent views. Beware of the trenches that lead along the rim, some are covered by rusty plates. There is a translator station round at the southern rim but getting there is very difficult.

Actually I don't think I got to the top. At the point where the official leaflet says there is a 'steep climb through bracken to the summit' I, for once in my life, got sensible and gave up. To my mind 'vertical' was a better description than 'steep'. The top disappeared into the clouds and I decided I'd rather have a cold beer! Two readers have subsequently written about climbing Te Kou, one gave up like me, the other reckoned he reached the top. Instructions from Kurt Eder, the successful climber, are integrated with my own above but I must admit I'm still puzzled as to where I went wrong!

Going down is, as usual, much easier

once, and then come into a second narrower valley of taro. At the end of this valley the trail is again to the right side but the valley is narrower and it's easier to find.

From here the trail winds back and forth across the stream and climbs steadily higher. It's fairly easy to follow – overgrown at times but you can always find traces of it. At times it climbs high above the stream but it frequently returns to it. If you have the Lands & Survey 1:25,000 scale Rarotonga map the trail seems to disappear at around the 200 metre contour line. Follow the riverbed on

You slither down the slope from the ridge with great rapidity and finding a way down through the taro swamps is much easier than finding your way up.

Raemaru (3 hours)

Raemaru (351 metres) is the flat-topped peak rising directly behind Arorangi on the west coast. From the coast road you can easily see the route to the top running up a sharp ridge line to the rock face below the final summit area.

Turn off the coast road to the Ara Metua just beyond the Cook Islands Christian Church and then turn right (south) on the Ara Metua. A track (accessible for motorcycles) turns off the Ara Metua to the Te Vai Uri reservoir. Alternatively you can turn off the coast road by the building marked 'Betela' (follow the sign to the Rose Flats) and then turn left (north) on the Ara Metua and take the steep but clear foot track which runs up to the south end of the same reservoir.

From the northern end of the reservoir look for trails leading up through the bracken ferns which stretch above the reservoir. These terraced slopes are all that remains of an abandoned project to grow pineapples. The trails are often very indistinct and there are a number of them – you'll often find yourself simply bashing through the brush but you soon come out above this and the way is clear.

An alternate way to get up here is to walk on the Avarua side of the reservoir and go left along the embankment beside the reservoir for about 10 metres, then up over the embankment. Walk straight up the hill through low bracken fern, veering to the left. Within 10 metres of leaving the embankment you'll hit an old disused and badly eroded road, which looks more like a creekbed than a road due to the deep erosion. Watching your footing, follow this road up the mountain.

A very distinct trail runs up the narrow ridge running directly towards the peak. If you've emerged from the ferns further to the south you'll find yourself on an alternative ridge with a wide, bare trail area along the top. It'll also get you there. On either ridge the trail eventually ends and you then have to turn to the right (south) across a slightly lower saddle to

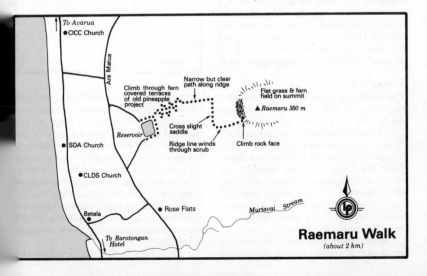

Raemaru Walk
(about 2 km)

another ridge which takes you right to the rock face of Raemaru. The vegetation here, and indeed all the way to the top, includes ferns but not exclusively as is the case on the lower slopes.

This second ridge trail winds through bush and scrub eventually running right along a sharp edge with fine views down into the Muriavai Valley. The Canterbury Museum in New Zealand has conducted a great deal of research in this valley and found evidence of various early settlements. Eventually the trail ends abruptly at the sheer rock face of Raemaru, well over to the southern edge of the face where it is lower than to the north. This is the hardest part of the climb as you have a tricky scramble up the face to the final plateau. The faint of heart or those who aren't experienced rock climbers may decide to call it a day here. If you press on take care, especially if the rocks are slippery as there's a bit of hanging on by the fingertips and scrabbling for toeholds on the way to the top.

Finally you emerge on an open grassy area which slopes gently to the top. From the far end you can look down across a valley to 519 metre Maungaroa and 413 metre Te Rua Manga, the easily recognised peak on the cross island walk known as the Needle. Looking back you can see along the coast all the way from south of Arorangi to the airport runway in the north.

Ikurangi (4 hours)

The ascent of Ikurangi (485 metres) is easier than Te Kou. The track starts from the Ara Metua just to the east of Arai te Tonga (see the Around the Island section). This is the same route as the trail to Te Manga, Rarotonga's highest mountain, along the Tupapa stream through taro plots but the Ikurangi trail soon branches off to the west. Finding where this trail starts is the most difficult part, if there are locals working in the taro patches ask them for the track.

The trail starts near some hills with low scrub on the western side of the stream.

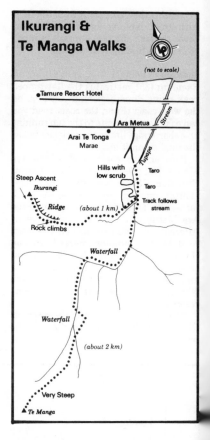

**Ikurangi &
Te Manga Walks**

(not to scale)

• Tamure Resort Hotel

Ara Metua

Arai Te Tonga
Marae

Hills with
low scrub

Steep Ascent
Ikurangi

Ridge   (about 1 km)

Rock climbs

Taro

Taro

Track follows
stream

Waterfall

Waterfall

(about 2 km)

Very Steep

▲ *Te Manga*

Take the third ridge on these hills and climb from the riverbed through the bush to the scrub then scan the ridge for the track. It can be a tiring struggle to get there but once you have found the track the route up to the top is fairly easy except for a short rock climb and then the final steep ascent. The track follows the narrow ridge through the bush moving to the left at the base of the rock summit. There's a steep and tricky climb round the south-west side of the peak then along the ridge to the top.

A Cook Islands flag awaits you on the

summit and there are fine views of Avarua, the north coast and the Takuvaine Valley. There's a sheer drop of nearly 300 metres from the summit so take care. From the top you may see white tropic birds, soaring by apparently without a wingstroke.

Te Manga (5 hours)
Rarotonga's highest mountain Te Manga (653 metres) is probably the most difficult climb on the island. An experienced local guide is probably a necessity if you want to reach the top. The trail starts off the same as the Ikurangi route, following the Tupapa stream through taro plots to the point where the Ikurangi trail branches off to the west.

The Te Manga trail follows the Tupapa stream further inland before branching off along a tributary just beyond a waterfall. The trail goes through plantations of wild bananas, round to the left (east) of a 13-metre waterfall and ascends a ridge marked by a cairn towards the summit. The final ridge to the top is very narrow and steep and great care must be taken. Kurt Eder, who supplied useful notes on Te Kou and Ikurangi for this edition, says he didn't attempt Te Manga after he met some climbers who'd spent eight hours trying to find a way to the top!

Hospital Hill
About the easiest way to climb up to a good viewpoint is to drive up the hill to the hospital, just behind the golf course, park in the parking lot there and continue up the hill on foot. It's an easy walk which even children and elderly people can do without a struggle. For those in good shape, the walk to the top takes about five minutes. The view from the top is beautiful and unobstructed, with the airport on one side, a lush agricultural valley stretching inland from there between mountain ridges and, on the other side, the village of Arorangi, pushing from the coast up to the sides of the mountains. The different colours of water in the lagoon, much deeper blue out past the reef, the wide vista of ocean stretching off into the distance and the fresh breezes blowing by up on the top of the hill, all make it a most refreshing change from the lowlands.

Valley & Beach Walks
The mountain walks on Rarotonga are hard work. If you want something easier consider the valley walks, such as the stroll along the Avana stream from Ngatangiia. You can drive quite a distance up the road beside the stream and then follow the trail, repeatedly crossing the stream until you reach a pleasant picnic spot at the water intake. A similar walk follows the Turangi stream a little north of Ngatangiia and there is also a trail beside the Muriavai stream in the shadow of Raemaru on the Arorangi side of the island. Be prepared for mosquitoes on these walks.

Two other beautiful valleys are Takuvaine, behind Avarua, and Avatiu, inland from Avatiu Harbour. See details on these under Inland Drives. They also have walking tracks extending up into the valleys and even across the island, beyond where the roads end.

Any beach on Rarotonga is pleasant for strolling. Start beside Muri Lagoon, for example, and walk towards Titikaveka for fine views of the *motus* on the edge of the lagoon.

A Request
I found the various climbs on Rarotonga rather harder than I'd anticipated. The trails were often difficult to find and then hard to follow. At times it was impossible to know where you were and more than once I failed to reach the final objective of the walk. If you do manage to find better ways up these mountains or have additional suggestions to make – both about these walks and other possible walks – I'd be very glad to hear them. Kurt Eder (Austria) supplied useful notes on Te Kou and Ikurangi for this edition.

Aitutaki & Manuae

Aitutaki

Population: 2391
Area: 18.1 square km

Aitutaki is another Cook Islands entrant in the 'most beautiful island in the Pacific' competition. It's the second largest island in the Cooks in terms of population although in area it only ranks sixth. It's also the second most popular island in terms of tourist visits. The hook-shaped island nestles in a huge triangular lagoon, 12 km across its base and 15 km from top to bottom. The outer reef of the lagoon is dotted with beautiful *motus* (small islands) and they're one of the island's major attractions.

The people of Aitutaki are particularly friendly and open, unfortunately their mosquitoes are also decidedly gregarious! Aitutaki has one of the best 'Island Nights' in the Cook Islands; try to arrange to be on the island on a Friday night to catch this authentic local occasion.

Apart from the beaches, *motus*, snorkelling, fishing and dancing Aitutaki is also historically interesting because this was the first foothold in the Cooks for the London Missionary Society. Only after converting Aitutaki's population did they move on to Rarotonga.

History

Various legends tell of early Polynesian settlers arriving at Aitutaki by canoe. The first settler was Ru, coming from the island of Tupuaki in what is today French Polynesia. Tupuaki had become over-crowded so Ru, his four wives, his four brothers and their wives, and a crew of 20 royal maidens sailed off in search of new land. Eventually they landed on Aitutaki at the *motu* Akitua, and decided to make this their new home.

Ru went to the highest point on the island, the top of Mt Maungapu, and surveyed the island. He divided the land into 20 sections, one for each of the 20 royal maidens, but completely forgot about his brothers! One brother had been killed as the huge canoe was hauled onto land, rolling it over logs. The three remaining brothers left the island in anger – they had come all that way to find a new land to settle, and yet Ru allotted no land for them. They continued over the ocean and eventually wound up in New Zealand.

The original name of Aitutaki was Ararau Enua O Ru Ki Te Moana, meaning 'Ru in search of land over the sea.' Later this long name was shortened to a more manageable mouthful: Araura. Still later the name was changed again to its present one of Aitutaki – *a'i tutaki* means 'to keep the fire going' – but the old names are still used in legend and chant. Akitua, the *motu* now occupied by the Aitutaki Resort, was the party's landing place and was originally named Uri Tua O Ru Ki Te Moana, or 'Ru turning his back to the sea.'

Various canoes came after Ru's party, from Tonga, Samoa and islands in French Polynesia, landing on different parts of the island. Each new people had to be accepted by one of the 20 maidens or their descendants in order to have a space on the island to settle. One explorer from a far-off land, guided to Aitutaki by Are Mangoa, the god of sharks, came ashore on the south part of the island and built the *marae* Tokongarangi to honour that god.

The island's European discoverer was Captain William Bligh on board the *Bounty* on 11 April 1789. The famous mutiny took place just 17 days later as the ship was en route to Tonga. Two years later in May 1791 Captain Edward Edwards came by in HMS *Pandora* searching for those mutineers, and in 179 Bligh paid his second visit to the island

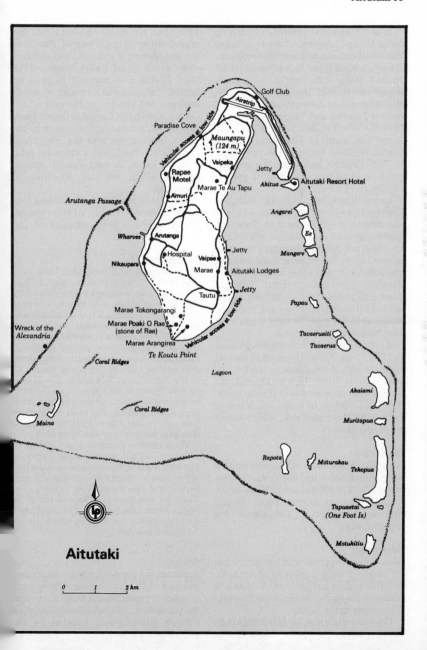

Aitutaki

0   1   2 km

In 1814 Captain Goodenough turned up with his ship *Cumberland* after his visit to Rarotonga came to its ill-starred conclusion. He left behind three Rarotongans whom he had taken with him on his sudden departure. In 1821 the missionary John Williams visited Aitutaki briefly and left behind Papeiha and Vahapata, converts from the island of Raiatea near Tahiti, to begin the work of Christianising the Cooks. Williams returned two years later to find Papeiha had made remarkable progress so he was moved on to greater challenges in Rarotonga.

Later European visitors included Charles Darwin on the famous voyage of the *Beagle* in 1835. The first European missionary took up residence in 1839 and the 1850s saw Aitutaki became a favourite port of call for the whaling ships scouring the Pacific at that time. During WW II Aitutaki went through great upheaval when a large American contingent moved in to build the island's two long runways, which until the mid-70s were larger than Rarotonga's airport runway.

Aitutaki suffered from a major hurricane in 1977. At the Rapae Hotel water washed right through the restaurant and kitchen area and the family unit up the hill was turned into an emergency dining room. The CICC church in town, which is well back from the waterfront, also suffered extensive damage.

Orientation

Arutanga is the main settlement on this large island, about halfway down the west coast. There are five other villages on the island. The numerous small *motus* around the edge of the lagoon are unpopulated.

Information

The Survey Department in Rarotonga has an excellent large scale map of Aitutaki. It's also widely available on Aitutaki. It shows all the roads and trails and the coral formations in the lagoon.

Cook Islandair and Air Rarotonga both have their offices on the road into the main town Arutanga. The post office is on the intersection of this road and the road down to the wharf, and a branch of the Cook Islands Development Bank is up behind that. You can't change money at the bank but you can at the post office! Once a month the Pacific & Orient Bank comes to Aitutaki and operates from the Te Ivi Maori store, near the post office, and offers a much better exchange rate. Aitutaki issues its own special postage stamps which are not available in Rarotonga.

Ask at your hotel if you should boil your water before drinking it. At some places, the water comes from underground and should be boiled first.

Dogs & Pigs

There are no dogs at all on Aitutaki and nobody is allowed to bring dogs to the island. There haven't been any for quite a few years and there are numerous stories as to what happened to them. Probably the best is that the Aitutakians, like the Tahitians, savoured dog-meat and eventually ate them all. Another is that the dogs were thought to be carriers of leprosy, which at one time was rampant on the island. Still another story is that a dog mauled an *ariki's* (high chief's) child and he then banned all dogs. Whatever the reason it's a relief not to be tripping over them all the time and not to have to worry about your shoes being stolen from outside your door at night. And Aitutaki does have some healthy looking stray cats!

There are also plenty of pigs – that most popular of Pacific domestic animals. South Sea pigs have learnt to make coconuts a major part of their diet although well-kept pigs also have papaya and taro mash! They're tasty pigs. There are even some pigs, kept on one of the *motus*, which have learnt to dig up and break open the *pahua* clam shells which are an Aitutakian delicacy!

Arutanga

Arutanga is a pleasant, sleepy little place redolent of the South Seas. There are a number of typical island trade stores and the weathered, old Cook Islands Christian Church picturesquely situated by the

Top: Rarotongan *ariki* investiture ceremony – the *ariki* is seated; his orator (taunga)
   is at his right hand (LB/C)
Left: Dancer, Rarotonga (CITA)
Right: Schoolboy drummer, Aitutaki (CITA)

Top: Baking bread on Aitutaki (LB/C)
Left: Near the Rapae Hotel, Aitutaki (TW)
Right: Signpost, Aitutaki Airport (TW)

playing fields next to the harbour. Built in 1828 the church is the oldest in the Cooks, and also one of the most beautiful, with red, yellow, green and white carved wood all around the ceiling, more dark woodcarving over the doorways, simple stained glass windows, and an anchor placed on the ceiling with the inscription Ebera 6:19 (Hebrews 6:19). A colourful mural over the altar shows angels announcing 'Tapu, Tapu, Tapu' ('Holy, Holy, Holy'). This church also has some of the best acoustics in the Cooks, wonderful

Arutanga

for enjoying the spirited hymn singing. In the churchyard there's a double-sided monument to the London Missionary Society's pioneering Reverend John Williams and to the Polynesian convert Papeiha who Williams left here in 1821.

The harbour is a quiet affair although there are often a few visiting yachts moored offshore. Larger ships have to be unloaded by lighters, outside the lagoon. You can get an excellent view of the island's whole western coastline from out on the tip of the jetty. A huge banana packing plant to handle the island's major export crop stands beside the harbour in front of the Post Office.

Around the Island

You can do a complete circular tour of the island in just a few hours, even on a pushbike. The road runs close to the coast most of the way, and you pass through several lovely villages. There's plenty to see – crabs duck into holes as you come by, ripe fruit lies under trees wherever it falls, exuberant children laugh and sing by every harbour jetty, the water glitters turquoise bright on sunny days. Look for the huge banyan tree arching over the road just north of the Aitutaki Lodges in the village of Tautu.

A round of golf at the nine-hole golf course by the airport costs NZ$5.

Marae

The Aitutaki *marae* are notable for the huge size of the stones. The road goes right through a big *marae* just north of the Aitutaki Lodges and the stones are along both sides of the road. One of the large stones on the south-west corner of this *marae*, on the inland side of the road, looks as though it could be the rough beginning of a carved figure. It's said that when the missionaries destroyed the old carved gods, some of which were very large, this stone had been in the process of being made into a carved human figure. Since it was not finished and the people had never yet worshipped it, the missionaries did not bother to destroy it.

On the inland road to the south of Aitutaki, you pass a sign saying 'Historical Sites' leading to some of the most magnificent *marae* on the island. Tokongarangi, near a watermelon patch just off this road to your right, is a *marae* built in honour of Are Mangoa, the god of sharks:

A huge and powerful warrior named Tairi Teranga came from Rarotonga to try to overpower Aitutaki. He started at the north of Aitutaki and worked his way down the island, defeating or killing everyone and everything in his path. As he forged southwards, the people became increasingly terrified, and the *taungas* (high priests) tried to divine, with a fortune-telling power they had using coconut shells, what the outcome would be. In place after place, the shells prophesied the victory of Tairi Teranga – all the way to the south of the island, to the *marae* Tokongarangi.

Since Tokongarangi is practically at the island's southernmost tip, if Tairi Teranga had prevailed there, it would have spelled the defeat of all Aitutaki. But when he arrived on the *marae*, a much smaller man, Pukenga, inspired with the divine power and assistance of the god of sharks, killed him, releasing the whole island from the reign of terror.

It's also an interesting story, how this *marae* came to be built. Ikaroa-O-Taua, a seafarer from far away in Raiatea in French Polynesia travelled with the carved god Are Mangoa on the prow of his canoe. As he headed across the seas in search of land, the carved god shifted directions. He kept sailing in the direction the god faced and eventually he was led to Aitutaki. He landed on the south part of the island and built this *marae* to honour the god who led him here.

Further along this same road, you come to Taravao – a sign nailed up on a tree announces the spot. From this crossroads, there are two *marae*, one on either side of the road. The one on the west side is Poaki O Rae ('Stone of Rae'), arresting your attention as you come over the hill with its

huge expanse and gigantic black volcanic stones. On the east side, the *marae* Arangirea is composed of long vertical stones. They're reminiscent of the single erect pillar at Arai Te Tonga in Rarotonga, only here there are many of them.

To fully appreciate any *marae*, you must know the story behind it. On Aitutaki Tunui Tereu knows the full histories of all the *marae* and takes visitors to them. His family runs the Tiare Maori Guesthouse and his historical tours last a couple of hours, visit several *marae* and cost NZ$15.

Mt Maungapu

Maungapu is the highest point on the island at just 124 metres. It's an easy 30-minute hike to the top which is marked by a rusty, fenced-off pylon. I squeezed through the gate and climbed part of the way up the pylon for a superb view of the island and the whole lagoon but a recent visitor commented that the pylon was now even rustier and quite unsafe to climb.

The route to the top takes off from directly in front of the Paradise Cove motel and is marked by a big sign on the road. It starts off gently and gets steeper as you near the top. Another Aitutaki legend relates how Maungapu came to be:

Apparently Aitutaki was once just a low atoll, and the inhabitants decided they needed a mountain for their island, so they went off across the sea in search of one. Coming to Rarotonga, they spotted Raemaru, the mountain just behind the village of Arorangi, and thought that one would be perfect. However, it was rather large for Aitutaki, so they decided they'd take just the top off and bring it home.

Late at night, they sneaked up the sides of Raemaru and encircled it, thrust their spears in until they had severed the top from the bottom and took off with it. They held it aloft with their spears as they set off for Aitutaki in their canoes, spread out in the sea all around the mountain.

When morning came, quite naturally the Arorangi villagers looked up and noticed something was wrong. They set off in hot pursuit of the Aitutakians to get their mountain back. But the fierce Aitutakian warriors beat the Rarotongans back, using only their single free hands while still holding up the mountain between them with their spears in their other hands. They succeeded in bringing the mountain top back to Aitutaki, and placed it in the north part of the island. Raemaru today has a distinctly cut-off, flat-topped appearance.

Around the Lagoon

The lagoon of Aitutaki is one of the wonders of the Cook Islands. It is large, colourful and full of life although fortunately not sharks. The snorkelling is magnificent. The lagoon is dotted with sand bars, coral ridges and 21 *motus*, many of them with their own stories.

Maina Maina or 'Little Girl', at the south-west corner of the lagoon, offers some of the lagoon's best snorkelling on the coral formations near its shore and around the large powder-white sandbars just to the north and east. It is also the nesting place of the Red-Tailed Tropic Bird, that bird which used to inspire Cook Islanders from as far away as Atiu to come seeking its red tail feathers for use in their spectacular headdresses. If you're here at the right time of year you may get to see them nesting on the island; their nesting season ends around December when they fly off to other lands.

Just north of Maina, out on the reef, is the shipwreck of the *Alexandria*, which crashed on the reef during the 1930s as it was carrying a load of Model T Fords from the United States to New Zealand. Fortunately, there was no loss of life. You won't see any old Model Ts around the wreck, but the skeleton of the ship is still there.

Rapota Rapota, a volcanic islet further east, was once a leper colony.

Akaiami Akaiami is the *motu* where the old flying boats used to land to refuel. You can still see their wharf on the lagoon side of the *motu*. There are some thatch houses not far from the wharf, used for short camping trips to the island.

Eastern Motus From Akaiama south the eastern *motus* are interesting to explore, but the snorkelling is not so good because there is little coral. If you visit them during the December to May wet season be sure to bring along your mosquito repellent.

Tapuaetai Perhaps the most famous *motu*, and certainly the one that most tourists visit, is Tapuaetai, or One Foot Island, with its lovely white stretch of beach. The brilliant pale turquoise colour of the water off this beach is amazing! The pure white sand of the lagoon is very shallow in the channel between One Foot Island and its neighbour Tekopua, causing the water to gleam. Since there is no coral the snorkelling is not so good but the clear water compensates.

One Foot Island, out of all the 21 *motus*, wasn't always the major tourist attraction. In 1978, a photographer working for Air New Zealand came to Aitutaki to take publicity photos and a photo of this islet's beautiful beach was used for a big promotional poster. Travel writers who came to the island sought out this idyllic stretch of beach and its fame soon spread. Technically, the name Tapuaitai means not 'one foot' but 'one footprint' and there are a couple of versions of how One Foot Island got its name.

One legend tells how a father and son, fleeing warriors from the main island, sought refuge on Tapuaitai. Upon reaching the *motu's* shore, the father picked his son up and hid him in a tree. When the warriors arrived they killed their father but having seen only one set of footprints leading away from his canoe did not realise his son was there. The son returned to Aitutaka and told the story of how the single set of footprints had saved his life.

In another legend, a seafarer from Tonga was crossing the seas with his sister. She died but he wanted to bury her on land, not throw her to the sharks, so he kept her body in the canoe until he sighted land. He came into Aitutaki's lagoon near Tapuaitai and landed there, hoping to bury his sister on the *motu*. As he alighted from the canoe, some fierce Aitutakians emerged from the bush and he jumped back into the canoe and sailed away, still bearing his sister and leaving only a single footprint in the sand.

Beaches, Snorkelling, Diving & Cruises

Beaches on most parts of the main island are not that good because the water is so shallow. From beside the Rapae Hotel you can walk all the way out to the outer reef on a natural coral causeway which starts only 50 or so metres from the shore – at low tide it's not more than knee deep all the way. There are interesting coral rockpools just inside the outer reef and there are places you can snorkel there. A little to the north of where this causeway gets to the outer reef you can fish in the Tonga ruta passage. The branches of the passage are very narrow – some as narrow as 30 cm – but they are over 15 metres deep and full of fish. This is one of the main passages through which the lagoon drains.

If you continue round the corner beyond the black rocks beside the Rapae there's a slightly better beach, with water about 1½ metres deep and some interesting snorkelling. Beware of stonefish in this area, however.

The snorkelling is actually pretty good along this same stretch of coast all the way up to the airport, even though the water is not deep, because the reef here is close in, with the coral formations supporting an abundance of life. Snorkelling is also good in the channel separating Akitua *motu* (where the Aitutaki Resort is) from the main island, especially on the outer side of the channel, towards the reef, and on the lagoon side, around the far tip of the *motu*. Lots of local children come to this channel to swim.

Anywhere there's a jetty – in the harbour, or around the jetties on the east side of the island – there's water deep enough to swim in, and you'll likely find lots of friendly local children doing just that.

The best swimming, snorkelling and beaches are found out on the lagoon *motus*. Numerous people offer trips on the lagoon and the best way of finding out who is going, and when, is to ask around, ask in your hotel, and keep an eye open for the many printed flyers advertising the various cruises and activities.

Ask exactly what is included in a cruise. Some go to only one island, some go to many; some include a barbecued fresh fish feast, with drinks and beer included, others provide only a sandwich lunch. Prices are all about the same at NZ$25 to NZ$35 for a full day with lunch.

One popular boatman is Tuatonga (tel 8M during business hours, tel 173M the rest of the time), a personable fellow who operates Tu's Moana Tours daily from 10 am to 4 pm. Clive Baxter (tel 25) is another boatman who operates a variety of tours, including a lagoon picnic tour to One Foot Island (NZ$35 adults, NZ$15 ages two to 12), a sunset cruise to Maina Island (NZ$25), snorkelling trips inside or outside the lagoon (NZ$18), and big game fishing trips (NZ$75). You'll see Clive's flyers everywhere and bookings can be made at Mike's Bikes, Big Jay's and the Cook Islandair office.

Lagoon Sailing Tours, operated by the very friendly and likeable Aussie Admiral Ben Grummels (tel 120 or 197U), offers the widest variety of aquatic tours and activities. You can pick up one of his pamphlets at the Sailing Centre on the main road, at your hotel or anywhere around town. He has a fleet of Hobie Catamarans, power boats, windsurfers and paddle boards and offers a wide variety of tours and activities. He also has a transparent 'goggle boat' enabling you to see everything beneath you as you sail around.

Lagoon Adventures on the main road also has sailing trips, with full-day trips including lunch for NZ$35, afternoon sailing and snorkelling only for NZ$20. Almost all the hotels and guest houses also offer their own lagoon cruises.

Scuba diving outside the lagoon is another attraction. Contact Aitutaki Scuba about their diving trips which cost NZ$55 if you use their gear, NZ$50 if you use your own. Diving in Aitutaki is relaxed, visibility is good, and it's suitable for everyone from novices to experts. The drop-off at the edge of the reef is as much as 200 metres in places and divers have seen everything up to, and including, whale sharks, humpback whales and an operating submarine! You must be a certified diver to go on these dives, but you can also pay just NZ$10 and go along to snorkel. Aitutaki Scuba also offers dive courses with NAUI certification (NZ$330, four day minimum), deep sea game fishing and water skiing.

Things to Buy

The Aitutaki Women's Development Craft Centre (tel 80), behind the post office, sells some of the most beautiful native crafts that you'll see in the islands. The fancy white rito church hats cost NZ$48; other rito hats are NZ$21. Pandanus purses sell from NZ$9 to NZ$20, exquisite shell-and-rito fans for

NZ$21 and there's also shell jewellery, kiko brooms and home-made coconut oil. It's open Monday to Friday, 8 am to 4 pm.

The Sailing Centre on the main road has T-shirts with many attractive island designs plus Aitutaki patches and other mementoes. Maina Traders, also on the main road, has beautiful tie-dyed Aitutaki T-shirts, pareus, perfumes and other items.

Places to Stay

The popular and pleasantly situated *Rapae Cottage Hotel* (tel 77, telex RG 62054) is set in lush gardens right beside the lagoon, about two km from the centre of Arutanga. The orange hotel cats and a motley collection of chickens (at least one rooster per room commented one visitor) roam the grounds. There are 14 rooms, 12 of them studio doubles in duplex units – they're simple but comfortable with bathroom, tea/coffee making equipment and a big shady verandah. Singles/ doubles are NZ$60/65.

The other two rooms are spacious family units which occupy the same space as a regular duplex, with separate bedroom and sitting room, beds for six people (they allow for large families) and full-size kitchen. The family units cost NZ$72 double. At both the double and family units, additional people cost NZ$8 each and children under five are free. The Rapae has a nice restaurant, the best Island Night on Aitutaki every Friday, and offers lagoon tours to One Foot Island (NZ$30) and three-hour round-the-island bus tours (NZ$12).

There are a number of guest houses in Aitutaki, most of them along the road between the Rapae Hotel and the centre of Arutanga. Two of the longest established ones, *Josie's Lodge* (tel 111) and the *Tiare Maori Guesthouse* (tel 119), are practically next door to one another and offer much the same facilities and standards – six or seven simple bedrooms each sleeping two, with common bathroom facilities and sitting areas. Prices are the same too at NZ$25/35 single/double, breakfast included. You can eat dinner there if you like (NZ$10 at Josie's, NZ$13 at the Tiare Maori), or use the kitchen facilities to do your own cooking for an extra couple of dollars a day. Both places offer lagoon cruises which for NZ$30 include a barbecue lunch on the *motus*. The Tiare Maori also offers round-the-island tours; at Josie's, you can hire pushbikes, motorcycles or cars.

The *Aitutaki Guest House* (tel 158) is south of Arutanga in the Reureu area. The *Paradise Cove* (tel 69M or 69K) is a five-bedroom house right on the beach between Arutanga and the airport, directly across from Mt Maungapu. Rates are NZ$15 per person, which may be discounted for longer stays. Each bedroom sleeps two and there are two bathrooms, a kitchen and common areas.

The best deal on the island for those on a budget or planning a longer stay is the *Torino Villa* (tel 136). There are actually two of them – one is a pleasant little two-bedroom house by the sea near Arutanga, the other is a large house, sleeping 10 people or even more, right across the road. Each house is only NZ$50 a week. If you can't find the owner around, look for him at Rino's Bar, opposite the Rapae – he owns that, too.

On the other side of the island *Aitutaki Lodges* (tel 106), opened in September '87, is a fancier place with six new A-frame chalets, each with a kitchenette, one queen-size bed and one single bed, and a large verandah with a splendid view of the lagoon and the *motus* stretching away in the distance. The view is unsurpassed on the island; the only drawbacks are that the beach here is not so good and you're a bit far from town, although you can hire a motorcycle at NZ$23 per day. Prices vary depending on how long you stay: for just one or two nights, it's NZ$106 single or double. For three nights or more, it's NZ$96 single or double, with extra adults costing NZ$21, children under 14 NZ$15. You can arrange

for cooked meals when you don't feel like cooking; a new bar and dining room are under construction.

At the far end of the airstrip, the *Aitutaki Resort Hotel* (tel 20-234 in Rarotonga, telex RG 62048) is on Akitua *motu*, across a narrow channel from the main island. The locals often call it the Akitua Resort, after the *motu*. The causeway joining the *motu* to the main island was washed away in Hurricane Sally in 1987, and now you get ferried across the channel on a little barge. The resort has 25 individual cottages, each with a double and a single bed, a sink and a fridge. The resort has all the modern conveniences including a restaurant, bar and swimming pool and many activities are on offer. Nearly everybody staying here will be on some sort of all-inclusive package deal, booked through travel agencies or airlines but the walk-in rates are NZ$115 single or double, NZ$35 for each extra person, children under 16 free. The major drawback is the resort's considerable isolation from the rest of the island.

Places to Eat

The restaurant at the *Rapae Hotel* has good food – their home-cured ham sandwiches are delicious and they have hot lunch and dinner main dishes for around NZ$10, sandwiches for under NZ$2. On Friday night their excellent Island Night Buffet (NZ$16) begins at around 7.30 pm and provides a varied spread of island specialities from octopus to roast pork, fried fish to taro, curried goat to clams. A floorshow and dance follows and on Sunday night beginning around 8 pm there's a barbecue for NZ$14.50. You should make reservations in advance for these popular functions. The restaurant is a beautiful, relaxed place, open-air with a thatched roof, right on the lagoon and white beach.

Across the road from the Rapae, the open-air *Rino's Bar* serves food Wednesday through Saturday, with some of the best prices on the island: fish & chips for NZ$3.50, hamburgers for NZ$1.80. The beer prices are the best in town, too, and the place is always full of friendly locals out to eat, drink, have a game of billiards or ping pong, and socialise with whoever stops by. It's open 9 am to midnight every day but Sunday.

Big Jay's Takeaways in town just past the post office and opposite the CICC church is a pleasant place with a counter inside and shaded picnic tables set around on the lawn. Fish or chicken, chips and salad come for NZ$5 a plate, various burgers for about NZ$3, and they have five flavours of milkshakes besides coffee, tea and sodas. When potatoes are in short supply on the island, they make breadfruit chips – try them, they're crunchy and delicious! It's open Monday through Saturday, 9.30 am until 9 or 10 pm, with a break between 4 and 6.30 pm.

The bar/restaurant at the *Aitutaki Resort* serves all meals and has a changing dinner menu served from 7.30 to 10 pm, with soups and starters for NZ$5, main courses for NZ$17 and desserts for NZ$5, tea and coffee at no charge. Saturday night is Island Night, beginning at 7.30 pm with a buffet, floorshow and dancing afterwards (NZ$25). The Sunday barbecue, served from 1 to 7 pm, is also open to the public and costs NZ$22. Wednesday there's an Island Feast, but it's for guests only.

The stores have the usual Cook Islands selection of tins and the usual limited variety of fresh fruit and vegetables. The choice is more restricted than on Rarotonga and the prices are higher. It's worth bringing some supplies with you, particularly if you plan to cook for yourself.

The shop opposite Aitutaki Scuba, near the Rapae Hotel, has excellent fresh-baked bread. Aitutaki's large lagoon supplies the best variety of fresh fish in the islands but you've got to catch them yourself or know somebody who has been fishing! If you go on a lagoon cruise you're likely to come back with some.

Entertainment

Island Night at the *Rapae Hotel* on Friday night is a social event only out-done by the Sunday church service. There's a buffet served from around 7.30 pm which costs NZ$16 and eating here, or simply being a Rapae Hotel guest, also gets you a ringside seat but if you don't want to eat there's no cover charge or entry cost.

The band starts playing around 8 pm and the dancing gets under way around 9.30 pm. It's an hour of raucous fun. Large matrons return from the bar through the dancers and show very clearly that they can still swing a hip as well as any upstart teenager! The finale involves pulling *papa'a* out of the audience and getting them to show what they've learnt. By this time most people have had enough to drink for embarrassment to be minimal. The band continues on until around 1 am with an increasingly unsteady but highly entertaining crowd.

Rino's Bar across the road also has entertainment – a local band and dancers on Thursday nights beginning at 9 pm or a band for dancing on Friday and Saturday nights from 7 pm to midnight. There's no entry charge, drinks are reasonably priced, and it's one of the best places to meet friendly locals.

The *Aitutaki Resort* has its Island Night on Saturday, beginning with a buffet at 7.30 pm, floorshow and dancing afterwards. Cost for the buffet is NZ$22, but again, if you wish to come for the entertainment only, there's no charge.

Getting There & Away

Air Aitutaki's large airstrip was built by US forces during WW II. It's the only airport in the Cooks with a two-way runway and it could handle much larger aircraft than those currently used. You could fly Boeing 737s into Aitutaki.

Aitutaki was the first outer island in the Cooks to have regular air links with Rarotonga. There are two flights a day (except on Sundays) with Cook Islandair and two more with Air Rarotonga. Round trip fares are NZ$198 with Cook Islandair (NZ$178 if you buy your ticket locally seven days in advance), NZ$220 with Air Rarotonga. See the introductory Getting Around section for details on discounts.

Stars Travel (tel 23-669 or 23-683) in Avarua, Rarotonga offers two-night package tours combining airfare and accommodation with rates beginning at NZ$217 per person (based on double occupancy) departing Rarotonga every day except Sunday. You may find it cheaper to book your stay this way than it would be to book your airfare and accommodation separately; five separate packages are offered, for five different prices, depending on the level of luxury you choose in your accommodation. You can stay longer simply by adding on extra days when you make your reservations. The price also includes round trip airport transfers on both islands.

Several companies offer day trips from Rarotonga to Aitutaki, departing in the morning and returning in the late afternoon. Trips include a lagoon cruise and lunch on Aitutaki, with a couple of hours available for exploring on your own. Cook Islandair and Air Rarotonga each charge NZ$225; with Stars Travel, it's NZ$210.

The Coral Route
Aitutaki had a pioneering role in Pacific aviation as a stopping point in Tasman Empire Air Line's 'Coral Route'. Back in the 1950s TEAL, the predecessor to Air New Zealand, flew across the Pacific: Auckland/Suva (Fiji)/Apia (Western Samoa)/Aitutaki/Papeete (Tahiti). The first leg to Suva was flown by DC-6s but the rest of the way was by four-engined Solent flying boats.

The stop at Aitutaki was purely to refuel, indeed this was carried out at the uninhabited *motu* of Akaiami. It took over two hours so passengers had a chance to take a swim in the lagoon. Flying in those days was hardly a one stop operation: one day took you from Suva to Apia and the next day required a pre-dawn departure from Apia in order to make Papeete before nightfall. The flying boats were unpressurised so they did not fly above 3000

metres and they sometimes had to descend to less than 500 metres.

The old Solents carried their 60-odd passengers in seven separate cabins and in some degree of luxury. Food was actually cooked on the aircraft, in contrast to today's reheated airline meals. At that time the fortnightly flight into Papeete was the only direct air link between Tahiti and the rest of the world and the aircraft's arrival was a major event.

Usually the trips were uneventful but on one occasion a malfunction at Aitutaki required off-loading the passengers while the aircraft limped on to Tahiti on three engines. It was a week before it arrived back to collect the passengers – who by that time had begun to really enjoy their enforced stay on hotel-less Aitutaki. On another occasion the aircraft was forced to return to Aitutaki when the Tahiti lagoon turned out to be full of logs. The trip to Tahiti was attempted twice more before the lagoon was clear enough for a landing. One of the TEAL flying boats is now on display in the transport museum in Auckland, New Zealand.

Solents were also used by British Airways (BOAC in those days) on routes from England through to India and Australia. A couple were still in use by Ansett Airlines in Australia for Sydney-Lord Howe Island flights right into the early '70s, but flying boat travel was really ended by WW II. Prior to the war most long-range commercial flights were made by flying boats as suitable airports for long-range land planes did not exist. After the war not only had large, long-range aircraft been greatly improved but there were airport runways capable of handling them all over the world. The flying boat days were over.

Ship One-way fares from Rarotonga on Silk & Boyd ships are NZ$37 deck class, NZ$75 cabin class. Round-trip from Rarotonga to Aitutaki and back again is NZ$55 deck class, NZ$115 cabin class. Although Aitutaki is a popular yachting destination the narrow reef passage is too hazardous for large ships to enter so cargo is normally taken by lighters outside the reef.

Getting Around
A minibus meets the flights and charges

NZ$3 into town. Around the island there's a reasonable network of roads although apart from a km or two through Arutanga none of them are paved. A road surfacing programme due to be completed in 1989 may extend the paved portions. Even the unpaved roads are in good condition, but if you're riding on a motorcycle, be careful! Many of the roads are surfaced with pebbles and the dirt roads can be exceedingly slippery after rain.

Motorbikes can be hired from a number of places on the island. Ask at your hotel to see if they rent them: the Aitutaki Resort, the Rapae, Aitutaki Lodges and Josie's all have them available. Josie's has the cheapest prices on the island at NZ$12 per day plus a NZ$5 deposit which is refunded if you return the bike full of petrol, and hires motorcycles to guests and non-guests alike.

In town, Mike's Bikes (tel 17M) hires Yamaha 50s for NZ$20 per day; if you're staying for a whole week, pay in advance and you get seven days for the price of six. Ben Grummels at the Sailing Centre (tel 120 or 197U) also hires motorcycles for NZ$20 per day including petrol. You can hire a car from Josie's for NZ$46 per day.

There are many places renting pushbikes, which is a fine way of getting around since distances are short and the roads are pretty flat. Many hotels rent them, usually from about NZ$5 to NZ$8 per day. In town, along the main road, you can also find them at Aitutaki Scuba (NZ$5 per day), Aitutaki Enterprises (NZ$4 per day), and Amuri Bicycle Hire (NZ$5 per day for a BMX, NZ$10 for a 10-speed).

Manuae

Population: unpopulated
Area: 6.2 square km

The two tiny islets of Manuae and Te Au O Tu are effectively unpopulated –

occasionally copra cutting parties visit from Aitutaki. The Cook Islands Government has suggested that in view of the unspoilt nature of the lagoon the islands should be declared an international marine park.

The two islets are actually the only parts of a huge volcanic cone which break the surface. The cone is 56 km from east to west, 24 km north to south. The other highpoint on the rim of this vast cone is the Astronomer Bank, 13 km west of Manuae. It comes to within 300 metres of the ocean's surface. Manuae is 101 km from Aitutaki and coconuts were often collected from the atoll by Aitutakians.

History
Cook was the European discoverer of the atoll. He sighted it in 1773 during his second voyage and in 1777 on his third voyage he paused to investigate but did not land. The islands were named the Hervey Islands by Captain Cook, a name which for a time was applied to the whole southern group, but fortunately that name is rarely used.

In 1823 the missionary John Williams

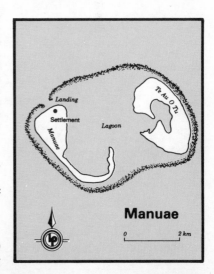

Manuae

visited the island and there were about 60 inhabitants. There were only a dozen or so in the late 1820s and the missionaries took them to Aitutaki. Later a series of Europeans made temporary homes. The best known was the prolific William Marsters who in 1863 was moved to Palmerston with his three wives. Today, that island's entire population is descended from him.

Atiu & Takutea

Atiu

Population: 955
Area: 26.9 square km

The third largest of the Cook Islands, Atiu is noted for its raised coral reef or *makatea*, a phenomenon also found on the islands of Mangaia, Mauke and Mitiaro. The island has had a colourful and bloodthirsty history as the Atiuans were the warriors of the Cooks and specialised in creating havoc on all their neighbouring islands.

Unlike all the other Cook Islands, including Mangaia with its similar geography, the villages in Atiu are not on the coast. The five villages – Areora, Ngatiarua, Teenui, Mapumai and Tengatangi – are all close together in the centre of the hill region. Prior to Christianisation, the people lived spread out around the lowlands, where the taro is grown. When the missionaries persuaded the people to come upland and move the original settlements together they effectively created a single village – the post office and church form the centre, and the 'villages' radiate out from this centre on five roads, like the five arms of a starfish.

Atiu is surprisingly interesting for the visitor – there are some fine beaches, magnificent scenery, excellent walks, ancient *marae* (pre-Christian ceremonial and religious sites) and the *makatea* is riddled with limestone caves, some of them used as ancient burial caves. You can also see coffee production, sample pineapples, visit the fibre arts studio and there's an excellent place to stay. Most people stay two days, the usual time between flights, and that really isn't long enough. Atiu is not, however, a place for easy lazing around – you have to get out and do things, burn some energy. This was one of my favourite places in the Cooks and the island really deserves more visitors!

History

Atiu was once known as Enua-manu which can be translated as 'land of birds' or 'land of insects'. Numerous legends tell of early settlers arriving by canoe or of visits by legendary Polynesian navigators. What is more certain is that some time before the first European arrival three *ariki* controlled the island and began to extend their power over the neighbouring islands of Mauke and Mitiaro.

The European discovery of Atiu is credited to Captain Cook on 3 April 1777. The previous day the Atiuans had made friendly visits to his ships the *Resolution* and *Discovery*. The Atiuans were uninterested in any items they were offered for trade but they did want a dog. They

Atiu Cross Section

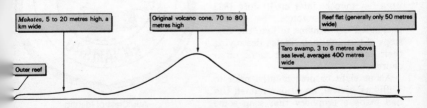

Makatea, 5 to 20 metres high, a km wide

Original volcano cone, 70 to 80 metres high

Reef flat (generally only 50 metres wide)

Taro swamp, 3 to 6 metres above sea level, averages 400 metres wide

Outer reef

had heard of but not seen such an animal and Cook would have been happy to oblige them for, 'We had a Dog and a bitch on board belonging to one of the Gentlemen, that were a great nusence in the Ship', but the gentleman was reluctant to part with them. Fortunately the Tahitian, Omai, who Cook had taken back to England on his previous voyage, offered one of his dogs.

The next day the captain sent three of his boats ashore to try to procure supplies. His men spent a long day being feted (and pickpocketed) by the Atiuans – they watched wrestling matches and dancing displays – but came back effectively empty handed. At one point when a large oven was being prepared Omai was so frightened it was intended for himself and his companions that he came straight out and asked the Atiuans if they were preparing to eat them! The Atiuans expressed shock at the mere thought of such an idea but subsequent tales of the Atiuans' eating habits amongst the people of Mauke and Mitiaro makes one wonder about their ingenuousness.

His men safely back on board, Cook 'resolved to try no more and thought my self well off that it ended as it did'. He sailed away and managed to find the necessary provisions, principally for the cattle he had on board, on the neighbouring island of Takutea, where he left 'a hatchet and some nails to the full Value of what we took from the island'.

Forty years were to pass before the next European contact when in late 1822 or early 1823 two Polynesian 'teachers' were sent from Bora Bora near Tahiti. They were singularly unsuccessful although when the Reverend John Williams turned up a few months later on 19 July 1823 searching for Rarotonga, he quickly persuaded the Atiuans to take the first steps of burning their 'idols', destroying their *marae* and starting work on a church.

About eight or nine months prior to Williams' arrival, an Atiuan named Uia had made a prophecy that soon some

people would arrive in Atiu in a huge canoe with no outrigger, their bodies, heads and feet covered, with a mighty God in heaven called Jehovah, and that the Atiuan gods would be burnt with fire. The chiefs were indignant and ordered that Uia be caught and punished, but he escaped the chiefs' wrath and was never heard of again. On board the mission ship were *ariki* from Rarotonga and Aitutaki, who told Rongomatane, the leading Atiuan chief, that many of their gods had already been burnt and this also influenced him greatly.

The day after Williams' arrival, Rongomatane took the mission party to his own *marae* and challenged them to eat the sugar cane from a sacred grove. When Williams, Papeiha and the rest of the group ate the cane and did not drop dead on the spot Rongomatane became an instant convert, ordered all the idols on the island burnt and told his people to come and listen to the missionaries' teachings.

Rongomatane told Williams that he had two other islands close by – Akatokamanava (Mauke) and Nukuroa (Mitiaro) – and that he would like the

Atiu Crest of Identity

people on those islands to receive the gospel as well. He accompanied Williams' ship to these two islands, converting the inhabitants with amazing speed. This conversion of Mauke and Mitiaro had a rather macabre sidelight. Some time before Williams' visit a dispute had evolved between Atiu and Mauke. Rongomatane had rushed off to Mauke bent on revenge and virtually wiped out the islands' inhabitants. Having killed, cooked and eaten their fill the Atiuans took back canoe-loads of cooked Maukeans for the rest of the Atiuans to sample.

This was not the first time Rongomatane had descended upon Mauke and the Atiuans had also worked off their appetites on the unfortunate inhabitants of Mitiaro. It's hardly surprising that shortly after, when Williams and his new Christian convert, only recently a blood-thirsty cannibal chief, turned up on Mauke the poor inhabitants of the island embraced Christianity with such alacrity and fervour!

After Williams' profitable visit to Atiu, Mauke and Mitiaro, he still had not found Rarotonga, the island he was looking for in the first place. Rongomatane had never been to Rarotonga, but he knew where it was and easily directed Williams towards it. Taking the ship to Orovaru beach on Atiu's western shore, they lined up the stern of the ship with the big rock in the lagoon and Williams sailed off in a bee-line to discover Rarotonga, arriving on 26 October 1823.

The missionaries subsequently made occasional visits to Atiu from Tahiti but in 1836 the Tahitian convert Papeiha was sent back from Rarotonga and started the serious work of Christianising the island.

Gospel Day is still celebrated in Atiu on 19 July every year, often with *nuku* plays acting out the drama of how the gospel came to Atiu.

Geology

Atiu's geology is fascinating. It's thought that Atiu rose out of the sea as a volcano cone around 11 million years ago. The cone was worn down to a shoal, then upheaval (or a drop in the sea level) raised the shoal to form a flat-topped island. Further eons produced a wide coral reef around the island but then, about 100,000 years ago, the island rose another 20 or so metres out of the sea. The coral reef then became a coastal plain, stretching back about a km from the new coastline to the older central hills. In the past 100,000 years a new coral reef has grown up around most of the island, but this is only 100 or so metres wide.

The island today is rather like a very low-brimmed hat with a flat outer rim. This outer rim or *makatea* is principally rough and rugged, fossilised coral. Although it's comparatively infertile the *makatea* is no barren wasteland; it's a veritable jungle, densely covered in scrub and coconut palms. The *makatea* starts off around five metres in height right at the coast and gradually slopes up to around 20 metres at its inner edge. Then instead of sloping up immediately into the central hills – the old volcanic core – there's a circular band of swamp. It seems that water running off the hills permeates the edge of the *makatea* and has eroded it away to form this damp swamp area. It's extensively used for taro cultivation but it's also a breeding ground for mosquitoes! Inland from the swamp is the inner plateau, the most fertile area of the island where coffee and pineapples are grown.

Information

There's electricity for 12 hours a day, running from 6 am to 12 noon and again from 6 pm to midnight. Atiu produces two important crops although both face numerous problems. Pineapples are grown and exported fresh to New Zealand. Coffee is also grown; the only commercially grown coffee in the Cook Islands.

Plans are now underway for a road to be completed all the way around the coast and it should be finished by the time you come.

Two important items to bring with you to Atiu are a torch (flashlight) and mosquito repellent. The Atiu Motel lends you a torch for cave exploring but you'll want a backup in case of emergencies when underground. And the mosquitoes in the swamp region are voracious and exceedingly numerous. At times you seem to have such a line of them across any tasty looking stretch of skin there seems to be no room for a single additional freeloader.

A couple of years ago there was an especially bad outbreak of mosquitoes following a period of rain. Everybody walked around in the streets carrying paint cans full of smouldering coconut bark, creating a smokescreen around themselves to keep the mosquitoes away!

It's amusing how wherever they are voracious tall tales concerning mosquitoes are soon concocted. The Atiuans relate that during this time a local doctor had some pigs which he kept down in the *makatea*, as is the usual custom. One pig died and its body looked horrible and emaciated. Could it be some kind of a serious pig illness that might spread to other pigs on the island? The doctor decided to perform an autopsy on the pig to find out for sure what had killed it. He found that the pig had died because 80% of its blood had been sucked out by mosquitoes!

Leave your restaurant gear behind in Raro. On Atiu you need old T-shirts, torn shorts, worn-out running shoes. Be prepared to get muddy, sweaty and tired! The big exception is if you plan to go to a dance or to church. Fancy dress is not needed, but you should be able to meet the demands of local modesty and women must wear a hat to church. Standards of modesty in Atiu, as in all the outer islands, are more conservative than in Rarotonga and locals have become upset about women wearing shorts in town, men going without a shirt and *anyone* wearing swimming gear in town.

If you want more information on Atiu there are a couple of interesting books to look for. *Atiu through European Eyes* (Institute of Pacific Studies, University of the South Pacific, 1982) is fascinating. It's subtitled 'A Selection of Historical Documents 1777-1967' and is a collection of references to Atiu from books and reports, reproduced in facsimile form. There are three sections: 'explorers' is principally from the logbook for Cook's visit in 1777; 'missionaries and traders' has accounts of Atiu by those early visitors; and the third section includes more modern academic reports on Atiu's archaeology, its fascinating geology and various customs and social systems.

Also published by the Institute of Pacific Studies *Atiu, an Island Community* (1984) is a modern study of Atiu's current conditions and customs, written by Atiuans. There's an impressive bibliography of 82 books in which Atiu makes an appearance.

The small paperback *Atiu Nui Maruarua*, also published by the USP's Institute of Pacific Studies (1984), is a bilingual collection of wonderful legends about Atiu told in Maori (Atiuan) and English. All the books published by USP are available at the USP's Rarotonga Centre, across from the Library in downtown Avarua.

The parts about Atiu and Atiuans in chapter four of Ronald Syme's book *The Lagoon is Lonely Now* (Millwood Press, Wellington, 1978) are particularly insightful and amusing.

Beaches & Coast

Atiu is not a great place for swimming – the surrounding lagoon is rarely more than 50 metres wide and the water is generally too shallow for more than wading and gentle splashing around. There are, however, countless beautiful, sandy bays all along the coast. You can easily find one to yourself and when you tire of sunbathing just slip into the water for a cooling dip. Some of them are easily reached but to get to others a little pushing through the bush is required.

although the coastal roads are rarely more than 100 metres from the coast.

On the west coast Orovaru Beach is thought to be where Cook's party made their historic landing. There's a large rock in the water just off the beach, which the chief Rongomatane used in directing John Williams to Rarotonga. Further south is the longer sweep of Taungaroro Beach, backed by high cliffs and sloping fairly steeply into the water. South again is Tumai Beach and there are plenty of others. The coast road runs all the way down to Te Tau at the southern tip. The water at Taunganui Harbour is clear and deep enough for good swimming and snorkelling.

The south-east coast takes the brunt of the prevailing northerly winds and the sea, washing fiercely over the reef, is often unsafe for swimming. There are, however, a series of picturesque little beaches including Matai at the start of the south-east coast road and Oneroa at the end. Oneroa is the best beach for finding beautiful shells; a surprising number of old shoes are also washed up!

About halfway along this road is the turn-off to Takauroa Beach, just by a stretch of old pig fence. If you walk back along the rugged cliff face about 100 metres there are some sink holes deep enough for good snorkelling. They are only safe at low tide or when the sea is calm.

On the north-east coast there's a km-long stretch where there is no fringing reef and the sea beats directly on the cliffs. At the end of the road Tarapaku is a rarely used emergency boat landing and there's a pleasant stretch of beach. There are more beaches south to Oneroa but there is no coast road, although there may be one soon.

Caves

The *makatea* is riddled with limestone caves, complete with stalactites and stalagmites. You'll stumble across many small ones in any ramble through the *makatea* so take a torch (flashlight). Take

your bearings too as it's very easy to get totally confused underground and when (if?) you finally find your way out it may be by a different exit.

It's necessary to take a guide (usually about NZ$10 plus a small charge for each additional person) partly because the caves can be difficult to find but also because most of the better known caves are on 'owned' land and permission must be obtained before you enter. Many of the caves were used for burials although when and why nobody knows. If you visit one of these caves do not move or take any of the bones. At the very least there will be a curse on you if you do! Roger Malcolm at the Atiu Motel can help you to arrange a guide.

The Te ana o Raka burial cave is one cave you can visit by yourself. You can approach it either by taking the road down from the central plateau or by taking the road which runs inland from about three quarters of the way down the airstrip. The cave is just off the road and very easy to find. There are, however, numerous entrances and exits to this extensive cave and it is very easy to get confused.

In the south-east of the island is the Anatakitaki or 'cave of the kopeka'. The cave is reached by a longish walk across the *makatea* from the plateau road. Kopekas are tiny birds, very much like swifts, which nest in huge numbers inside the cave. When they come out to hunt insects they are never seen to land, only in the cave do they rest. Inside the pitch dark cave they make a continuous chattering, clicking noise which they use to find their way around like bats. Try to dissuade your guide from catching the birds, a trick they perform by throwing a shirt or jacket over the sleeping birds on the roof of the cavern.

Some of the chambers in this extensive cavern are very large. Although this is the main kopeka cave they do nest in smaller numbers in at least one other cave. There's a legend that relates how a

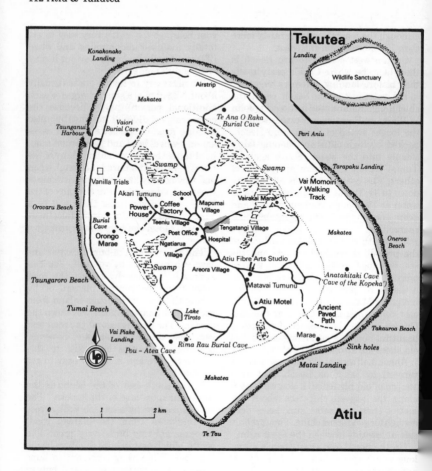

Takutea

Landing

Wildlife Sanctuary

Atiu

Konakonako Landing

Airstrip

Makatea

Vaiori Burial Cave

Te Ana O Raka Burial Cave

Pari Aniu

Taunganui Harbour

Swamp

Swamp

Tarapaku Landing

Vai Momoiri Walking Track

Vanilla Trials

Akari Tumunu

School

Vairakai Marae

Orovaru Beach

Power House

Coffee Factory

Mapumai Village

Teeniu Village

Tengatangi Village

Makatea

Burial Cave

Post Office

Oneroa Beach

Orongo Marae

Ngatiarua Village

Hospital

Atiu Fibre Arts Studio

Anatakitaki Cave ('Cave of the Kopeka')

Taungaroro Beach

Swamp

Areora Village

Matavai Tumunu

Tumai Beach

Atiu Motel

Lake Tiroto

Ancient Paved Path

Takauroa Beach

Vai Piake Landing

Marae

Sink holes

Pou – Atea Cave

Rima Rau Burial Cave

Matai Landing

Makatea

0   1   2 km

Te Tau

Polynesian hero, Rangi, was led to this cave which concealed his missing wife, by a kingfisher bird.

In the south-west the Rima Rau burial cave is a smaller cave reached by a vertical pothole. There are many bones to be seen in this cave and nearby there's a very deep sink hole with a deep, cold pool at the bottom.

Vai Momoiri Track & Vairakai Marae

From Tarapaku Landing on the north-east coast a walking track leads inland all the way to the central villages. It's best to arrange transport round to the landing so you can walk the whole way inland. At first the track winds across a wonderful stretch of *makatea* with thick vegetation, colourful flowers and impressive outcrops. Much of the track is paved with stone slabs and there are numerous small caves very close to the path. At one point you can see the Vai Momoiri, a deep canyon off the track to the left, filled with brown water. A short stretch of tunnel connects this water to a second, similar sink hole.

Top: Outrigger on the lagoon, Aitutaki (TW)
Bottom: Spearfishing in the lagoon, Aitutaki (LB/C)

Top: Cave entrance from the *makatea*, Atiu (TW)
Left: Pineapple plantation, Atiu (NK)
Right: Making a canoe in the traditional way, Atiu (LB/C)

Eventually the path heads into the swamp and if the log bridge has not been repaired you may have to wade through knee-deep water and mud for about 100 metres before reaching drier ground. The path follows irrigation ditches and at one point turns sharply across a cement culvert. Look to your left at this point to the 37-metre-long wall of the Vairakai Marae. It's somewhat overgrown but stands parallel to and only a metre or so away from the path. There are 47 large limestone slabs, six of which have been cut with curious projections on their top edge. Very shortly after this impressive wall the path climbs steeply up to the plateau and enters Tengatangi village.

Other Marae

Atiu has a number of interesting *marae* remains. One of the best known is the Orongo Marae near Cook's landing place. An international Earthwatch party came in 1985 to clean up the *marae*, which was practically an excavation project since it had become so overgrown it was almost lost in the jungle. You must have a guide, because it's difficult to find and it's on private land.

Teapiripiri Marae where Papeiha is said to have first preached the gospel in 1823 is behind the tennis courts and house opposite the post office. There's little left of the *marae* apart from some stalactites or stalagmites lying on the ground but there's a memorial stone to mark the spot. A little north of here, behind the park opposite the CICC church, there's another small *marae*.

Coffee

Atiu is the only place in the Cooks which grows coffee commercially – but it has been a precarious activity. Private planters began growing coffee in 1955 but by 1974 the industry had dwindled to the point where coffee was simply picked for local home consumption. Coffee plants were still growing when German-born Juergen Manske-Eimke moved from

Nigeria to Atiu and changed his occupation from economist to coffee grower. The Atiu coffee business is now rebounding and Juergen hopes that the five tonnes of coffee the island currently produces annually will expand to twice that level. At present there are about eight hectares of coffee being grown but that could potentially be expanded to around 50 hectares, which could yield up to 33 tonnes of coffee annually.

The supermarkets and fancier restaurants of Rarotonga alone use about 2½ tonnes of coffee a year and Atiuan coffee is now being exported to New Zealand and Tahiti as well. Juergen entered Atiuan coffee in a coffee competition in Hawaii recently (Atiuan coffee is similar to the renowned Hawaiian Kona) and it came third out of 16 entrants.

The coffee is usually picked from February to May. Because of the small scale of production and relatively low labour costs Atiuan coffee is 100% sun dried and 100% hand selected. Coffee growing in Atiu has its problems – wild pigs, too much sunshine and the perennial Cook Islands land-ownership questions all cause hassles. It's good coffee though, and you can buy a half kg package from the factory for NZ$8.50 (NZ$12 in Rarotonga shops).

Juergen gives tours of the coffee plantations, pulping factory and the new factory where it's hulled, roasted and packed. They cost NZ$10 (additional people NZ$5). The tour ends with a cup (or two) of Atiuan coffee. His wife Andrea, who runs the Atiu Fibre Arts Studio, is an embroidery and fibre artist and the Atiuan coffee package is her work.

Atiu Fibre Arts Studio

The Atiu Fibre Arts Studio specialises in traditional arts and crafts of Atiu, all hand-made by local women using local materials such as pandanus, coconut palm, tapa bark cloth and shells found on Atiu's beaches. It's also about the only place in the Cooks that you can purchase a real *tivaivai*, the colourful patterned bedspread normally made only for home use. Cost for a machine-sewn double to queen-size *tivaivai* is about NZ$400 to NZ$600; a hand-sewn one, requiring countless hours to make, costs NZ$800 and up. You can get one there or custom order it in the pattern and colours you want. Also on display in the studio are artwork, jewellery, pandanus mats, purses and other items, all of exceptional quality.

Andrea, originally from Germany, can tell you everything you want to know about the local arts and crafts. You can usually find her at the studio in Areora village Monday to Saturday. Andrea is interested in promoting cultural exchange, inviting artists and craftspeople to come and share their skills with the studio and

Handcrafted articles from the Atiu Fibre Arts Studio. Illustrated by Judith Künzle.

learn Atiuan crafts. She can arrange for accommodation, craftsmaking facilities and anything else you'd need. Work from the Atiu Fibre Arts Studio is also on display at the Colonial Craft House in Matavera village, Rarotonga.

Dances

A dance is held at the Town Hall, just across from the CICC church, every Friday night most of the year, particularly at Christmas. Sometimes it's disco music, but at other times there's a rousing local band. People of all ages appear and it's always good fun.

However, between 1 January and 31 March there's an interesting twist, a holdover from the 'blue laws' days. The original London Missionary Society missionaries who founded the CICC church managed to convince the people of Atiu that if they held dances during the hurricane season, it could cause a hurricane to strike the island! The CICC, which owns the Town Hall, will still not permit dances to be held there at that time. The Roman Catholics, however, have no such compunctions so the Friday night dance usually goes on at some other location. The dances are often a fundraiser for some project or occasion.

Other

There are a couple of dusty display cases with some Atiuan artefacts in the library of Atiu College. The CICC church in the centre of the villages has walls over a metre thick and is in the traditional island style.

The villages have a surprising number of tennis courts – a few years ago the five villages got into a tennis court building competition, each attempting to build a better one than the next!

Lake Tiroto is noted for its eels which are a popular island delicacy. On the western side of the lake is a cave which leads right through the *makatea* to the sea. You can crawl through it for a considerable distance if the water in the lake is low enough. Be prepared to get very muddy, however. And watch out for eels.

Tutaka & Tivavae

Twice a year, a committee goes around to inspect all the houses in Atiu for their condition, cleanliness, etc. This *tutaka* is done in many of the Cook Islands, but in Atiu it's made into a big occasion, with the local ladies bringing out all their best handicrafts to put on display. The major *tutaka* of the year is just before Christmas; there's another one in the last week of June. It's easy to spot the inspection committee going around, since they're all in uniform, and if you ask permission you can join them. All the handicrafts of Atiu are proudly on display in the homes. The *tutaka* inspection is held on a Wednesday and Thursday, and that same Friday there's a big ball, with prizes handed out for the village that wins the competition.

Exhibitions of tivaivai, the colourful patterned bedspreads and cushions which are one of the most distinctive local handicrafts, take place during the last week of May and the last week of November in the Sunday School hall of the CICC.

Bush Beer Schools

Don't miss the opportunity to visit a *tumunu*

while you're in Atiu. It's a direct descendant of the old *kava* ceremony of pre-missionary times. *Kava* was a drink prepared from the root of the pepper plant *piper methysticum*. It was not alcoholic but it certainly had an effect on its drinkers – ranging from a mildly fuzzy head to total unconsciousness! Drinking *kava* was always a communal activity with some ceremony involved; you could not be a solitary *kava* drinker. In Fiji *kava* is still popular today but in the Cook Islands the missionaries managed to all but totally stamp it out. During that missionary period, however, when drinking was banned, the *tumunu* came into existence and men would retreat to the bush to drink home-brewed 'orange beer'. The 'tumunu' is the hollowed out coconut palm stump which was traditionally used as a container for brewing the beer.

Tumunu are still held regularly at various places on the island although the container is likely to be plastic these days and the beer will be made from imported hops, much like any western home brew, rather than from oranges as in the old days. Technically, however, the bush beer schools are still illegal. If you stay at the Atiu Motel, Roger will arrange an invitation for a visit to the local *tumunu*. Traditionally the *tumunu* is for men only, and women rarely participate, but for tourists the rules relax somewhat and any visitor, male or female, is welcome.

There's still quite a tradition to the beer schools. The barman sits behind the *tumunu* and ladles the beer out in a coconut cup. Each drinker swallows his cup in a single gulp and returns the empty cup to the barman who fills it for the next in line. You can pass if you want to but by the end of the evening everybody is decidedly unsteady on their feet. Including, on the night I went, the barman who is supposed to stay sober and keep everyone in line! At some point in the evening the barman calls the school to order by tapping on the side of the *tumunu* with the empty cup and then says a short prayer. Guitars and ukeleles are usually around to provide music and accompaniment to song. As a visitor to the *tumunu* you should bring a kg of sugar or a couple of dollars, the equivalent in cash.

Places to Stay & Eat

The *Atiu Motel* is the only organised accommodation on the island. Roger and Kura Malcolm have three units at NZ$53/

60/67 for singles/doubles/triples. They're delightful, individual, A-frame chalets that make maximum use of local materials. The main beams are sections of coconut palm trunks retaining the outer bark. Coconut palm wood is used extensively inside (it's a beautiful wood) and drawer and cupboard fronts are made with hibiscus wood. So much of the accommodation in Rarotonga makes absolutely zero use of local materials and has no 'Pacific' feel at all; this place should be a real object lesson.

The rooms have a single and double bed and on top of the bathroom there's a mezzanine area where you could sleep another person or two. There's a verandah in front and a kitchen area. There is no place to eat on Atiu so you have to fix your own food – each unit comes with a fridge and cupboard full of food and at the end of your stay you're simply billed for what you've used.

The motel has a lawn tennis court with a thatch pavilion off to one side. Roger is planning to open a bar and try Saturday night counter meals in the pavilion.

The Atiu Motel is a great place to stay and Roger is helpful and informative, helping to organise your stay, arrange guided trips and make sure you have plenty of things to do. Air Rarotonga, Cook Islandair or the Rarotonga travel agents can book you a room at the Atiu Motel. Should it be full up you could no doubt find a place to stay with one of the villagers. Roger could probably suggest something.

There are a several trade stores on Atiu, two bread bakers and three places that bake doughnuts. The amount of bread produced is quite amazing, as on all the islands. Doughnuts are supplied on a loop made from a strip of leaf and you can hang it from the handlebar of your motorcycle and ride off. *Maroro* or flying fish are an Atiuan delicacy; they're caught in butterfly nets on the 10th, 11th and 12th nights after the new moon during the spawning season, from June to December.

Getting There & Away

Air Air Rarotonga and Cook Islandair fly to Atiu about three times a week each. The 40 minute flight costs NZ$200 return with Air Raro, NZ$174 return with Cook Islandair (NZ$156 return if you purchase your ticket locally seven days in advance). Cook Islandair also has connecting flights between Atiu, Mitiaro and Mauke: rates are NZ$58 from Atiu to Mitiaro, NZ$68 from Atiu to Mauke.

Stars Travel in Avarua, Rarotonga organise package tours either to this island alone or as part of an Island Combination tour to Atiu, Mitiaro and Mauke. See the Outer Island Tours section in the Getting Around chapter for details.

Atiu's airport is on the north-east corner of the island. It was built in '83 as the old airstrip, itself built only in '77, was too small. The new strip's coral surface is also better. Roger Malcolm from the Atiu Motel meets incoming guests and drops off outgoing ones.

Sea Silk & Boyd also sail here. The all weather harbour at Taunganui was built in 1974 but it's still too small to take ships so they have to be unloaded onto a barge while they're standing offshore. Prior to '74 getting ashore on Atiu could be a pretty fraught business. In fact some say the Atiuans, once the terror of Mauke and Mitiaro, could have been the terror of many more places were it not for their lack of harbour facilities. As it was the Atiuans could never build really big ocean-going canoes. Instead they used smaller canoes and once offshore lashed two together to make a larger and more stable vessel.

Day Tours Day trips from Rarotonga to Atiu are planned and will include visits to one of Atiu's more spectacular caves, with a hike through the *makatea* along the way; pineapple plantations; a tour of the Atiu Island Coffee plantation and factory; the beach; a local foods lunch; the five villages and the top of the island; and finally to the Atiu Fibre Arts Studio for some local Atiu coffee and refreshments before heading back to Raro.

Getting Around

Atiu is great for walking but you definitely need a motorcycle to get around – the Atiu Motel rents motorcycles for NZ$20 a day or NZ$100 a week. Take great care when walking across the *makatea*. The coral is sharp as hell. It's often like walking across razor blades and if you slipped and fell you'd be sliced to pieces. Wear good shoes too; if you stubbed your toe while wearing thongs you'd probably cut it right off.

Takutea

Population: unpopulated
Area: 1.2 square km

Clearly visible from Atiu this small sand cay is only six metres above sea level at its highest point. The island has also been called Enua-iti which simply means 'small island'. Cook visited Takutea in 1777, shortly after he left Atiu, and paused to search for food for the livestock on his ship.

It's only 16 km north-west of Atiu and copra collecting parties used to come from that island. Today it is unpopulated and rarely visited. Many seabirds including frigates and tropic birds nest on the island.

Margaia

Population: 1235
Area: 51.8 square km

The second largest of the Cook Islands, Mangaia is not much smaller than Rarotonga although its population is much less and has declined sharply in recent years. The island is a geological oddity very similar to Atiu. Like Atiu the central hills are surrounded by an outer rim of raised coral reef known as the *makatea*. The lagoon inside the fringing coral reef is very narrow and shallow.

Only scrub and coconut palms grow on the makatea although Oneroa, Tamarua and Ivirua, the three main villages, are all right on the coast. Taro swamps are found around the inner edge of the makatea where water collects between the hills and the coral flatlands. The central hills are the most fertile part of the island and they're planted with pineapples. Although the geography is basically similar to Atiu's it is much more dramatic. The makatea rises rapidly from the coast and in most places it drops as a sheer wall to the inner region. There are places where you can climb to the top of the cliff for impressive, uninterrupted views.

Since all the streams and rivers running down from the central hills run into a dead end at the inner cliff of the makatea the Mangaia villages all have water problems. You'll see water tanks beside many houses, storing the rainwater from the roofs. A World Health Organisation dam and water reservoir was built in 1986. The inner cliff of the makatea is such a major barrier that some of the routes through it are quite spectacular, one of the ones through to Ivirua in particular.

History

Captain Cook claimed the European discovery of Mangaia during his second Pacific voyage. He arrived on 29 March 1777 but since the reception was not the friendliest and it was not possible to find a place to land boats the *Resolution* and *Discovery* sailed on to a more friendly greeting at Atiu.

The reception was even less inviting when John Williams turned up in 1823. The pioneering missionary had left Aitutaki to search for Rarotonga, which he eventually found by way of Atiu. Coming first upon Mangaia he attempted to set Polynesian 'teachers' ashore but the Mangaians were so unfriendly that he quickly dropped the idea and sailed off again. In 1824, however, two Polynesian missionaries were landed on the island and, as elsewhere, the conversion to Christianity was soon underway.

The Mangaians have a strange legend of their early history. Most Polynesian islands have some sort of misty legend about a great ancestor arriving on a fantastic canoe. Not the Mangaians: nobody sailed from anywhere to settle

Mangaia Cross Section

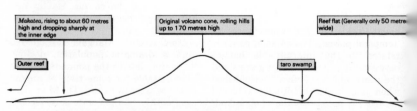

Makatea, rising to about 60 metres high and dropping sharply at the inner edge

Original volcano cone, rolling hills up to 170 metres high

Reef flat (Generally only 50 metres wide)

Outer reef

taro swamp

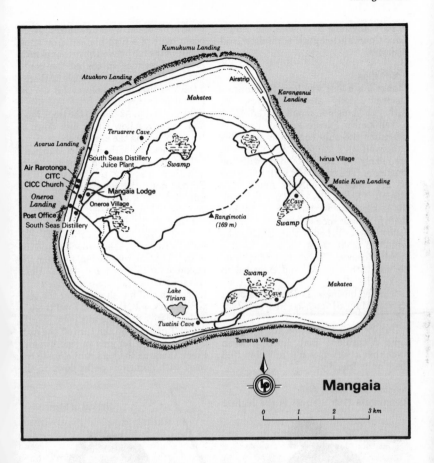

Mangaia. Rongo, the father of Mangaia, simply rose from the deep complete with his three sons, to found the island.

The island's name is comparatively recent – it's thought to have been bestowed upon the island only a few years before Cook's visit and means 'peace' or 'temporal power'. The name apparently relates to the interminable battles between the island's various groups and the peace which was finally established when one leader eventually achieved *mangaia* or power over the whole island.

The Mangaians have a reputation for being a dour, unfriendly lot, an attribute which perhaps helped to keep the aggressive Atiuans at bay. The warriors of Atiu wreaked havoc on Mauke and Mitiaro but never had much success against Mangaia.

More recently Mangaia has suffered from a dramatic population decline. Since the mid-70s the population of the island, stable for some time at around 2000, has fallen by a third. The Mangaians have positively and consistently refused to have anything to do with the central Land Court's attempts to administer land disputes.

Information

Mangaia is a long way from Rarotonga – electricity only arrived in late '85. Although Mangaian ceremonial adzes are a well-known Pacific artefact in world museums the only commonly available handiworks are the *pupu ei's* which you are likely to be garlanded with on departure. The tiny shells with which the *eis* are made can only be found after rainfall. They're black and are found on the makatea, not by the the water. Boiling them in caustic soda produces the typical yellow colour although they can also be grilled to make them white, or dyed a variety of colours. They're then individually pierced with a needle and threaded to make the finished *ei*. It's a time consuming business. In Rarotonga *pupu eis* from Mangaia fetch as much as NZ$25 a dozen.

Despite their reputation and although some Mangaians may initially seem somewhat reserved you'll probably find them quite friendly!

Rangimotia & Island Walk

Rangimotia (169 metres) is the highest point in the island. It's not a straightforward peak, more of a high plateau. You know you're at the top but you have to explore in several directions to see all the coast. From the Oneroa side of the island there's a track – suitable for motorcycles, 4WDs, even regular cars with a little difficulty – right to the top. At the top the track forks and you can follow either fork down to Ivirua village on the east coast.

The tracks follow the ridges of Mangaia's rolling hills and even when they're indistinct it's easy to find your way. Further down the houses in Ivirua come into view and if you take the right track you reach Ivirua through a spectacular cut through the makatea.

From Ivirua you can turn south and walk to Tamarua, the third village on the island. The trail runs just inland from the makatea for most of the distance. Along this stretch the makatea is not edged with much of a cliff but shortly after the trail climbs back onto the raised coral there is an impressive drop and at a point shortly before Tamarua you can turn off the road for a view over an area of taro swamp. From Tamarua the road runs close to the coast with numerous paths down to the

Natives of Mangaia

Mangaian hut

reef. Or you can take the shorter direct route back to Oneroa.

This a pleasant but quite long day's walk. It's probably more than 25 km in total. There's no chance of going thirsty or hungry along the way as long as you have your Swiss Army Knife handy – coconuts, papaya, passionfruit, bananas and, of course, pineapples, can be found along the way.

Caves

The makatea is riddled with caves but the largest and most spectacular is Teruarere. George Tuara who works at the Cook Islands Trading Company is the guide for this cave. He charges NZ$10 and you may have to ask his boss to let him off work to go with you! The caves were used for burial in the distant past but were rediscovered in the 1930s by George's grandfather and Robert Dean Frisbie – see the introductory Books section. Teruarere means 'jump' (because people used to jump down into the cave opening?).

You do have to climb down into the opening. There's a tree whose branches

emerge at ground level and at the other end of this opening chasm there's a fine and frightening view out from the makatea cliff. As you enter, the high, narrow cliffs seem to close overhead. At first there are several small openings high above you and a tree root winds down through one to floor level. Then you have to slither through a low, muddy opening and the cave becomes much more enclosed.

This is a very dramatic cave and most of the time it is very high although fairly narrow. There are glistening-white stalactites and stalagmites but the most interesting feature is simply how far it continues. There are no major side chambers but the main cavern simply continues on and on. It fact it goes so far you have to start out fairly early in the day if you want to explore a reasonable amount. George reckons that it continues at least two km. Although he has been going into the cave for nearly 50 years he has never reached the end.

There are numerous other caves all over the island and several legendary ones no one has yet discovered. One is said to contain the bones of ancient Mangaians of gigantic size. Another, the legendary cave of Piriteumeume, is said to be filled with the skeletons of countless Mangaian warriors, each with his weapons laid beside him.

Other

There are typical, old CICC churches in Oneroa, Ivirua and Tamarua. Look for the sennet rope binding on the roof beams in the Tamarua and Oneroa churches. In front of the Oneroa church is an interesting monument detailing the ministers, both *papa'a* and Maori, of the church and also the Mangaian ministers who have worked as missionaries abroad.

Mangaia has numerous pre-missionary *maraes* but you'd need a local expert to find them. There are countless little beaches and bays around the coastline although nowhere is there good swimming. The reef is very shallow and generally close to the coast. Lake Tiriara is the one lake on the island but it's difficult to distinguish it from the surrounding swamp. There are several landings around the coastline but Avarua, just

north of Oneroa towards the airport, is the main shipping harbour.

South Seas Distillery, which makes 'Mangaia Ara' and 'Rum Ara' liquors out of the fresh Mangaia pineapples, has its fields, juice plant and offices here in Mangaia (see map) and you're welcome to drop in for a look. To taste the finished product, however, you must visit the tasting room in Avarua, Rarotonga, where the final blending and bottling is done.

Places to Stay & Eat

Oneroa consists of one road along the coast, a road up from the coast through a cutting in the makatea and a couple of roads along the coastal edge of the makatea. The government run *Mangaia Lodge* is on the edge of the makatea, with prices of around NZ$20 to NZ$30 per person. Bookings can be made through Air Rarotonga. There are also several families who take paying guests, typically charging NZ$25 a night including meals. Ask around about this once you get to the island; you can try Mrs Karereoa or Mr Kaokao Raeora, both on the road up from the makatea cutting.

If you're staying long you might want to

Mangaia

bring some of your own food with you.
There's a Cook Islands Trading Company
store down on the coast road and several
other trade stores around. There's a
bakery by the school and the steps up from
the coast road to the top of the makatea.

Getting There & Away
Air Air Rarotonga fly to Mangaia four
times a week for NZ$200 return. The 203
km flight takes 40 minutes.

Sea You can also use the Silk & Boyd
shipping services.

Getting Around
There's no regular motorcycle hire on
Mangaia although you could probably
arrange something as there are plenty of
motorcycles about. Walking is fine,
especially the route across the island via
Rangimotia, but the distances around the
coast are quite long and you can't count on
getting a ride from a passing vehicle as
there is so little traffic. I walked all the
way from Ivirua via Tamarua to Oneroa,
several hours' walk, and only saw one
truck passing by – the wrong way.

Mauke

Population: 687
Area: 18.4 square km

Mauke is the most easterly of the Cook Islands. It's one of the more easily visited islands since there is a fairly regular flight schedule and it can be combined with a visit to Atiu, its physically similar and once dominant sister island just 92 km away. Mauke, Mitiaro and Atiu are sometimes referred to by the collective name Nga Pu Toru, 'The Three Roots'.

History

Mauke takes its name from its legendary founder Uke but there are several versions of what the name means. The most obvious is simply 'land of Uke' but another relates that it means 'clean Uke.' This legend tells of Tangiia, one of the two famous mariners who settled Rarotonga (the Ngatangiia district of Rarotonga still bears his name today), coming to ask Uke's aid in going to war against the Samoans. Uke replied, 'my hands are clean' – he did not want war. It is said that Uke came to Mauke in search of a peaceful place to live, and he wanted to continue to live in peace.

Prior to this, Mauke was known as Akatokamanava, which means 'my heart is at rest, is at peace.' These were the first words uttered by Uke when he arrived from the legendary homeland Hawaiiki, landing at Arapaea on the eastern coast in the huge canoe *Paipaimoana*, carrying 2000 settlers. Mauke is still referred to as Akatokamanava in song, dance, legend and in formal address.

Uke arrived on Mauke with a wife he had brought from the Vanuatuan island of Erromanga – the same island where the missionary John Williams would later be

killed and eaten. They had six children, four boys and two girls. The two girls were renowned for their exceptional beauty, and when the two famous Rarotongan settlers, Tangiia and Karika, came seeking these girls for marriage, they went to live in Rarotonga. Uke's sons also went to other islands, and thus Uke became a common ancestor for all the islands of the Southern Group.

Prior to the arrival of Christianity Mauke was totally dominated by the island of Atiu. The Atiuans would descend on murderous, cannibal raids. Akaina, an Atiuan chieftain, settled on Mauke and spirited away the wife of an island chief. Swearing revenge the jilted chief killed Akaina and most of his

Te Rongo & his three sons

ompatriots but one escaped and in a mall canoe made the perilous crossing to Atiu. Incensed by this affront to Atiuan ower Rongomatane, the great chief of Atiu, set out for Mauke at the head of a leet of 80 war canoes. The terrified Maukeans took refuge in caves but many of them were hauled out, beaten to death with clubs, cooked and eaten. Satisfied hat justice had been done Rongomatane nstalled an Atiuan named Tararo as chief and sailed back to Atiu.

The surviving islanders regrouped, however, and under Maiti attacked the Atiuans. Unfortunately for the Maukeans Tararo survived and once again an emissary sailed off to alert Rongomatane. And once again the Atiuan war canoes sallied forth to Mauke. This time the Atiuans showed at least some restraint and spared a number of the women and children, taking them back to Atiu as slaves, the cooked flesh of their husbands and fathers accompanying them in the canoes.

The European discovery of Mauke is credited to the pioneering missionary John Williams who arrived on Mauke on 23 June 1823. And who accompanied Mr Williams? Why none other than that unpleasant previous visitor, Rongomatane! It's hardly surprising that the Maukeans were converted to Christianity with an ease and speed that astonished the western visitors. Despite western influence Mauke remained subject to Atiu with ariki appointed from Atiu.

Author and island personality Julian Dashwood (*Rakau*) lived for years on Mauke where he ran the island store. See the introductory Books section for more information. His second book, *Today is Forever*, is largely about Mauke.

Geology

Like Atiu, Mangaia and Mitiaro this island is a raised atoll with a surrounding *makatea*. Inland from this fossil coral reef there is a band of swampland surrounding the fertile central land. Mauke is like Mitiaro as the central area of the island is flat, rising virtually no higher than the *makatea*. In contrast to Atiu and Mangaia where the central area is hilly, Mauke rises barely 30 metres above sea level at its highest point. Like Atiu and Mangaia there are numerous limestone caves in the *makatea*, which is densely forested with lush jungle-like growth.

Economy & Crafts

Mauke's economic development has been erratic. Growing ginger has been a failure and citrus plantations have also been unsuccessful. A handful of cattle are raised. Mauke is noted for its pandanus mats and hats and the *kete* baskets. Bowls shaped like the leaves of the breadfruit tree and carved from *miro* wood are another traditional Maukean craft.

The People of Mauke

On one of their murderous forays to Mauke the Atiuans tempted the unfortunate inhabitants out of their cave hideaways by claiming they were on a friendly visit and inviting them (the Maukeans) to a feast that they (the Atiuans) were setting up. This was not totally untrue, as the foolish people of Mauke found, but they did not anticipate their role at the feast. They were henceforth labelled *Mauke kaa-kaa* or 'Mauke the easily fooled'.

Some say that when deciding which women to eat, the Atiuans always ate the ugliest and spared the most beautiful, which accounts for the extraordinary beauty of Maukean women today!

Information

The electricity schedule on Mauke is similar to that on Mitiaro: the power comes on from 6 to 9 am, from 12 noon to 3 pm and from 6.30 pm to midnight.

The Divided Church

Mauke has two villages in the centre, Areora and Ngatiarua, and one on the coast, Kimiangatau. The coastal village was built in 1904 because some of the Maukeans had decided to become Roman Catholics and could no longer tolerate living with those who still followed the London Missionary Society.

Religious disputes were nothing new to the Maukeans as the 1882 CICC church illustrates. At that time there were still just two villages and they got together to build the church. When the outside was complete, however, the two sides could not agree on how the inside should be fitted out. Eventually the argument became so acrimonious that the only solution was to build a wall down the middle and let each village have it's own church within the church.

A new pastor eventually managed to convince his congregations that this was hardly the spirit of neighbourly Christianity, and the wall was removed, but the two sides of the church are still decorated in different styles and each village has its own entrance. Inside, the two villages each sit on their own side of the aisle and they take turns singing the hymns! The pulpit, with old Chilean dollars set into

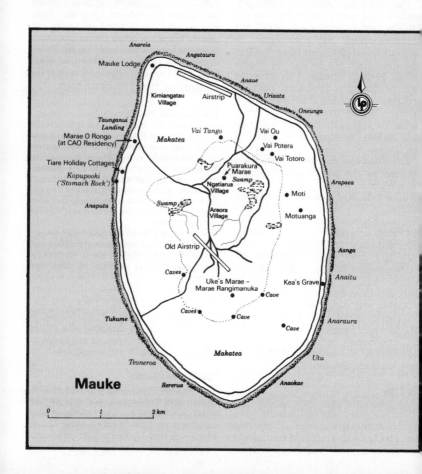

Mauke

0   1   2 km

the railing, is centrally placed but there's a dividing line down the middle and the minister is expected to straddle the line at all times. The interior of the church is painted in soft, pastel colours.

Today, Mauke's population is about 50% CICC, 50% Roman Catholic, with a few families of Mormons, Seventh Day Adventists and Baha'is.

Beaches

A road runs right around the coast of Mauke, a total distance of 18 km. The fringing reef platform is narrow but Teoneroa beach is fairly good as is the beach at Arapaea Landing on the east side of the island. The beaches on the south side of the island like Anaokae are pleasantly secluded. Some beaches, like Anaraura and Teoneroa, have picnic areas with thatched shelters providing welcome shade on a hot day. Oneunga is also a nice little beach for a picnic. All around the island, the waves have beaten the shoreline cliffs into an overhanging formation.

The very first turn-off towards the sea after you pass the Tiare Holiday Cottage, just a few hundred metres to the south, leads you to Kopupooki ('stomach rock') beach. The name comes from a cave located just to your left as you face out to sea – go just past the last outcrop of rock that you see from the beach and you come to this lovely cave full of fish, good for swimming and snorkelling. It's about the only place deep enough for a good swim, since the reef all around the island is quite shallow. You can only reach it at low tide, at other times, the pounding waves make it too dangerous. There are many more little coves and beaches around the island.

Anaiti One of Mauke's beaches, Anaiti, has a special history. Up on the cliff to the right of the beach as you face the sea is a mound of grey coral stones. This is the grave of Kea.

Kea's husband, Paikea, was out fishing one day

in his canoe when Kea, up on the cliff, saw a huge storm coming across the sea. She shouted to her husband to come back to land, but he didn't hear her. The storm caught him at sea and blew him further and further away from the island. Kea believed her husband was dead, and she cried and cried on that cliff overlooking the sea until she died of grief, and the people buried her there.

In the early 1970s, after a severe storm, Kea's bones became exposed, the surrounding sand having been washed away but they have been covered again with big coral stones.

Paikea had not died at sea, however. He was blown very far by the storm, but he finally did reach land – the island of Mangaia. The people there did not want him to stay and were on the point of killing him when a woman who was half-Maukean took him under her protection. With her help, he escaped Mangaia, and sailed to Rarotonga. On Rarotonga, Paikea stayed in Ngatangiia, and finally left on a canoe for New Zealand. There is some doubt as to whether he sailed with the first seven canoes that left Ngatangiia to populate New Zealand in 1350 AD, or if he went later.

The people of Mauke did not know the ultimate fate of Paikea until the 1940s. During WW II some New Zealand Maoris were visiting Mauke, and shared with them their legends and histories. One told of Paikea, who had come from a far-off land after being blown by a storm from his home island. The Maukeans were electrified – it fitted exactly with their legend of Paikea, the husband of Kea, who had been blown away in a storm and never seen again!

In the mid-1980s, New Zealand descendants of Paikea came to the Cooks to trace their family history. They went first to Rarotonga and were told, 'No, he's not from here, he came here from Mangaia.' In Mangaia the historians said, 'He came here from Mauke.' And so they finally traced their ancestor back to his homeland. The Paikeas are now a big family in New Zealand – apparently Paikea went on to have many children and grandchildren in the new land.

Caves

Like Atiu and Mangaia the *makatea* is riddled with limestone caves, many filled with cool water, wonderful for a swim on a hot day. Walking through the *makatea* to the caves is like walking through a lush jungle, with coconuts and other shady trees, pandanus, mosses, ferns and 'tropical houseplant-greenery' in wild profusion. The shade is also welcome on a hot day.

The easiest cave to reach, and also one of the larger ones on the island for swimming, is Vai Tango, just a short walk from Ngatiarua village. You'll probably need someone to show you how to get there the first time, but that's no problem as everybody knows where it is. It's often full of children on Saturdays and after school but at other times you may get it all to yourself.

Other interesting caves in the north part of the island, just a short walk off the main road, are Vai Ou, Vai Totoro and Vai Potera. Vai Ou is in a beautiful, lushly tropical grotto, with an ancient coral pathway leading to it. Vai Totoro is also known as the Crawling Cave – you have to crawl down through a slit in the rockface to get in! It opens up into a big cave inside, but the pools are small, although deep, and they taste like saltwater. Be especially careful walking around in this one, as the rocks are wet and very slippery. Just a little further on is Vai Potera.

Motuanga Cave or the 'Cave of a Hundred Rooms', each with its own pool, is the best known cave on the island. You must ask permission from the landowner, Inepo Temaeva, if you want to visit it. The cave is entered on land and extends out toward the sea and under the reef. In some of the last rooms you can reach, the waves can be heard crashing above you.

There is nobody around today who has reached all of Motuanga's 100 rooms; they say that nowadays you can only get into 12 of them. But there is a legend of one man, Timeni Oariki, who did swim through all of them, finally emerging out into the sea where he was eaten by sharks. So he never got to tell anybody what it was like!

Other important caves are Vai Tunamea and Moti Cave near the old airstrip.

Marae

Mauke, like all the other Cook Islands, has many *marae* or ancient religious meeting grounds. The three most important are those associated with the three *ariki*.

The best preserved, and still used for ceremonial functions, is the Puarakura Marae, in the village of Ngatiarua. There's a triangular area enclosed within a rectangle within another larger rectangle, with seats for the *ariki*, the *rangatira* and the *mataipo*. All the stones are white-washed, just for decoration.

Out past the old airstrip is Marae Rangimanuka, the *marae* of Uke, Mauke's famous ancestor and namesake. It's hidden in an overgrown area but it's not difficult to get to with a guide who knows the way. There's a thatch house over the *marae's* altar and white sand inside but the rest of the site is quite overgrown.

Down near the harbour, behind the CAO Residency, the Marae O Rongo was once a huge *marae* but all you see is one large stone and a coral platform under a very big tree. According to tradition, this is the only *marae* on Mauke where anyone was killed and eaten.

Kovitoa Ariki had two sons, Koumu and Kaivaiva, and when his wife died he remarried to a woman who had five small children. Because he wanted to be sure that his own two sons, who were away in Atiu at the time, would inherit his title, he concocted a plan to get rid of the five small children of his wife.

He took the children out to his plantation on successive occasions, and each time sent them off on various errands, keeping one with him to help him. When the rest of the children returned, they found their father had prepared meat in an *umu* (underground oven) and their little brother or sister was gone. Each time, Kovitoa told the children that he had killed a pig in the bush and that their brother or sister had gone home. When the child was not at home upon their return, he said it must be those Atiu people who had spirited him away.

Finally, when there were only two children left, the older one was getting very suspicious. When Kovitoa sent him away, he hid in the

Top: Cave by candlelight, Mauke (LB/C)
Left: Stalactite or stalagmite from an ancient *marae*, Atiu (TW)
Right: Skulls, Rima Rau Burial Cave, Atiu (TW)

Top: Stalagmites in Teruarere Cave, Mangaia (TW)
Bottom: Waves breaking on the reef, Mangaia (TW)

bush, and saw his brother killed. He ran back to the village and told the people what Kovitoa had done. Not long after that, when Kovitoa was sleeping, someone bashed his head with a coconut grater, and he was roasted and eaten on his own *marae*.

As the people were washing Kovitoa's body down at the present-day harbour, with the roasting oven blazing away, one of Kovitoa's two sons arrived in a canoe from Atiu. He ended up avenging the death of his father by killing his assassin in his sleep with the same coconut grater that had been used on his father, and he took over his father's title.

Places to Stay & Eat

The *Tiare Holiday Cottage* is right on the coast, near to the village and to Kopupooki, one of Mauke's nicer beaches. It has three simple cottages, each with cement walls, a thatch roof and its own fridge. You can do your own cooking in the separate kitchen/dining area, or have meals prepared for you. Showers are in a separate area nearby. Room only costs are NZ$25/35/45 for singles/doubles/triples. You can book directly, by telegram, or through travel agents or Cook Islandair.

The *Mauke Lodge*, also sometimes known as the *Cove Lodge*, is a huge old three-bedroom house at the edge of Kimiangatau village on the north side of the island. It can hold up to 10 people, but is always rented out as one complete unit. Amenities include a washing machine, freezer, library, chord organ and a motorcycle to get around on, and someone comes daily to clean. Singles/doubles are NZ$45/60 plus NZ$15 for each additional person. Special rates are offered for stays of one week or longer and you can book through Air Rarotonga, but it's 20% cheaper if you book directly by telegram, addressed to Mr and Mrs Guinea, Mauke.

Getting There & Away

Air Cook Islandair and Air Rarotonga each fly twice a week between Rarotonga and Mauke; Cook Islandair also has connecting flights between Mauke, Mitiaro and Atiu. Prices from Rarotonga are NZ$200 return

on Air Raro, NZ$198 on Cook Islandair (NZ$178 if you purchase your ticket locally seven days in advance).

You can also visit Mauke as a part of the seven-night Island Combination tour offered by Stars Travel in Avarua, Rarotonga, visiting the islands of Mauke, Mitiaro and Atiu. See the Outer Island Tours section in the Getting Around chapter for details.

Mauke now has a new airstrip on the island's north coast, replacing the older one in the centre of the island.

Sea Silk & Boyd ships also operate to Mauke.

Getting Around

The Tiare Holiday Cottage has motorcycles for hire at NZ$15 per day. Both places to stay provide free airport transfers.

Mitiaro

Population: 272
Area: 22.3 square km

Mitiaro is not one of the Cooks' most physically beautiful islands, but there are a few very enjoyable things you can do there to pass a pleasant few days. The people do not initially appear very happy to see a new face but everyone will greet you as you walk around, and when you stop to talk to them they are wonderfully friendly. You'll find that many people whom you have met only once will remember your name and greet you every time they see you.

To see the sights of Mitiaro, especially the caves and the *marae*, you'll need a local person to guide you. This does not present any problem; people are not in a hurry or so busy with their own affairs that they have no time to show you the beautiful parts of their island. Mitiaro's eels are a renowned delicacy.

History

Like Mauke the island of Mitiaro was subject to repeated raids from Atiu, but unlike the Maukeans the Mitiaroans did not hide in caves. They stoutly defended their fortress Te Pare but were, nevertheless, eventually overcome by the Atiuans.

The Reverend John Williams arrived on Mitiaro on 29 July 1823 accompanied by Rongomatane as he had been on Mauke. The small and declining population that lives on Mitiaro today is thought to be almost entirely descended from raiding Atiuan warriors. Atiuan raids continued, even after the arrival of Christianity, into the 1840s.

Before Christianity came to Mitiaro, the people lived in inland villages – Taurangi, Atai, Auta, Mangarei and Takaue. As in Rarotonga, when the missionaries came, they moved the people out to live on the coast, where they built a village centred around the church. Today the old village sites are the plantation areas, where all the food is grown.

Geology

Mitiaro is another of the southern islands with a raised outer coral limestone plain or *makatea*. Like Mauke, but to an even greater degree, the interior of the island is very flat – the *makatea* rises to a maximum of 9 metres above sea level, the interior foodlands to about 12 metres. Much of the interior of Mitiaro is swampland, just one metre above sea level. Two parts of this swamp are deep enough to be labelled as lakes: Rotonui, which is the larger, and Rotoiti.

People & Culture

All the inhabitants of Mitiaro are related to one another in some way. The local ladies sometimes bemoan the situation, saying, 'We'll *never* find a husband on this island! All the men here are our cousins!' In fact Mitiaro, Mauke and Atiu, known collectively as Nga Pu Toru, are all in much the same situation and a great deal of intermarriage has taken place among

them right down through the years. Everybody on Mitiaro seems to have family on Mauke, Atiu and even further afield and there's much visiting back and forth.

With everyone on Mitiaro being a relative, it makes for a high degree of cooperation. There's not much money around, but everyone gets what they need. The Mitiaro schools only go up to about age 12, after that children must go to Atiu or even to Rarotonga or New Zealand. Usually there are relatives for the children to stay with.

This system breaks up the families on Mitiaro and is certainly a cause of the small population figure as children rarely return to the narrow economic horizons of the island. Plantation work or fishing is about all Mitiaro has to offer and usually they only return for occasional Christmas visits.

Economy & Crafts

Although most people now live in western-style houses, they usually have outbuildings made of traditional thatch which may serve as cookhouses, fishermen's shacks, etc. Women weave long pandanus strips into floor mats, fans, handbags and other craftwork. Big bowls are carved of solid wood and canoes are still made in the traditional way. Fishing and planting are done according to the phases of the moon. Boys grow up learning the habits of each type of fish – at what phase of the moon it will be found, where, at what depth, doing what and so on. The traditional arts are still taught to both boys and girls.

Terevai

The women of Mitiaro have a delightful custom known as the *terevai*. A group of women get together and go to one of the island's pools, often to Vai Naure or Vai Tamaroa. Along the way, they sing the old bawdy songs of the ancestors – many of which are action songs with very graphic movements accompanying the lyrics. The mood gets exuberantly racy and by the time the women have trekked out to the pool, everyone is in high spirits. At the pool a prayer, a hymn and a chant precede a synchronised leap into the water.

Information

Progress has arrived very recently in Mitiaro. The island road has recently been completely overhauled and by now should extend right around the island. Bring your sunglasses, the white surface is very reflective. Electricity is another recent arrival. Once only available from individual generators power is now available on a similar schedule to Mauke:

5 to 9 am, 12 noon to 2 pm and 6 pm to midnight.

Mitiaro has a telephone system but you can only dial directly to other numbers on the island. Outside calls must be made through the phone at the post office. When a call comes in from outside the operator calls the person receiving the call to tell them to come down to the post office!

The CICC Church

The inhabitants of Mitiaro are now concentrated in one settlement on the

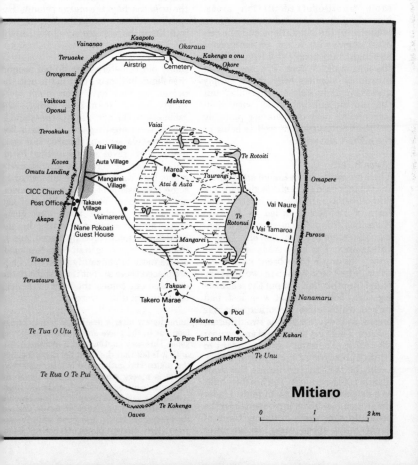

Mitiaro

0   1   2 km

west coast. The white-painted CICC church (the third church that the London Missionary Society built in the Cooks), with its blue trim, parquet ceiling decorated with black and white stars, and stained-glass windows is a fine sight and the singing on Sundays is superb. There's also a small Catholic church.

Plantations

In the old days people made their villages where they grew their food. Even after moving the houses to the seaside village in the 1800s, they have continued using the same traditional plantation areas. Nowadays there are roadways across the *makatea* to the plantations and one can drive there with a car or motorcycle although many people still have to make the long walk on foot. The new visitor invariably wonders why don't simply grow their produce closer to the village but the old agricultural areas with their surrounding peat deposits are probably the most fertile spots as well as being at the highest elevation.

Marae & Fort

There are *marae* in the inland areas where the villages used to be although many are now overgrown. In 1988 an international team of archaeologists led by Dr Hiro Kurashina of Japan located and excavated the Takero *marae*, in the old Takaue village area. The huge stone seat of the *ariki* – he must have been quite a big fellow! – had been broken in two and they found the other half and put the seat back together. The side that was lost had turned white while the other side was brown, so today the seat is two different colours. There are several old graves near the *marae*. The same team had plans to return and excavate a *marae* in Atai in 1989.

Off the trail to Te Unu are the stone remains of the ancient Te Pare fort, built as a defence against Atiuan raids. Under the ground is a shelter large enough for the people to congregate in during times of danger while above was a lookout tower

from which approaching canoes could be watched for. Footsteps could be easily heard on the loose stone pathway to the fort. The important *marae* in the fort complex ensured there was spiritual as well as physical protection. Despite all of this, the fierce Atiuan warriors eventually did overpower the island. The present three *ariki* of Mitiaro are descended from the foremost Mitiaro warriors, who were appointed by the Atiu conquerors to represent the people.

To visit the Te Pare fort and *marae*, you must first ask permission of Tiki Tetava the *ariki* to whom the *marae* belongs. His speaker will take you to the fort, the long walk across the *makatea* is well worthwhile.

Cemetery

Many old cemeteries are dotted around the island, indicating that in the past the population may have been much more widely spread than it is today. The cemetery on the north side of the island is the most interesting one. It has a few modern-style cement tombs, but also many older graves simply marked by an upright slab of coral. At almost every grave, both the old and the modern ones, some possessions of the deceased person are left at the headstone. Most of the graves have a plate, bowl, cup, glass, bottle and/or silverware sitting by the headstone – some carefully placed, just as if someone was going to sit down to a meal, others more haphazardly piled up. They are placed there so that if the spirit of the deceased one comes, they can eat a meal on their own dinnerware!

Immediately after a death, the family brings food out to the grave and leaves it until it is gone. This may continue for a month or two until it is felt that the spirit has departed, but the plates and cutlery are left permanently There is a very strong belief that the spirit continues to live on after death, and every effort is made to ensure that the spirit will not become angry with the living. At older graves, you see tin or enamel bowls and cups while newer graves have modern plates and cutlery. I saw one grave with a whole box full of what appeared to be medicine bottles, some with the medicine still in it, as well as a baby bottle and a tiny pair of baby shoes.

Beaches, Caves & Pools

Mitiaro has some fine stretches of beach and the reef at low tide is excellent for walking on all around the island. In common with the other islands with *makatea* it also has a number of beautiful caves, with pools of fresh water that make great swimming holes. The *makatea* looks parched and dry, you would never guess that out there, somewhere, are these cool, clear pools, hidden under the ground! The water in the pools, as well as in the lakes and the swamp, rises and falls with the tides. There's no trace of saltwater in the pools but they must somehow be connected to the sea.

Just a 10-minute walk from the village on the Takaue road, Vai Marere is the only sulphur pool in the Cook Islands. All you see from the road is a big hole in the ground but it opens up into a large cave with stalactites. The water is darker than in other pools, possibly due to the sulphur content. It's refreshingly cool and makes your skin and hair feel wonderfully soft.

Vai Tamaroa and Vai Naure are on the eastern side of the island, reached by walking across the *makatea* off from the main road. Vai Naure is about a 15-minute walk in; Vai Tamaroa is further in. You'll need a local to take you there, since the trails across the *makatea* are faint.

Vai Naure is a large, brilliantly clear pool in a big cave. You can reach the water either by climbing down one side and wading in, or by going around to the other side and jumping off the three metre cliff, like the locals do! It's beautiful to sit peacefully and listen to the water dripping down from the stalactites on the ceiling, falling down like rain.

Vai Tamaroa is another large pool, but open to the sky. All around it are cliffs about 10 metres high, and the locals love to jump down into the water, climbing

back up the cliffs again for another leap. The women hold their *terevai* gatherings at both Vai Tamaroa and Vai Naure.

Vaiai or the Sandalwood Cave, named for the sandalwood that grows there, is in the north of the island and also has a good freshwater swimming hole. It's reached by a winding track.

Lakes

It's hard to tell where the surrounding swamps end and the lakes begin. They're hard to approach and although the water is clear the lake bottoms are horribly muddy. As you get closer to the lakes the ground becomes increasingly soggy and wallows unsteadily under your feet.

It's easier to approach Lake Rotonui than Lake Rotoiti as there's a walking trail there from Parava. The trail can take about two hours to traverse, what with crossing the *makatea* and a few places with big rocks to get over, but a road there may be completed in 1989. Where the pathway arrives at the lake there's a boat landing and a pleasant picnic spot.

You can also approach the lakes from the Taurangi plantation area, which is quite easy since there is no *makatea* to cross – only a wide strip of very black mud! At least until the other road is built this is the fastest way with a motorcycle since you can take it all the way to the end of the Taurangi area pathway. From there it's only a 15-minute walk to the lake but the mud you have to cross may deter you.

The local men often fish in the lake for the prolific small fish and the famous eels. The eels are caught at night by blinding them with a light then hitting them with a bush knife. In a couple of hours 10 or more eels can be caught.

Peat

There are many areas of natural peat on the island, principally around the lakes, adjacent to the foodlands and in the swamp. A particularly rich strip is located by the Parava boat landing on Lake Rotonui. A 1988 study concluded that the peat could not be efficiently used for energy but farmers do use it to enrich the soil.

When you walk near the lake, or on the roads through the swamp towards the plantation lands, there is a pleasant peat smell in the air. Crossing the peat to the lake is quite an adventure as it can wobble like jelly beneath your feet. In places logs have been placed to spread the weight.

Places to Stay & Eat

The *Nane Pokoati Guesthouse* is the only place to stay on the island and it can only take three or four visitors at a time. It's run like a large family home by Nane, a wonderfully friendly lady. Singles/doubles are NZ$25/35 including all meals and children are free. You can bring your own food and do your own cooking but Nane's food is delicious. You can use the family motorcycle to get about on and one of Nane's relations will show you around the island.

Bookings are made through Stars Travel in Rarotonga or Cook Islandair or by calling Nane direct. Her number in Mitiaro is 36-107. The post office call her at home and she has to come down to the post office to receive your call but it's only two houses away.

Pieres – dried bananas wrapped in banana leaves

Limited food supplies are available at the island stores but it's wise to bring some with you, particularly bread. Mitiaro's dried bananas wrapped in banana leaves (*pieres*) are a delicacy in Rarotonga. The local eels are delicious and there's a good variety of fish and fresh produce. Passionfruit and mangoes simply fall on the ground under the trees and there are coconuts everywhere.

Getting There & Away

Cook Islandair fly to Mitiaro twice a week, with connecting flights to Atiu and Mauke. The price from Rarotonga is NZ$198 return, or NZ$178 if you buy your ticket seven days in advance.

You can also come to Mitiaro as a part of the Island Combination tour offered by Stars Travel in Avarua, Rarotonga. See the Outer Island Tours section in the Getting Around chapter for details.

Palmerston

Population: 66
Area: 2.0 square km

Palmerston is something of a Cook Islands oddity: it's only a little north of Aitutaki, otherwise the most northerly of the southern group, but it's also far to the west of the other southern islands. Furthermore it's an atoll like the northern group islands and unlike the other southern islands. As a result it sometimes gets treated as part of the northern group.

The lagoon is 11 km wide at its widest point and 35 small islands dot the reef. At low tide the lagoon is completely closed off. Visiting ships have to anchor outside the reef.

History

Captain Cook sighted the island in 1774 when it was unpopulated. He did not stop on that occasion but in 1777 when he passed by on his third voyage his ships did

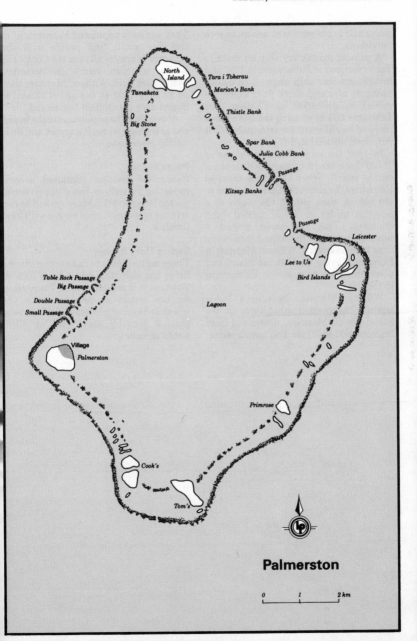

North Island
Tara i Tokerau
Marion's Bank
Tamaketa
Thistle Bank
Big Stone
Spar Bank
Julia Cobb Bank
Passage
Kitsap Banks
Passage
Leicester
Lee to Us
Bird Islands
Table Rock Passage
Big Passage
Double Passage
Small Passage
Lagoon
Village
Palmerston
Primrose
Cook's
Tom's

Palmerston

0   1   2 km

pause and boats were sent ashore to seek provisions.

A passing missionary ship en route to Tahiti stopped at Palmerston in 1797 and in 1811 another ship stopped to collect bêche de mer and shark fins, which are valued as delicacies by Chinese. The Tahitians talked of using the island as a place of banishment for criminals but it remained uninhabited.

In 1850 the crew of the *Merchant of Tahiti* discovered four starving Europeans on the island. When they took them to Rarotonga the ship's captain laid claim to the island, then passed the claim to a Scottish trader in Tahiti named John Branden. This gentlemen placed a representative on the island and some time later discovered William Marsters, a European, living on Manuae island and persuaded him to move to Palmerston in 1863.

William Marsters became a living legend. The present inhabitants of the island are all Marsters, descended from William and his three Polynesian wives.

They not only populated Palmerston: to this day you'll find people with the surname Marsters all over the Cooks and it's a common name on cemetery headstones. Old William Marsters died on 22 May 1899 at the age of 78 and is buried near his original homestead.

At one time the population of the island was as high as 150 but it's a quiet and little visited place today.

Places to Stay

Palmerston has no organised accommodation for visitors, but if you do come, see the Reverend Bill Marsters and he can arrange accommodation for you with local families.

Getting There & Away

There are no flights to Palmerston. At one time, the shipping schedule of Silk & Boyd made it possible to visit Palmerston for one week; at present, since the schedule has changed again, you'd have to plan a lengthy stay (two or three weeks or more).

The
Northern
Islands

The Northern Islands

The northern islands of the Cooks are scattered coral atolls, specks of land in a vast expanse of sea. They are all low-lying and from a ship cannot even be seen from much more than 10 km away. On many of the islands severe hurricanes will send waves right across the islands. Although atolls such as these are the romantic image of a Pacific island – complete with sandy beaches, clear and shallow lagoons, swaying palm trees – in actual fact life is hard on an atoll. Fish may be abundant in the lagoon but atoll soil is only marginally fertile and the range of foodstuffs which can be grown is very limited. Fresh water is always a problem. Shallow wells are often the only source of drinking water and the supply is generally limited and often not very pleasant to drink.

In the modern world atoll life has another drawback apart from these natural ones and that is sheer isolation. Today people want economic opportunity, education for their children and contact with the outside world. On a tiny island where the only physical contact is a trading ship coming through about six times a year these things are clearly not available and at the same time returning islanders and the radio whet the appetite for the outside world. Many of the northern islands are suffering from a declining population.

If you want to visit islands of the northern group the only regular way of getting there is on the Silk & Boyd ships - see the introductory Getting Around chapter for fare details. The ships generally unload and load at the islands by day so if you're doing a circuit of the islands you can spend a day or more on a number of islands. If you want to stay longer you're generally stuck with waiting until the next ship comes by – which may be months away.

Although there is no regular accommodation on any of the northern islands the infrequent visitors are usually made

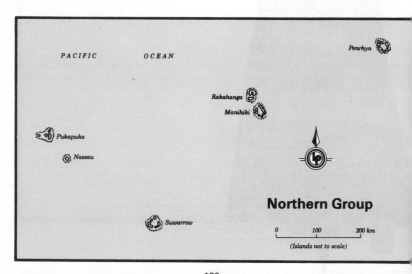

PACIFIC   OCEAN

Penrhyn

Rakahanga
Manihiki

Pukapuka

Nassau

Northern Group

Suwarrow

0   100   200 km

(Islands not to scale)

welcome and some arrangement will always be made. Plan to pay your way, however, both in cash terms and with food or other supplies. Food supplies are always limited on the islands and the arrival of a ship is always a major occasion.

For an account of a short visit to various northern islands via the Silk & Boyd ships look for *Lost & Found in the Cook Islands* (Pukapuka, Nassau and Palmerston) or *Across the South Pacific* (Manihiki and Rakahanga).

Manihiki

Population: 508
Area: 5.4 square km

This is reputed to be one of the most beautiful atolls in the Pacific. Nearly 40 islands, some of them little more than tiny *motus*, encircle the four km wide and totally enclosed lagoon. The main village is Tauhunu but there is a second village, Tukao.

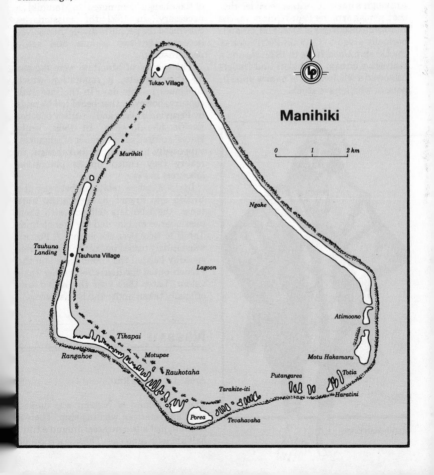

Manihiki has no safe anchorage for visiting ships which consequently stay offshore. What it does have is pearl shells which are the mainstay of the island and a significant export for the Cook Islands. The abilities of the island's pearl divers are legendary – they can dive effortlessly to great depths and stay submerged for minutes at a time. Manihiki was formerly owned by the people of Rakahanga – see the Rakahanga section for more details.

History

Although some authorities consider that the Spanish explorer Pedro Quiros was the European discoverer of Manihiki, credit is normally given to Captain Patrickson of the US ship *Good Hope* in 1822. He and a successive stream of whalers and traders bestowed a whole series of names upon it, none of which have stuck.

Manihikian bride

The missions came to Manihiki in 1849 after a Manihiki canoe en route to Rakahanga was blown off course, rescued by a whaler and left at Manuae. The missionaries took the canoe passengers back to Manihiki and left two Polynesian teachers at the same time. They also left disease. The ensuing epidemic quickly convinced the islanders that they had not been behaving themselves and should embrace Christianity.

Manihiki at that time was more-or-less a subsidiary of Rakahanga and the people of Rakahanga 'commuted' to Manihiki as necessary. In 1852 the missionaries convinced the people to divide themselves between the two islands and settle permanently.

The women of Manihiki were famous for their beauty, a reputation which continues to this day. In the late 19th century, however, that belief led to raids by Peruvian slavers and a variety of other Pacific n'er-do-wells. In 1869 'Bully Hates' spirited off a number of islanders, supposedly for a visit to Rakahanga; in reality they ended up as plantation labourers in Fiji.

In 1889, when relations between the British and French in the Pacific were tense, the islanders fell out with their missionaries and invited the French from Tahiti to take over the island. A French warship duly turned up but the missionaries speedily hoisted the Union Jack and the French opted for discretion rather than valour. Later that year the island was officially taken under the British wing.

Nassau

Population: 118
Area: 1.2 square km

The tiny island of Nassau was named after an American whaling ship. There's no atoll, just a fringing reef around a tiny, half km long sand cay. There is a coconut plantation and taro is grown in the centre of the island.

History

Only 88 km south-east of Pukapuka the island was effectively the property of the Pukapukans. It was probably first discovered by Europeans in 1803 and each successive visitor gave it a new name, usually that of the discovering ship. For some reason, however, it was the American whaler *Nassau's* visit, comparatively late in the day in 1835, which gave the island its present name.

The island did not have a permanent population although occasional groups from other islands stopped for longer or shorter periods. An American attempted to grow coconuts and other plants from 1876 and in later years a number of European-owned copra plantations were established. In 1945 these were sold to the colonial government for £2000. Six years later they were sold to the chiefs of Pukapuka for the same figure; their temporary work groups have become a virtually permanent population.

Wreck of the Manuvai

The Scandinavian-built 50 metre (164 foot), 400 ton *Manuvai* carried freight and passengers throughout the islands for the Silk & Boyd shipping company. There was space for 20 passengers in five four-berth cabins and 70 passengers on deck. On 27 December 1988, at around midnight, the *Manuvai* ran onto the reef on Nassau as it was returning to Rarotonga from a northern group loop. No storm, no wind, it simply ran onto the reef!

It was windy for the next four days and the seas pushed the ship further and further up the reef. The old ship was damaged beyond repair; a Silk & Boyd team came up to salvage whatever was useful off the vessel, but its remains will probably be sitting on the reef for the next 100 years. It was quite an adventure for all, including the 100-odd population of the remote island who suddenly found themselves hosting the stranded 30-to-40 passengers and crew for the next two weeks, until an emergency ship could be brought up from Rarotonga to retrieve them.

Penrhyn

Population: 496
Area: 9.8 square km

Penrhyn is the most northerly of the Cook Islands and its lagoon is unlike most of the other Cook atolls in that it is very wide and easily accessible. From Omoka, one main village, Te Tautua, the other main village, isn't visible except for its church roof. Not only is the lagoon accessible to ships, it also has plenty of sharks although most are harmless. For an interesting account of the island's history during the last century see *Impressions of Tongareva – 1816-1901* from the University of the South Pacific (Suva, Fiji, 1984).

Penrhyn was famous throughout the Pacific at one time for its natural mother of pearl which is still found to this day. Some interesting shell jewellery is also produced and Penrhyn is noted for its fine *rito* hats.

History

Polynesian legends relate that the island was fished up from the depths of the ocean by Vatea, the eldest son of the great mother in Avaiki. He used a fish-hook baited with a star but when that did not work he tore a piece of flesh from his thigh, baited the hook with that and promptly pulled up the island from the deep. He then hung the hook in the sky. Although the local name Tongareva is still widely used the atoll takes its most un-Polynesian name from the British ship *Lady Penrhyn* which dropped by in 1788 on the way back to England from Australia. The ship was one of the 11 which carried the original convict settlers out to Sydney in Australia. The Maori name Tongareva could

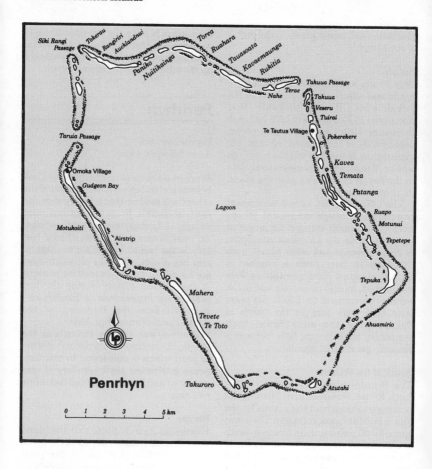

Siki Rangi Passage
Tokerau
Rangiiri
Aucklandnui
Torea
Ruahara
Paniko
Nuitikainga
Tawasoata
Kavaemaunga
Rukitia
Takuua Passage
Nahe
Terae
Takuua
Veseru
Tuirai
Te Tautua Village
Pokerekere
Kavea
Temata
Patanga
Ruapo
Motunui
Tepetepe
Taruia Passage
Omoka Village
Gudgeon Bay
Lagoon
Motukoiti
Airstrip
Tepuka
Mahera
Tevete
Te Toto
Ahuamirio
Penrhyn
Takuroro
Atutahi

0   1   2   3   4   5 km

translate as something like 'to the south of the great emptiness' – there's a lot of nothing to the north of Penrhyn – or 'Tonga floating in space'. Another Maori name, Mangarongaro, is also sometimes used although some people say it was originally only the name of one of the islands in the atoll. There is no direct translation but a *mangaro* is a kind of coconut.

After the *Lady Penrhyn* it was 28 years before a visit by the Russian ship *Rurick* in 1816. The earliest western accounts of Penrhyn all comment on the unusual fierceness and erratic behaviour of the inhabitants of Penrhyn. The following extract is a typical description from a visit by the US ship *Porpoise* in 1841:

.... each and all of them were talking in a language altogether unintelligible and in voices peculiarly harsh and discordant accompanying their words with every unimaginable contortion of the body and with the most diabolical expressions of countenance every muscle being brought into play and made to quiver apparently with rage & excitement, and their eyes fairly starting from their heads. It is utterly impossible for the mind to conceive and altogether out of my power to find words to express or convey any adequate idea of a scene so savage . . . .

None of these early visitors dared to go ashore and they all tried to keep the inhabitants distinctly at arms length. Despite this impression when the American ship *Chatham* ran onto the reef in 1853 to the surprise and relief of the crew and passengers they were treated well. Some of them were to remain on the island for almost a year before being rescued. E H Lamont, the trader who had chartered the unfortunate vessel, wrote *Wild Life among the Pacific Islanders* about his time on the island. He obviously entered into atoll life wholeheartedly because he married three women while he was there! Dr R in his account was the Dr Longghost of Herman Melville's *Omoo*.

The first missionaries arrived in 1854 and those warlike and terrifying islanders quickly became obedient churchgoers. So obedient that the four Polynesian teachers landed by the missionaries 'sold' their flock to Peruvian slavers in 1862-63. They netted $5 a head and went along to South America as overseers for a salary of $100 a month. The island's population was decimated by the activities of the slavers who dubbed the island 'the island of the four evangelists'. That disastrous slaving foray left Penrhyn with a population of only 88 – down from an estimated 700 before the trade began, with around 472 persons taken to Peru, and another 130 to Tahiti. The population had rebounded to 445 by 1902 but the entire chiefly line disappeared during this period so today Penrhyn is the only island in the Cooks with no *ariki* or paramount chief.

Like Rakahanga, Penrhyn has an unused airstrip as a result of its use as an American, WW II airbase. The airstrip is near Omoka village but it's too far from the southern islands to be flown to regularly. The remains of the *Go-Gettin'* *Gal*, a four-engined bomber, still remain there although it's gradually being used up as a source of scrap metal.

Pukapuka

Population: 760
Area: 5.1 square km

Shaped like a three-bladed fan Pukapuka's atoll has an island at each 'blade end' and another in the middle. The northernmost island gives its name to the whole atoll although it is also known, usually in parentheses, as 'Wale'. The only landing place is reached by narrow and difficult passages through the reef on the western side of Wale Island.

There are three villages – Ngake, Roto and Yato – all on Wale Island. Copra and

Soul traps in Pukapuka

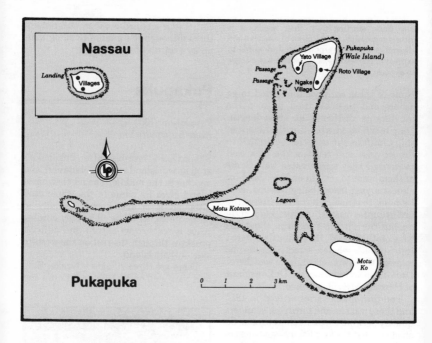

smaller quantities of bananas and papayas are grown. The relative proximity to Samoa has resulted in the islanders' customs and language relating more closely to Samoa than to the rest of the Cooks. There is a notably decorated Catholic church on the island and excellent swimming and snorkelling, particularly off the central island of Kotawa. Pukapuka is noted for its finely woven mats.

History

Early legends relate tales of the island rising from the deep with men inside it or of great voyages. Another tale tells of a great tidal wave about 400 years ago which left only two women and 15 men alive on the island; with considerable effort (on the women's part!) they managed to repopulate it. There may have been some truth in this tale as the islanders recall that it was during the rule of the fourth

chief after the great disaster that the first western visitors arrived.

That first western visitor was the Spanish explorer Alvaro de Mendana who, with his navigator Pedro Fernandez de Quiros, sailed from Peru in 1595 and later that year discovered an island which he named San Bernardo. Although they did not attempt to land nor did they see signs of life it is generally accepted that the island they sighted was Pukapuka. Over 150 years later in 1765 the British ships *Dolphin* and *Tamar* again sighted the islands and again decided against attempting a landing due to the high surf. They named the atoll the Islands of Danger and Pukapuka is still sometimes referred to as Danger Island.

Further sightings and namings continued and finally in 1857 Polynesian missionaries were landed, followed in 1862 by a visit by the pioneer missionary William Wyatt Gill. A year later the population of the island was decimated by slave raids from Peru. In 1865 the London Missionary Society ship *John Williams* which had spent so much time in this region was wrecked on Pukapuka's reef.

During this century South Seas character Robert Dean Frisbie lived for some time on the island and wrote *The Book of Puka-Puka* and *The Island of Desire*. His daughter Johnny Frisbie also wrote of the island in *Miss Ulysses from Puka-Puka*. Modern maps of Pukapuka are still based on Robert Dean Frisbie's 1925 survey.

Robert Dean Frisbie

Robert Dean Frisbie never achieved his dream of writing a great book, a modern *Moby Dick*, but his accounts of life in the Pacific are still classics and if his life was hard it was also colourful. Born in 1896 in Cleveland, Ohio his parents were strict and Frisbie was a frail weak child. He joined the US army during WW I but was discharged as medically unfit in 1918 with a warning that he was unlikely to survive another North American winter.

Two years later Frisbie, living in Tahiti with a Tahitian mistress named Terii, had become known as Ropati to his Polynesian neighbours and was running a small plantation and dreaming of that great book. In 1923 with two partners he set off on a sailing trip which would take them to Manihiki, Penrhyn and Suwarrow in the Cook Islands, to the Samoas and finally to Fiji where the now penniless adventurers had to sell their boat. Back in Tahiti Frisbie learned that his first magazine article had been sold.

In 1924 he sailed to Rarotonga where he got a job running a trading store on Pukapuka and wrote of his experiences in a series of magazine articles which established that idyllic vision of warm seas, swaying palm trees and romantic and beautiful women! Many were published by the *Atlantic Monthly* and came out in book form as *The Book of Puka-Puka* in 1929. Frisbie spent four years on Pukapuka and married Ngatokorua, with whom he had five children.

In 1928 Frisbie and his wife travelled to Rarotonga and in 1930 his first child, a son named Charles was born. Frisbie made a brief trip back to the US but quickly returned to his beloved Pacific islands where he lived with Nga on Tahiti and continued to write magazine

articles. In 1932 his daughter Florence was born in Papeete and was soon nicknamed 'Johnny', a name which stuck. Moving to Moorea he went into poultry farming and had a second son, William who was always known as 'Jakey'.

In 1934 the Frisbie family, all except Charles who had remained in Rarotonga since his birth with a grand aunt, returned to Pukapuka and lived on the southern *motu* Ko where two more daughters, Elaine and Nga, were born. For a spell he had difficulty selling his articles but now his writing was again in demand. Then in 1938 his wife became so ill with tuberculosis that she had to be evacuated to Western Samoa for treatment. The Frisbies soon returned to Pukapuka where she died in early 1939.

That same year Frisbie's first novel, *Mr Moonlight's Island* was published and in December 1941, unaware that the Japanese raid on Pearl Harbour had taken place earlier in the month, Frisbie and his four children set off on a Pacific cruise that was soon interrupted by a lengthy pause on the atoll of Suwarrow. The five Frisbies were soon joined by three New Zealand surveyors accompanied by three islanders from Manihiki and then by two yachtsmen. On 19 February 1942 the island was struck by an exceptionally severe hurricane. Waves as high as five metres swept right across the low-lying island, parts of the atoll which the New Zealanders had recently surveyed were totally reshaped and the yacht disappeared completely. Remarkably the nine adults and four children all survived and Frisbie was to write of this experience in *The Island of Desire* which was published in 1944. Desire was his late wife, Nga, and her island was Pukapuka but Suwarrow also features in this South Seas classic.

The later years of Frisbie's energetic life are told not only in his own writings but also in those of his daughter Johnny who, with help from her father, wrote *Miss Ulysses from Puka-Puka* when she was only 15 years old. It was published in 1948 with support from no less a Pacific luminary than James Michener. She also wrote *The Frisbies of the South Seas* which was published in 1959. His long time friend James Norman Hall also wrote of Frisbie in 'Frisbie of Danger Island' in his book *The Forgotten One* (1952) and he features in James Michener's book *Return to Paradise*

From Suwarrow the Frisbies sailed to Manihiki where he remarried then moved on to Rarotonga where his new wife soon left him.

In Rarotonga his decidedly able children had their first experience of school but soon the Frisbies were on the move again first to Manihiki then to Penrhyn from where he was rescued by a US Navy aircraft and taken to Pago Pago in American Samoa dying from tuberculosis. On board the aircraft was James Michener. The well travelled Frisbie children soon joined their remarkable father who proceeded to make an equally remarkable recovery and added schoolteacher to his list of occupations. From American Samoa the Frisbies moved to the quieter surroundings of Western Samoa, then on to Tahiti and back to Rarotonga where he completed his last work before he died of tetanus in 1948. It was not the great South Pacific novel he dreamed of but no matter, he'd led a full life and left works he will be remembered by. Robert Dean Frisbie's grave can be found by the CICC church in Avarua, Rarotonga.

Rakahanga

Population: 283
Area: 4.1 square km

Only 42 km north of Manihiki this rectangular atoll is almost completely enclosed by two major islands and a host of smaller *motus*. Without the pearl wealth of Manihiki the island is conspicuously quieter and less energetic. Copra is the only export product although the islanders grow breadfruit and a taro-like vegetable. The *rito* hats woven on Manihiki are particularly fine. The population is concentrated in the village of Nivano on the south-west corner of the atoll.

Rakahanga has an airstrip but in common with Penrhyn, the other northern island with this luxury, the cost of flying from Rarotonga is so excessive that it is rarely used.

History
Legends tell of Rakahanga being hauled up from under the sea by three brothers and the island of Manihiki breaking off from the island and drifting away. There

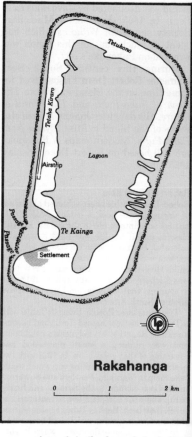

Rakahanga

0   1   2 km

are a variety of similar legends including one which tells of the island subsequently being populated entirely by the offspring of one man and his wife, the man taking his four daughters as additional wives.

In 1606 the commander of the ships *Capitana* and *Almiranta*, Pedro Fernandez de Quiros, who as navigator to Mendana had already discovered Pukapuka 10 years earlier, sighted the island. He reported that the islanders were:

the most beautiful white and elegant people that were met during the voyage.

urthermore, he continued, the women
vere exceptionally beautiful and:

f properly dressed, would have advantages
ver our Spanish women.

3uch reports were no doubt the genesis for
nany romantic notions of the South Seas!
De Quiros was not the only member of the
xpedition to be impressed. A Franciscan
riar accompanying the expedition named
he discovery the island of Gente
Hermosa, 'beautiful people'. At this time
Rakahanga and Manihiki were both
owned by the people of Rakahanga who
ased to 'commute' between the two
islands.

Over 200 years were to pass before the
island was again visited by western ships,
first a Russian expedition in 1820 then a
series of whalers and trading ships. As
usual a number of easily forgotten names
were bestowed on the island. In 1849
Polynesian missionaries arrived on
Manihiki, although at that time it was
still only settled by temporary groups
from Rakahanga. The often hazardous
journey between the two islands resulted
in numerous deaths at sea and in 1852 the
missionaries convinced the islanders to
divide themselves between the two atolls.
Travelling between Manihiki and Rakahanga can still be dangerous.

Lost En Route

Although missionaries tried as early as 1852 to
put an end to voyaging back and forth across
the 40-odd km between Rakahanga and
Manihiki, people continue to shuttle back and
forth, sometimes with harrowing results. In
June 1953, for example, nine islanders set out at
night to sail from Manihiki to Rakahanga.
Come the dawn they were lost: a squall had
blown them off course and where they were
relative to the two islands was a mystery.
Where they were relative to Pukapuka, 500 km
downwind, didn't seem to be such a mystery
because they set out to sail there. Five days
later, in an extraordinary navigational feat,
they arrived in Pukapuka.

In 1965 another small boat from Manihiki

suffered engine failure midway between the
islands and was swept away to the west by the
steady three to four knot current that runs
between the islands. Sixty-five days and
almost 3500 km later the crew landed at
Erromanga in Vanuatu. The book *The Man
who Refused to Die* recounts the tale of this
extraordinary voyage and the persistence of
Techu Makimare, the hero of the crew.

Suwarrow

Population: 6
Area: 0.4 square km

The usually unpopulated atoll of Suwarrow
is one of the best known in the whole Cook
Islands group due to a prolonged visit by
one man. Between 1952 and his death in
1977 New Zealander Tom Neale lived on
the island for extended periods as a virtual
hermit and his book, *An Island to Oneself*
became a South Seas classic. If you want
to know all about how to live on an atoll
then this book is a must.

Although Tom Neale is long gone – he is
buried in the cemetery opposite Rarotonga's
airport – his memory lives on and yachties
often call in to the atoll. It's one of the few
in the northern Cooks with an accessible
lagoon. Tom's room is still furnished just
as it was when he lived there. Visiting
yachts fill in a logbook left in the room.
Pearl divers from Manihiki also visit
occasionally.

Tom Neale wasn't the only writer to live
on, and write about, Suwarrow. American-
born Robert Dean Frisbie survived a
terrible hurricane in 1942 and wrote of it in
Island of Desire. His daughter Johnny
Frisbie also wrote about the same
hurricane in *The Frisbies of the South
Seas*. Although the lagoon is large the
scattered islands of Suwarrow are all very
small and low-lying. Hurricanes have
brought waves which wash right across
even the highest of the islands and in 1942

the Frisbie group only survived by tying themselves to a tree.

History

Suwarrow's curious name is neither English nor Polynesian. It was named by the Russian explorer Mikhail Lazarev in 1814 after his ship *Suvarov*. Nor has it always been uninhabited. There was an unsuccessful attempt to produce pearl shell here in the early part of this century while in the '20s and '30s copra was produced until a devastating termite infestation halted production. 'Coast watchers' from New Zealand kept an eye on Japanese activity from Suwarrow during WW II and the remains of their buildings can still be seen on Anchorage Island.

There may well have been earlier visitors. In the mid-19th century the American whaler *Gem* was wrecked on the reef. A ship came from Tahiti to salvage the whaler's oil cargo and one of the visiting ship's officers dug up a box containing $15,000. Where this cache

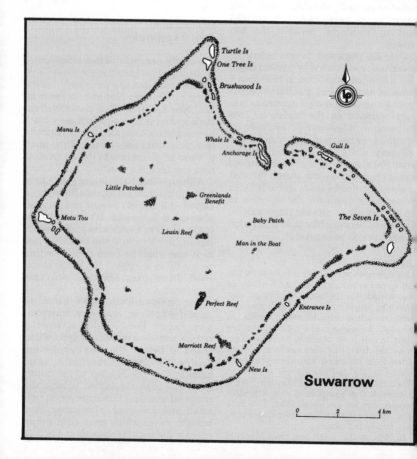

Suwarrow

Turtle Is
One Tree Is
Brushwood Is
Manu Is
Whale Is
Anchorage Is
Gull Is
Little Patches
Greenlands Benefit
Motu Tou
Baby Patch
The Seven Is
Lewin Reef
Man in the Boat
Perfect Reef
Entrance Is
Marriott Reef
New Is

0   2   4 km

came from has never been satisfactorily explained although the coins were thought to date from the mid-1700s and may have been connected with the first British Pacific expedition under Commodore George Anson in 1742. In 1876 another visitor found Spanish coins dating from the 1600s.

In 1860 the atoll was the scene of a dramatic and tragic dispute. First, a group of eight people, one of them an Englishman, drifted to Suwarrow after an abortive Manihiki-Rakahanga voyage. Later a group of Penrhyn pearl divers with a European boss turned up and later still another European visitor was left on the atoll. Shortly after the arrival of the third European an argument broke out between the pearl divers and their leader and all three Europeans were murdered.

In the mid-1870s more evidence of an early European visit was discovered when signs of habitation, various artefacts and skeletons were unearthed. Were they left by shipwrecked Spaniards? Or were they the remains of the English crew lost on a cutter from the ship *Pandora*, sent to the Pacific in 1791 to search for the mutineers of the *Bounty*?

Glossary

adze – axe like hand tool with ceremonial importance in the Cook Islands.
Ara Metua – ancient Polynesian road around the circumference of Rarotonga: many parts of it still remain, inland from the newer coast road.
ariki – high chiefs: traditional head of a district or tribe.

beer school – communal drinking session where bush beer is consumed.
bush beer – locally produced, moonshine beer brewed from oranges, bananas, or pawpaws.

CICC – Cook Island Christian Church, the protestant church which continues from the original London Missionary Society churches.
copra – coconut 'meat' from which coconut oil is produced, an important product throughout the Pacific. The problem with copra is the price is very volatile – it has reached as high as US$450 a tonne but currently is much much lower.

ei kaki – flower leis draped around visitors on arrival or departure.
ei katu – flower tiaras.
eke – octopus.

ika – fish.

koutu – ancient Polynesian open-air royal court used for meeting and political functions.

LMS – London Missionary Society, the original missionary force in the Cook Islands and in many other regions of the Pacific.

mataiapo – head of a sub-tribe, a rank down from an *ariki*.
makatea – raised coral reef which forms a coastal plain around several islands of the southern group including Mangaia and Atiu.

mana – power or influence.
Maori – the Polynesian people of the Cook Islands and also of New Zealand, also the language of these people. Literally means 'indigenous' or 'local'.
marae – family or tribal temple.
maroro – flying fish.
mate – die.
motu – lagoon islet.

pandanus – type of palm leaf used for thatching the roofs of traditional houses and for baskets, bags and *rito* hats.
papa'a – westerners, also the English language.
pareu – wrap around sarong-type garment.
puku – mollusc which produces pearlshell.

rito – hats woven of pandanus or bleached, young palm leaves.

tamanu – banyan tree.
Tangaroa – corpulent but phallic figure variously known as the god of fertility or the god of the sea; appears on the Cook Island one dollar coin.
taramea – crown-of-thorns starfish but colloquially used to refer to bar girls or prostitutes.
tiki – symbolic human figure.
tivaivai – colourful and intricately sewn applique works which are traditionally made as burial shrouds but are also used as bedspreads or simply as wall hangings. They're very rarely seen for sale.
tumunu – hollowed out stump of a coconut tree used to brew bush beer. Also refers to bush beer drinking sessions.

umukai – traditional Polynesian food (*kai*) cooked in an underground (*umu*) oven.

wale – traditional house on the island of Pukapuka.

MAPS

Temperature

To convert °C to °F multiply by 1.8 and add 32

To convert °F to °C subtract 32 and multiply by ·55

Length, Distance & Area

	multiply by
inches to centimetres	2.54
centimetres to inches	0.39
feet to metres	0.30
metres to feet	3.28
yards to metres	0.91
metres to yards	1.09
miles to kilometres	1.61
kilometres to miles	0.62
acres to hectares	0.40
hectares to acres	2.47

Weight

	multiply by
ounces to grams	28.35
grams to ounces	0.035
pounds to kilograms	0.45
kilograms to pounds	2.21
British tons to kilograms	1016
US tons to kilograms	907

A British ton is 2240 lbs, a US ton is 2000 lbs

Volume

	multiply by
Imperial gallons to litres	4.55
litres to imperial gallons	0.22
US gallons to litres	3.79
litres to US gallons	0.26

5 imperial gallons equals 6 US gallons
a litre is slightly more than a US quart, slightly less
than a British one

Guides to The Pacific

Australia – a travel survival kit
Australia is Lonely Planet's home territory so this guide gives you the complete low-down on Down Under, from the red centre to the coast, from cosmopolitan cities to country towns.

Bushwalking in Australia
Australia offers opportunities for walking in many different climates and terrains – from the tropical north, to the rocky gorges of the centre, to the mountains of the south-east. Two experienced and respected walkers give details of the best walks in every state, plus notes on many more.

New Zealand – a travel survival kit
Visitors to New Zealand find a land of fairytale beauty and scenic contrasts – a natural wonderland. This book has information about the places you won't want to miss, including ski-resorts and famous walks.

Tramping in New Zealand
Call it tramping, hiking, walking, bushwalking, or trekking – travelling on your feet is the best way to come to grips with New Zealand's natural beauty. This guide gives detailed descriptions for 20 walks of various length and difficulty.

Fiji – a travel survival kit
This is a comprehensive guide to the Fijian archipelago. On a number of these beautiful islands accommodation ranges from camping grounds to international hotels – whichever you prefer this book will help you to enjoy the South Seas.

Solomon Islands – a travel survival kit

The Solomon Islands are the Pacific's best kept secret. If you want to discover remote tropical islands, jungle-covered volcanoes and traditional Melanesian villages, this book will show you how.

Tahiti & French Polynesia – a travel survival kit

The image of palm-fringed beaches and friendly people continues to lure travellers to Polynesia. This book gives you all the facts on paradise, and will be useful whether you plan a package holiday, or to travel the islands independently.

Micronesia – a travel survival kit

Amongst these 2100 islands are beaches, lagoons and reefs that will dazzle the most jaded traveller. This guide is packed with all you need to know about island hopping across the north Pacific.

Papua New Guinea – a travel survival kit

Papua New Guinea is truly 'the last unknown' – the last inhabited place on earth to be explored by Europeans. This guide has the latest information for travellers who want to find just how rewarding a trip to this remote and amazing country can be.

Bushwalking in Papua New Guinea

Papua New Guinea offers exciting challenges for bushwalkers. This book describes 11 walks of various length and difficulty, through one of the world's most beautiful, rugged and exotic countries. Specific and practical information is provided.

Also Available:
Papua New Guinea phrasebook

Lonely Planet Guidebooks

Lonely Planet guidebooks cover virtually every accessible part of Asia as well as Australia, the Pacific, Central and South America, Africa, the Middle East and parts of North America. There are four main series: 'travel survival kits', covering a single country for a range of budgets; 'shoestring' guides with compact information for low-budget travel in a major region; trekking guides; and 'phrasebooks'.

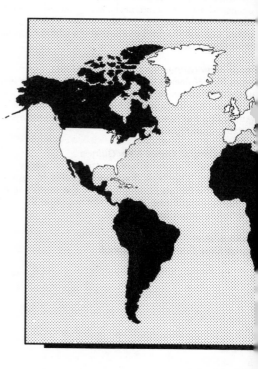

Mail Order

onely Planet guidebooks are distributed worldwide and are sold by good bookshops verywhere. They are also available by mail order from Lonely Planet, so if you have ifficulty finding a title please write to us. US and Canadian residents should write to mbarcadero West, 112 Linden St, Oakland CA 94607, USA and residents of other ountries to PO Box 617, Hawthorn, Victoria 3122, Australia.

Lonely Planet

Lonely Planet published its first book in 1973. Tony and Maureen Wheeler had made a lengthy overland trip from England to Australia and, in response to numerous 'how do you do it?' questions, Tony wrote and they published *Across Asia on the Cheap*. It became an instant local best-seller and inspired thoughts of a second travel guide. A year and a half in South-East Asia resulted in their second book, *South-East Asia on a Shoestring*, which they put together in a backstreet Chinese hotel in Singapore in 1975. The 'yellow book', as it quickly became known, soon became *the* guide to the region and has gone through five editions, always with its familiar yellow cover.

Soon other writers came to them with ideas for similar books – books that went off the beaten track with an adventurous approach to travel, books that 'assumed you knew how to get your luggage off the carousel,' as one reviewer put it. Lonely Planet grew from a kitchen table operation to a spare room and then to its own office. It's international reputation began to grow as the Lonely Planet logo began to appear in more and more countries. In 1982 *India – a travel survival kit* won the Thomas Cook award for the best guidebook of the year.

These days there are over 70 Lonely Planet titles. Over 40 people work at our office in Melbourne, Australia and another half dozen at our US office in Oakland, California.

At first Lonely Planet specialised in the Asia region but these days we are also developing major ranges of guidebooks to the Pacific region, to South America and to Africa. The list of walking guides is growing and Lonely Plan now has a unique series of phrasebooks 'unusual' languages. The emphasis continu to be on travel for travellers and Tony an Maureen still manage to fit in a number of tri each year and play a very active part in th writing and updating of Lonely Planet guides.

Keeping guidebooks up to date is a consta battle which requires an ear to the ground an lots of walking, but technology also plays i part. All Lonely Planet guidebooks are no stored and updated on computer, and som authors even take lap-top computers into th field. Lonely Planet is also using computers draw maps and eventually many of the map will be stored on disk.

The people at Lonely Planet strongly fe that travellers can make a positive contributio to the countries they visit both by bette appreciation of cultures and by the money the spend. In addition the company tries to make direct contribution to the countries and regio it covers. Since 1986 a percentage of the incom from each book has gone to aid groups an associations. This has included donations famine relief in Africa, to aid projects in Indi to agricultural projects in Nicaragua and othe Central American countries and to Greenpeace efforts to halt French nuclear testing in th Pacific. In 1988 over $40,000 was donated b Lonely Planet to these projects.

Lonely Planet Distributors

Australia & Papua New Guinea Lonely Planet Publications, PO Box 617, Hawthorn, Victoria 3122.
Canada Raincoast Books, 112 East 3rd Avenue, Vancouver, British Columbia V5T 1C8.
Denmark, Finland & Norway Scanvik Books aps, Store Kongensgade 59 A, DK-1264 Copenhagen K.
India & Nepal UBS Distributors, 5 Ansari Rd, New Delhi – 110002
Israel Geographical Tours Ltd, 8 Tverya St, Tel Aviv 63144.
Japan Intercontinental Marketing Corp, IPO Box 5056, Tokyo 100-31.
Netherlands Nilsson & Lamm bv, Postbus 195, Pampuslaan 212, 1380 AD Weesp.
New Zealand Transworld Publishers, PO Box 83-094, Edmonton PO, Auckland.
Singapore & Malaysia MPH Distributors, 601 Sims Drive, #03-21, Singapore 1438.
Spain Altair, Balmes 69, 08007 Barcelona.
Sweden Esselte Kartcentrum AB, Vasagatan 16, S-111 20 Stockholm.
Thailand Chalermnit, 108 Sukhumvit 53, Bangkok 10110.
Turkey Yab-Yay Dagitim, Alay Koshu Caddesi 12/A, Kat 4 no. 11-12, Cagaloglu, Istanbul.
UK Roger Lascelles, 47 York Rd, Brentford, Middlesex, TW8 0QP
USA Lonely Planet Publications, PO Box 2001A, Berkeley, CA 94702.
West Germany Buchvertrieb Gerda Schettler, Postfach 64, D3415 Hattorf a H.
All Other Countries refer to Australia address.